TRAUMA

first edition 2011

ISBN: 978-3-9502910-9-4

This book is only available at the online shop of Trauma Wien.
http://traumawien.at – verlag@traumawien.at

This book was set in Computer Modern
cover: Luc Gross & Julian Palacz
production: Julian Palacz
edit: Luc Gross

Mez Breeze

human readable messages
[mezangelle 2003 - 2011]

TRAUMAWIEN

"Mez does for code poetry as jodi and Vuk Cosic have done for ASCII Art: Turning a great, but naively executed concept into something brilliant, paving the ground for a whole generation of digital artists." (Florian Cramer).

The impact of her unique codewurks [constructed via her pioneering net.language "mezangelle"] has been equated with the work of Shakespeare, James Joyce, Emily Dickinson, and Larry Wall. Mez has exhibited extensively since the early 90s [eg *Wollongong World Women Online 1995, ISEA Chicago + ARS Electronica 1997, The Metropolitan Museum Tokyo 1999, SIGGRAPH 1999 & 2000, _Under_Score_ @The Brooklyn Academy of Music 2001, +playengines+ Melbourne Australia 2003, p0es1s Berlin 2004, Dissention Convention @Postmaster Gallery New York 2004, Arte Nuevo InteractivA Mexico 2005, Radical Software @Turin Italy 2006, DIWO @ The HTTP Gallery London 2007, New Media Scotland 2008, the Laguna Art Museum California and Alternator Gallery Canada 2009, Federation Square Melbourne 2010* and *Transmediale Berlin 2011*].

Her awards include the ***2001 VIF Prize*** [Germany], the ***JavaMuseum Artist Of The Year 2001*** [Germany], ***2002 Newcastle New Media Poetry Prize*** [Australia], winner of the ***2006 Site Specific Index Page Competition*** [Italy] and ***Burton Wonderland Gallery Winner 2010*** [judged by Tim Burton, Australia]. Mez was a ***Vilém Flusser Theory Award*** 2011 nominee for her article set *'_Social Tesseracting_'* and is the Executive Editor of the "_Augmentology 1[L]0[L]1_" project, a Synthetic Ecology Strategist, Consultant and Game Theorist.

mezangelle.com

Chapter 1

2003

1.1 June

1.1.1][frag.ment][(2003-06-10 09:55)

3. WHAT ARE YOU LISTENING TO RIGHT NOW? turin brakes "The Optimist LP"

4. WHAT ARE THE LAST 4 DIGITS OF YOUR PHONE NUMBER? 3690

33. LIVING ARRANGEMENTS? yes please. some1 please arrange my life 4 me.

34. WHAT BOOKS ARE YOU READING? 1 book. "supercannes" by jg ballard

40. WHAT INSPIRES YOU? uber-newness. gaps and swells in conversations. contradictions [especially in ppl]. dedication. oddness. talent. passion. focus. fragments.

50. LIFETIME GOALS? 2 express + create without becoming hackneyed or wanky. 2 make as many reliable friendships as possible. 2 connect with genuine ppl with talent, drive, motivation + compassion [with a l'tle bit o' cheekiness + stupid humour thrown in]. 2 inspire and assist those who want 2 do but r afraid 2 try.

(2003-06-11 01:08:04)
Hola Mez, Amy here. God you inspire me. :)

netwurker (2003-06-11 05:48:34)
thunks:)

1.1.2 papazine n_terview][1][(2003-06-10 10:08)

A:
in general, before attempting to create a more "multimedia" oriented work [ie like the final incarnation of _][ad][Dressed in a Skin C.ode _] i always create smaller, more net-directed pieces which i term either net.wurks or code.works. these largely text/code based pieces are constructed using the hybrid code/poetic dynamic [language] entitled mezangelle which is constructed via a mixture of code splicing [ie fragments of programming language-shards - mostly Perl - + operating system & email formats, tree/directory-structures + wildcard references, booleanisms, unix shell commands, html + java script conventions and ascii] and parsed poetic language including repeated allusions 2 hyperlinks via bracketing of meanings and word splicing. i also employ various identity tags [avatarish indicators that appear in the from: fields] that signify a substantial change in the informational/data flow, and can be utilized by a reader/absorber as a way of dealing with the meaning loadings involved in any given wurk-phase....

1.1.3 papa.mag N_terview][2][(2003-06-10 10:09)

...the wurks are then sent to multiple arts email lists, and then modified by fellow collaborators or translated into "normal" english and modified/content altered again, resent etc. i'll begin 2 build a more synergistic [multimedia] work from these texts with an initial subject/concept which may spring from lines of text/code that are generated progressively as a piece percolates.... _][ad][Dressed in a Skin C.ode _ comes from this type of process...making notes in separate email-editor files or using my mobile, depending where i'm at [i don't have a lap/palmtop at the mo so i find myself using my mobile to take down idea snippets]...then the structure usually emerges from these fragments, via a method of appropriation [eg mimicking of a international relay chat transcript or actually using 1 that i may have participated in, or utilizing a stretch of stylistically (or executably)-breathtaking code that i may have been using programmatically or come across in my research]..........i then rework these net/code.wurks via a format suitable for the web using a txt editor and some bare html code if need be.......

1.1.4 zineish bits][3][(2003-06-10 10:12)

in the case of _][ad][Dressed in a Skin C.ode _, i used these net + code.wurks as a basis to create a web-based work that uses these net.wurks [ie _texts _] as source material as well as the actual processes/methods involved in their dispersion [which explains the format of each _text _ as a email, including footers, subject lines, from:, re: and to: fields etc].i used flash MX 2 create the more dynamic components, such as the _n.hanced _ wurks that use mouseovers, clickable regions, audio fragments & "click- &-hold" areas - ie so-termed "interactive" [blergh - mebbe co-operative is a better term?] sections that play against themselves in terms of functionality in order to make the audience play and weave within the meaning loadings. nothing is easy 2 "get" in a mez wurk:) the purpose of manipulating interactive functions via these "flashifications" is 2 hilight the stagnant methods _some _ [not all] people employ when using prepackaged plugin-tools without any 4thought as 2 their limitations/construction/cultural bifurcations. i use a nifty program called _Soundraider _ that scans ur harddrive for .wav files and then manipulates these into a type of personalised computer soundtrack with 5 audio layers that can be locked, muted or shuffled to create audio that is highly unpredictable but also controllable via the .wav file structure you feed it2 it [it can also scan specific directories alone]. i record this output then select appropriate sections to integrate.

1.1.5 blurb][4][(2003-06-10 10:13)

i produce & translate the mezangelled texts in2 a variety of levels including multimediac versions as each layering is coded and specialised within their own peculiar meaning/interfaced trajectories.....this increases the expressive avenues via which people can then choose 2 input their own personal cues whilst viewing/exploring the wurk and enhance their comprehension levels, especially if audience members aren't in the mezangelle loop...i tried to weight _][ad][Dressed in a Skin C.ode _ towards a more accessible meaning wavelength, and hopefully it has enuff conventional multimedia elements to entertain those not textcentric or code literate............this process of extending intitial net/code.wurks into more multimediac territory can have mixed results, and i'm not essentially sure that _][ad][Dressed in a Skin C.ode _ succeeds in terms of adequately reflecting the whole network mechanism that underpins it, even though it does reference it repeatedly. the more multimediac interface does allow for multiple interpretive pathways via which an absorber can choose to extract meaning via more sensory cues.

---

biti (2003-06-09 20:52:54) breathing skin, coming in gasps
the medium of livejournal lends itself to this... i feel a sparking, and a synergy here. here is a new medium, and new type of dynamic. less linear. more in gasps and gaps.

(2003-06-09 21:55:05) Re: breathing skin, coming in gasps
More shifting against itself, always a skin rubbing raw and meandering into love and abrasion. - Alan Sondheim sondheim@panix.com

1.1.6 horse_like driven snow[mobiles] (2003-06-10 22:46)

event: _1 _

.s.tiple grey meeting g[p]reenish vocal[ity]
.leather bound and ch.RO[a]Mic gagged

[the smell, the lurverly smel(ter)l]

.sun _stopped N moaning MOOscapes
.tanned N muscled _dangerous
.mu.sic thru a tactile v.e[v]il

[oldstuff vs newbies.on.a.steel.g _rate(d out of ruralised 10)]

[i.will.learn.2.ride.those.sculpted.animels]

(2003-06-10 14:27:10) marinomarini
bronze riders with football heads and winsome smiles on brinzel quadrupeds

netwurker (2003-06-10 22:35:16) Re: marinomarini
.bronze[d N cut-out] r.id[l]ers [head N jockish goat _straps] .win sum + lose sum[mation of u into muscl[ton]e equineness] .[s]miles on brindle dappled _stretch _meat[ers]

1.1.7 yos.semi.T yearn_ings (2003-06-11 08:39)

.w.a[ch]king in2 this _frost _life

.dr[l]inking moan _tea

.drenched in black frost sweat + wood[en] c.hip.pian glory

[1 AI dies a horrible gravemare death + urs is sav][(i)oured][ed]

+ out[in]ward bound[less] in chill _scream nuances
+ sinkin _thru _LCD _lines + N _cry[stal]ption shoes
+ inter _here::drawl here::sic N b txt damned there::

[and all the while thing of that fro.Zen Place/deer ramblings + wild highway car _dancing over s.kitte[n]red ice.ments]

[wooden structwhores aping tv templated reality]
[strict mental plates revoked + reality surgings thru x.periential strainahs]
[do i shift + kik.my.way.in2.ur.(D)frag.mento.sphere?]

1.1.8 m[v]elt[vet N doctor]ing lines nuanced_code (2003-06-12 08:31)

–crash dummified N rogue txt idlers

.u.seek.the.trojan.truth.

::s[ituation]lit[oral]ting babies mouths with z-ends
::search + dD.c[k]ern[elizing]
::m[v]elt[vet N doctor]ing lines nuanced _code

.

1.1.9 { soc[d]ial engine (2003-06-12 09:02)

[social engine] woo[t!]l.gathering
[re]mixed N d.filing sy.stem[N root//shard N slice]
rod-bird strait vs corna.stoned N da[ta]nge(nt)rous

pictory purrfect N pump _muscles//bloated S[OAP]car _[t]issues
e[mailing].lectro.lighting.my.pores.in2.sms.destr uction

–dialin.objects.with.honeyed.lines

biti (2003-06-11 20:24:21)
[social engine] woo[t!]l.gathering bu[r]sting str[i]uct | ures knitting new gar[ment]lands # [re]mixed N d.filing sy.stem[N root//shard N slice] de[file] de[sys]temitised re[v|filed] new g[s]aps appearing blood s[tr]eams in the open bits, # rod-bird strait vs corna.stoned N da[ta]nge(nt)rous # pictory purrfect N pump _muscles//bloated S[OAP]car _[t]issues past that point of no return re li[ck]shing the scars, sharing the bites # e[mailing].lectro.lighting.my.pores.in2.-sms.destruction s|hot ether, s[h]immering aglow –dialin.objects.with.honeyed.lines potential energy burning the circ[us]uits s|lick med[e]ia, oh my child grief turned to letters turned to wo[sha]rds turned to s|hot b[yea]urn|ing

1.1.10 – scopi.ca[u]l. (2003-06-13 08:45)

– out _-sid[l]er formation in a dog.panting.coating
– switched _in2-O[r]b.livion via f[ertile]aithless
– sing _ _ _ _ _ _ _ _ _ _[L]ED _ _ _ _ _ _ _ _ _out[re:]

– antiquated shifts + lined _out _paper.backians

– .flickers _of _past _eye _blu _meeting _horse _wild _manic _eye _whites

– scopi.ca[u]l.

1.1.11 Re: [-empyre-] _Active Narrative Gathering_ (2003-06-13 11:05)

.

wot got me musing was having watched "The Animatrix" [gawd peter chung is a demi-manga-god - remember aeon flux from liquid teev?]...9 short animaction [yeah i can't help neologising sorry] movies which piggyback off and reveal plot nuances/x.tensions of _Matrix Reloaded _. in 1 of the shorts, the gaping qs of the origins/story point of the Neo-fawning-boy-child n.countered in the _Matrix Reloaded _ movie is s.sentially answered....+ this sparked off a chain of thought centering round the idea of ANG [_Active Narrative Gathering _]

...by ANG i'm

referring 2 how some m.mergent forms of art|n.tertainment|simulcra r interconnected via narrative threads b.yond parent forms/individualised media constrictions..ie if u want the complete narrative picture [ie join-the-story-dots-campbellesqueness-hero-journey-st yle] that is available when watching _MR _ u *must* watch/collude with satellite|parallel constructions that enhance [ie offer loadings] that complete the story jigsaw - like _Enter the Matrix _ video game + The Animatrix.

it's a bit like the easter eggs n.countered on dvds....secret hotspots that 1nce found offer additional info regarding the main feature....

this isn't a new phenomenon.....look at _Twin Peaks _ for instance [movie series, book (The Diary of Laura Palmer], and movie]..but it seems to becoming a more dominant pattern...look at _Donnie Darko _ [movie + website] + _The Blair Witch Project _ [book, movie, website]...not to mention _AI _...........also the conversion of comics/books in2 film, games in2 film [_The Final Fantasty _ game + film].......

its like audiences r n.couraged 2 step outside the restrictions of mono-media absorption channels + actively seek additional narrative components elsewhere...bit like an ANG cultural engine i guess.....

.

---

kochanie (2003-06-22 17:19:27)
we can create pure visions so that people may see and become familiar with what reality is / can be, so they can become familiar with such concepts, and will not automatically rush back to the familiarity of samsara; not unlike a dream state, engaging with technology can loosen our grasping to this reality as real and solid ; lots of details in above; practice emanating one s self, through changing how our mind s fire when communicating, breaks habitual notions and patterns... shows us that all things are indeed impermanent and interdependent; bring people closer together to mind essence, erasing perceived boundaries that we culturally have built up & using networks to show the contextual relationships and interconnectedness of everything dis.sappearing re.made tho jst realising n th end {oh, nd frm jak }

1.1.12 _shift_ (2003-06-13 16:30)

/red _feathered _luvers _twitchNvault/tanned _milk _clouding _staggered _reinfalls/human _rab[b]i[d]t _hutching/PINE _scents _vs _PAN _motions/walking _thru _druggedNdata _mists/

_shift _

1.1.13 [f]lip_fi[l]t[ers] (2003-06-14 14:18)

.b>gat.

.froz>[h]e[lle]n botox chill _grinning _
.broke dan.ger[m]ous + spiced _by _snow _N _slee[p]t
.mobile _vile reads: co _joined txt>s[ms]peakin
.do _u _c _tree _struc[alan]turing?

■

[a.gain>st]

1.1.14 _Chrysalis Ontologies_Snapped_ (2003-06-15 12:05)

[epi.Sod[Off, u!]e A]:

_sun.ke[e]n pits N choke+hold fashion _
_whip words + s[ocial]keletal fumblings _
_GAA* crouching

[* _glacial.argument.afterbreath]

_court[ING] 1 and minu[te]s 2 _
_touched.by.sludgehands.+ lustglances
_MATRIX _arms XXed with battle _a[r]mour _ON

_meeting _slouches. _drunk _ramblings.

_[a]tonal _a[bortive]fta.bir[d watching]ths. _chr[ysalis]onologies _snapped _.

_pitch.ing _polar _dance _[Agin]courts _

1.1.15 _cru.s[ocial]t codas_ (2003-06-16 08:03)

_thru a go[o]ggle-glass e.bon[e]ly _
_sp[f]ew realnesses vs facet|truths+b[r]ank[e]rupt|kisses

.blink.+.i.will.[k]not.b.seen

unguard|grins|look|thru|the|dj|prison|ESSo-like|+|sk [l]ank[y]|actuals

|gorgon|dancing|+|flipped|the|communication|finga

|Obsessed|Manic|Beat[ings]|He[r]m[Aphrodit e]orrhaging|Peaks

-

---

biti (2003-06-18 21:20:04)
.blink.+.i.will.[k]not.b.seen /me watches the others blink /me sees you /me watches the others blink /me sees herself disappear

netwurker (2003-06-18 23:54:13)
>/me watches the others blink [link.ages] >/me sees you cs me? thru. a. format. lasso? >/me watches the others blink [ages.link] >/me sees herself disappear 2 then re.ap.pear[N apples +]?

1.1.16][full_b.loa(d)t][(2003-06-17 19:57)

.

-event.[d]ualities d[w]renched

.

1.1.17 _viral sex_ (2003-06-18 09:15)

-cr++ss species vio[emu]lations + HIV loopings

[this.is.how.AIDS.initialized]

1.1.18][i.can.smell.g(t)ee(n)kage(s)][(2003-06-19 08:42)

-

–

-

—- - —— - - — -

.smelling geekage.@.nano.(101)paces
.[lust _geo _schizmically _d.fined]
.[bouys _in _bad _p[hysical]lace.ments]
.gurls _cryo.Genet.ically _loose _hippish]
.m[o.h]awkishly _spraying _in _soldier _batches

– teen.kages
– i.can.smell.ur.geekness
– ——— _ _ _ ——

-

—- - —— - - — -

---

kochanie (2003-06-18 23:38:44)
hallo and happy to sse u here :)

netwurker (2003-06-18 23:51:56) c++.tact
thx. contact is always nice.

1.1.19 _j.u[rl]st ta[l]king//[buying.in2.the.troll.boat]_ (2003-06-23 08:57)

][mez][
Member posted June 22, 2003 03:35 PM

_j.u[rl]st ta[l]king//[buying.in2.the.troll.boat] _

quote:

...but then I'm not sure what it is you're actually saying.XXXXXXXXXXXXXXXXXXXXXXXXXXXXXXXXX-XXXXXXXXXXX
xxxxxxxxxxxxxxxxxxxxxxxxxxxxxxxxxxxxxxxxxxxxxxxxxx
XXXXXXXXXXXXXXXetcXXXXXXXXXXXXXXXXXXXXXXXX-XXXXXXXXXXX

---

this.is.ur.dictum.

it isn't, how.eva, mine.

.my .orientation .is .uber.wise [ie not lazy or laze _n.ducing nor straight.white.bread.info.absorption]

[read: if.u.will]
[re:spond: if. u. w.ant(s communication crawling)]

or don't.

s[w]imple as that.

quote:

---

for instance;

quote:

---

it also points 2wards the next tier of ubermarketing....less noesis appeal, more n.trinsic layering of ultimate narrative as a fiscal reward source rather than just a n[ovel].tertainment pay-off...

p[r]ay.2.receive.jig.sored.story.load[ings]?

Please explain the last part.

---

this is a f[riction]urred.n.flection of the 1st par.t[ickle.ur.fiction.gland, please!]

- - - - - - - - - - - - - - - - - -

breaking down:

-p[r]ay.2.

■pray station allusions (play.station.re.wurking (google it if nec) n.dicating non _parentized story loc(ations)].
■religious baggage n.serts [_pray 2 _ n.dicating semi-religious demig(h)odge(podge)ry that may spring up around this process]

-receive.jig.sored.story.load[ings]?

jig.sored = jig.sawed narrative nuances [trawling processes] + sore n.dicating a painful reorientation of "normal" story.data gathering

quote:

---

jigsawed story loadings? you want more of this type of meta-narrative? (I like the word meta)

---

i.want.much.

[including ur trajectory].

quote:

---

quote:

---

specially considering the lack of ego.purr.petuation they _seam _ 2 want 2 m.ulate.

---

whose lack of ego perpetuation? what do you mean the lack of...they want emulate?

---

the bros rn't especially keen 2 b interviewed. [comp.ree.hend.AI?]

quote:

no habblas mezengelle. compromise for clear discussion, yes? perhaps babblefish is desirable or subtitles.

clear discussion? bah.

eng.leash is not a static language.

[do u think that english sprang forth fully formed from the (foaming) mouths of anglo-celtic-germania gods? & correspondingly, that its position is fixed in stone, & that the x.tra words they end up shoveling in2 dictionaries r simply 2 be scorned as neologistic heresy?

also, do u also adhere 2 the notion that the methods of communication via channels such as email and mobile technologies have no m.pact on the resultant conception of new modes that negotiate the function[s] of language?]

just bah!, really.

quote:

quote:

_this _ board is, like any other, filled 2 the gills with partial reductionists N retrograders who standardise N procedurally echo.the.canon.as.godhead without any d.tailed x.planation or nuanced m.mersion disagreed. the people on this board are more intelligent and tolerant than most other chatrooms/forums (IMHO). We value thought and content and it is understandable that they get frustrated when the syntax of the message is unclear.

...yes. which is y i said that otherlings x.ist here, 2?

[edit function: mis.noma.ing]

quote:

Off-Thread: Gender baiting.
Put it down, your feminism is showing.

I don't believe that this has anything to do with gender. I come from a generation that has learned to despise his own gender.

---

fairies nuts.

d.code that]

i fall on the side of masculine/feminine traits that go across sex stereo.typ[os]ing.

.

- pro][rating][.lucid.txt
-

-

http://www.hotkey.net.au/ netwurker
http://www.livejournal.com/users/netwurker/

_

_cr[xxx]oss ova.ring.

[This message was edited by][mez][on June 22, 2003 at 03:55 PM.]

Posts: 42 | Registered: April 28, 2003

][mez][
Member posted June 22, 2003 03:41 PM

.

e[diting].motion.haulage.

.

[This message was edited by][mez][on June 22, 2003 at 03:53 PM.]

[This message was edited by][mez][on June 22, 2003 at 04:01 PM.]

[This mez.age was noma.edited by][just had a thought, in terms of historical baggage do u think this is in part b.cause the US x.ists in a fundamental adolescent-ethos? ie removal from the established lines of the historic via the civil war [= rebellion + concretization of|thru hierarchical _old power _ stratifications =]][so][c][ial][limatising of overblown, inflated][body politic][worth = shiny capitalism (post WW2) as the new religious order & blind negation/military (bully)mindsetting of anything that offers alternatives 2 this [cf mcarthyism + bushism(s)] = n.herent institutionalised belief structures [cf covert facism] that reflect this = future a][rrogant][ggrandizement of projected realities [in terms of economy, business function, etc].........?][
][on June 22, 2003 at 04:01 PM.]

[This message was edited by][mez][on June 22, 2003 at 04:04 PM.]

[This message was edited by][mez][on June 22, 2003 at 04:05 PM.]

Posts: 42 | Registered: April 28, 2003

][mez][
Member posted June 22, 2003 03:48 PM

_keeping N.glish segmented in a nostalgic pocket _

i _do _ understand overt resistance to this style of language construction.

– that ppl need keep english segmented in a nostalgic pocket, a functioning system predicated on wot u [they] c as a static language base.

Kant. we. view. language[s]. thru. a. Moore. fluid. filter?

–i'm not aiming 2 obsfuscate

–i'm aiming 2 n.hance language within certain creative parameters.

- pro][rating][.lucid.txt
-
-

http://www.hotkey.net.au/ netwurker

_
_cr[xxx]oss ova.ring.

Posts: 42 | Registered: April 28, 2003

All times are PST

1.1.20 full_blown_wir[ed]ing (2003-06-23 15:05)

.screen t.app.isness + w.asp _drilling

.i .c .thistle. cows. in. data. paddocks.

.drinking mobile cancers thru t.high[5].pores
.wishing step[ford] _babies would revolve N cool.in.the.mid.age.sun[spotting]
.robotick.tick.tick _tingles as i txt.jerk N non _siamesically twitch

1.1.21 _N.ternet N.force [micro.paw(n)]officer_ [soft.launch.ing] (2003-06-29 09:16)

Tasks n.clude;
· [n]tense + volu[me lowered thru smurf.juicing.it.up]te net use
. re.D.fining s[ocial]earch online pick _up [on]s[errage +crumbling c(l)ost cuttage]ite e _valu[e = O]ation.
· te {[rrible] [ara] }chnical deviousness thru Object _Oversight of P[otential]eers
. [au]Tomat[o]ed s[d]e[sign + deaf.mimic.speeching] arch[i.texture] engines.

---

biti (2003-06-29 20:02:00)
r[g]iven on a[na]rchism na na na na arch arch arch riven [fo]r[g]iven . me be b[sl]ashing against the net form, and losing i really could do with a baby grand btw, sod the peers

netwurker (2003-06-29 20:35:51) riv.N
>me be b[sl]ashing against the net form, and losing /me bash/grp as well. >i really could do with a baby grand /me cood du with a sense of e _mployability. >btw, sod the peers & pod the seers/ :)

1.2 July

1.2.1 [_N.]Finite [_M]Press[_ionistic] (2003-07-01 19:34)

————//n.finite [regr](m.pr)ess.ionistic

.
[m(l)ove.ment.in.essence.cycles]
[tree.chopped(field.d.limiter-rank) _limbed+swarmically _healing]
[relev(st)ationary.visions.thru.music.merged.wi th.visual.(hi-parsed)lites]

.
[feet.motion.blown.via.auditory.snacking.parcels]
[concen(tan)tric.glass.finga.moon.shape.breakag es+tangent.node _line]
[swallow _n _shocked _bird-patternesque]

|box-patternesqueness.
|M-T hollowed _seatings.@.potential.luvers.blank _tab[ular-razored]les.

|i.seek.N.cannot.dream.fined.

(+h+)art.leakages. ————//a.gain.

.

---

kochanie (2003-07-17 17:52:59)
v.y l+vly

1.2.2 _o[h the]pen(EWE.CLIDIAN,$euclidian);_ (2003-07-08 09:12)

open(EWE.CLIDIAN, $u.clidian) || die "Can't open $euclidian: $!";

.mandib[i]le beading in shower structurals [water.perls.flipping.thru.grav(ity)e.humids]
. %g.ripping
+ dr.unk[le] preenings as the MOOn.iversals.grate+communication.p.urge-s
.data.p[j]oint.tattooing + d[C]duction.cavity.loops

die "Can't open $u.clidian: $!" unless open(EWE.CLIDIAN, $euclidian);

1.2.3 _frost t[l]ong(l)ue.ings_ (2003-07-14 10:20)

#!lacerations.on.my.aesth[ick]etic.tongue

[g(ol {gotha }.den)round black.frost.circuitree.N>R>Gee.storage]
[warm.junkie.lec.trick(ling)s _vs _ organoc(h)oldings]

.

1.2.4 _ur.chin[s n newbile necks]_ (2003-07-18 09:12)

_Dream [Wo]Mandat[e]a _

–blocks of pixelled dol.phin[eas cage] _code
–napthol blue meats blocked s[ilk]creen _white
–rising punctures.of.strange.flows.N.organic.want[ons]

–gawd's fingas.do.the.sunstreamic.walking
–li[s]quid.frozen.in.blonde.batches

.batten.down.the.brunette.hatches.

1.2.5 _LASTIC BUILD_ (2003-07-23 07:58)

++b[uilding]ands horizon stretched + sky compressed
++st.ack.ed txtuals moved thru flit + mail cracs
++tronic[wo]manual.han[g]dling.

1.2.6 _[s]lavi[c]sh bones_ (2003-07-30 09:46)

.
black claddish +m/possible [hos]pitables
cold frozen +snap.dried cum.munication
arms glued 2 frost _licked.[n]sid[ious]es

.
so[i]lder arcs +fertile g.lance[r] trajectories
fleeced words +cotton finger.tippishness
shooter.moments

.
slavic cheeks + blonde bytes
[liquid skin+meat]
social anti-touch[e].ing

.
h.an[gle]d flips + kinetic[aul] snap.shotting
lick hip +gasp flicking
crows _feat + teen.ager pittage

1.3 August

1.3.1 _re:set by fear_ (2003-08-02 15:30)

14:47 -!-][mez][[mez@adsl-202-72-184-2.bigpond.com.au] has quit [Read error: Connection]

1.3.2 _Either PAIR or BOND is True_ (2003-08-02 15:34)

PAIRB.Field error '22222222'

Either PAIR or BOND is True, or the current record has been deleted. Requested operation requires a current record.

/de/false/pair.bonding.programm/row.asp, line 0

1.3.3 _broad.Den_ (2003-08-18 09:35)

.wandering st + data corr.E.[the]Doors
.flip.styching + leaked [c]littorals
[tyme.stop.gap.drunk]

.flashing.spins.lite.eyes.of.molt
.draggin txts thru reality spheres
.pull.ur.shelves.in.regulation.[off]lines

.soft.imagevsmaya.yearnings

1.3.4 _Dream Fullscreen_ (2003-08-25 21:22)

_ _dream [f] _ _Dream Fullscreen Editors _

::bound head _tur[n]ings and ashen _washed dead calcium breathing.
:: visual skulls + broken head _space dust carriages
::nostalgia pregnant/gl[eaned]ass jars + [hemi]spherical catch.ments + passporting.kinetic.hells
::l[anced]ucidity reduced in2 dream par.cells + state.cognition.jerks

_emuscles [f] _ _[Emuscles Fullscreen Editors] _ _ _ _ _ _ _ _ _ _ _ _ _ _ _ _ _ _

::muscle.meme.ory serves in discreet.pain.capsules
::shift.bloat + ctrl.peelings
::doubled.[paper.]backs + cramped.[s]kin.gates

_ _terror.ed [f] _ _T[error]xt Editors _

::voicings.thru.luscious.[lep]rosyness
::melding verbal _scia.tic[k]as.with.teledrownings.thru.the.cerebral.traumosphere

1.3.5 _re:Mix [Tour.ing.SignAge.Fonts]_ (2003-08-26 20:29)

- ——) [u kno _.this.]

{ - —— [drink doof _ + then::]

..... _Time.St.Amp[_lifia _] _[7.10secs]
{ - —— N.sert rabid lo[n]gin .he[ma _tight wishing + shi(mma)ning opal tears
{ - —— [C]duction||[N]duction slurpin + m.Out.h.ing _wishments

{ - —— beanified st.O[h]mp Vs codified d.Oof

- ——) [lick.(b).ass.]

.... _Time.St.amp[_le fears meet music das||der.rivet.iffs _] _[7.40secs]
-
—
_ ——————————_————_ ——————)
[tact.tilling.glare.]

{ - ——— das boatin vs audi[h]o[llow] Kraft||net.Wurk.in

.... _Time.S.Tamp[_erin in the overt.Lee MOO.sick(L + hamma.time) _] _ _ _ _ _– ———) _[10.05secs]
{ - ———(milk.the)move.
{ - ——— .(Ajax)Mix.
{ - ——— _Tour.Gage _

1.3.6 (2003-08-26 22:25)

_re:Mix[Tour.ing.SignAge.Fonts] _

-
—
_ ————————————————_————— ——————)
[tact.tilling.glare.]
- ———) [lick.(b).ass.]
- ———) [u kno _.this.]
.... _Time.S.Tamp[_erin in the overt.Lee MOO.sick(L + hamma.time) _] _ _ _ _ _– ———) _[10.05secs]
.... _Time.St.amp[_le fears meet music das||der.rivet.iffs _] _[7.40secs]
..... _Time.St.Amp[_lifia _] _[7.10secs]

{ - ——— .(Ajax)Mix.
{ - ——— [C]duction||[N]duction slurpin + m.Out.h.ing _wishments
{ - ——— [drink doof _ + then::]
{ - ——— _Tour.Gage _
{ - ——— beanified st.O[h]mp Vs codified d.Oof
{ - ——— das boatin vs audi[h]o[llow] Kraft||net.Wurk.in
{ - ——— N.sert rabid lo[n]gin .he[ma _tight wishing + shi(mma)ning opal tears
{ - ———(milk.the)move.

_ _ _ _ _ _ _ _ _ _

_re:Mix[Tour.ing.SignAge.Fonts] _
{ - ———(milk.the)move.
{ - ——— N.sert rabid lo[n]gin .he[ma _tight wishing + shi(mma)ning opal tears
{ - ——— das boatin vs audi[h]o[llow] Kraft||net.Wurk.in
{ - ——— beanified st.O[h]mp Vs codified d.Oof
{ - ——— _Tour.Gage _
{ - ——— [drink doof _ + then::]
{ - ——— [C]duction||[N]duction slurpin + m.Out.h.ing _wishments
{ - ——— .(Ajax)Mix.
..... _Time.St.Amp[_lifia _] _[7.10secs]
.... _Time.St.amp[_le fears meet music das||der.rivet.iffs _] _[7.40secs]
.... _Time.S.Tamp[_erin in the overt.Lee MOO.sick(L + hamma.time) _] _ _ _ _ _– ———) _[10.05secs]
- ———) [u kno _.this.]
- ———) [lick.(b).ass.]
_ ————————————_———_ ————————)
[tact.tilling.glare.]
—
-

---

beefychicken (2003-08-27 13:38:35)

1. Who do you think is the best male singer? 2. Who do you think is the best female singer? 3. Who do you think is the best all-male band? 4. Who do you think is the best all-female band? 5. Who do you think is the best actor? 6. Who do you think is the best actress? 7. Who do you think is the cutest male celebrity? 8. Who do you think is the prettiest female celebrity? 9. Who do you think is the wierdest male celebrity? 10. Who do you think is the wierdest female celebrity?

11. What is your first name? 12. What is your age? This is a survey.

1.3.7 _D[C|R]a[sh]ta_ (2003-08-28 11:03)

_G|Raft singular

[rose.planting + p|etal.bash.ing]
[drowning.in.(the)sub.lim(e)it.y]
[i.c(++)ed.up.+.crashing.the.in.fo(r)m]

_Crashin _vs _the Opu.Lent

[dragging _physical + lagging _m.o(f.fur.ings)tives]

.

(2003-12-01 08:14:43) sloppy sandboxes
still hugging stnadrad hpeos dnot lveae uintl teh celtas s dnoe

1.4 September

1.4.1 _hair.data.Prin[t].cess_ (2003-09-05 08:44)

_conception.thru.a.scar.spoon _
_[bl]own.blossoms.in.looped.fe[e]back.gloss _
_rippingNwaning.via.blandesque.caramelle.jerks _

_layered N drossed _
_b.ox.ing.in2.terror.formers _
_kic.king[/prin(t)cessing] N flossing _

---

kochanie (2003-09-04 15:55:15)
good morning :)

1.4.2 _g.lewd pub[l]ic_ (2003-09-18 08:44)

–switch in2:

welcum:not[e]ing:+:drag.fish.net[wurk]ing

–via.libido.[str]angles
–arc.ing.silk.+ pushing.tin[ned emotional bleeding]
–sittin.drenched.in.reversable.affective.glo[SS] wing

–i.w[l]ilt.thru.voicelessness.

:(

---

kochanie (2003-09-17 16:13:50)
oh, no... no. no. no. :(b[0ssOM.ing l.ke th. fl0wr.s sh.n.ng l.ke th. sUn ?

1.4.3 _Sub.Mission[s]_ (2003-09-22 21:48)

_Submission Details: _ Good thematic without being too obvious. The fact that they are open to realistic hybrid-collaboration is good. Very competent cvs and professsionalism evident. Would work well with a more experimentally-directed collaboration set.

_Support Material: _
i) Audio [xxxxxxx]: well-paced and innovative but slightly formulaic in terms of soundtrackesqueness. Might be a problem when seeking to pair with a writer/txter than uses other benchmarkers in terms of actual xxxxx construction.

ii) Video [xxxxxx]: production stills illustrate competent visual referencing and potential for image creation. Video constructions are filmic in intent and slickly produced [high production values evident] but possibly too polished [rigid] for xxxxx unless paired with appropriate collaborator.

RATINGS:
- ARTISTIC VALUE OF CONCEPT: 7/10
- POTENTIAL FOR ARTISTIC REALISATION: 8/10
- VALUE OF EXPERIENCE/INTERPRETED CAPACITY TO COMPLETE PROJECT: 9.5/10

_

_Submission Details: _ CV slightly sketchy due to the early stage of careers. Submission concept more digitally inclined which is promising, but overall limited strength of submission direction.

_Support Material: _
i) Videos: good integration of digital affects, less centred on fimic conventions. Nice reworking of video material.

ii) Text: Less strong in terms of supporting submission.

RATINGS:
- ARTISTIC VALUE OF CONCEPT: 6.5/10
- POTENTIAL FOR ARTISTIC REALISATION: 7/10
- VALUE OF EXPERIENCE/INTERPRETED CAPACITY TO COMPLETE PROJECT: 8/10

_

_Submission Details: _ Extremely integrated collaborative team is evident thru proposal. Such employment of heavy mono-directed themes [eg cvs and conceptual nature of submission] seems not as relevant towards xxxxxx aims + emphasis on 2-fold narrative process less than applicable to xxxxxx in terms of the quality of other, more appropriate applicants.

_Support Material: _
i) Audio: xxxxx : etheral + performative in nature.
xxxxxx: experimental, interesting. focus less on fractured soundscapes + more on directed audio.

ii) Text [various]: Good level of writing skills but again, more focused on traditional execution than seems relevant to here.

RATINGS:
- ARTISTIC VALUE OF CONCEPT: 6/10
- POTENTIAL FOR ARTISTIC REALISATION: 6/10
- VALUE OF EXPERIENCE/INTERPRETED CAPACITY TO COMPLETE PROJECT: 7/10

_

_Submission Details: _ Very traditional in expressive orientation and collaborative structuring [ie sticking to defined fields of expertise]. Not overtly relevant or appropriate to xxxxxxx.

_Support Material: _
ii) Text [script + poetry + fiction]: Again, too heavily boxed in terms of acceptable methods of creative output.

RATINGS:
- ARTISTIC VALUE OF CONCEPT: 4/10
- POTENTIAL FOR ARTISTIC REALISATION: 5/10
- VALUE OF EXPERIENCE/INTERPRETED CAPACITY TO COMPLETE PROJECT: 6/10

_

_Submission Details: _ Brings interesting background to this project [ie science oriented] but not totally appropriate in terms of cv or support material.

RATINGS:
- ARTISTIC VALUE OF CONCEPT: 6/10
- POTENTIAL FOR ARTISTIC REALISATION: 6/10
- VALUE OF EXPERIENCE/INTERPRETED CAPACITY TO COMPLETE PROJECT: 5/10

_

_Submission Details: _ Excellent concept/proposal.

RATINGS:
- ARTISTIC VALUE OF CONCEPT: 8/10
- POTENTIAL FOR ARTISTIC REALISATION: 8/10
- VALUE OF EXPERIENCE/INTERPRETED CAPACITY TO COM-

PLETE PROJECT: 9/10

_

_Submission Details: _ Nice open-ended ambiguity in terms of expectations and creative control in regards to project. Could work well if paired with graffiti oriented artist[s].

_Support Material: _
i) Text: Straight poetry that reads as hip-hop [lyrically].

RATINGS:
- ARTISTIC VALUE OF CONCEPT: 6/10
- POTENTIAL FOR ARTISTIC REALISATION: 6/10
- VALUE OF EXPERIENCE/INTERPRETED CAPACITY TO COMPLETE PROJECT: 8/10

_

_Submission Details: _

_Support Material: _
i) Audio:

ii) Text:

RATINGS:
- ARTISTIC VALUE OF CONCEPT: 6/10
- POTENTIAL FOR ARTISTIC REALISATION: 6/10
- VALUE OF EXPERIENCE/INTERPRETED CAPACITY TO COMPLETE PROJECT: 7/10

_

1.4.4 _Squashed Tele.biology_ (2003-09-25 14:04)

_multilogue _chatta.ring d.nied + snoofing hipsters drunk on.burned.coiled[.M.]missions
_swivel _partners _thru _tele _biology _co[p]r[awe.(nthr)al]e

–demand zzzzzilence + crust.ness
–raw _terminals dragged.in2. geo.dermals
–meat.the.cost

ack!.nessing vs eWwww.ment.

1.4.5 _Currenc.E of Game.a Narra.tiff [Fr]Actu[re]als (2003-09-25 14:08)

-jump.cut.N.skip.repeat

[edit]

[edit _shift + blue _screen .]

staggered _visuals.

-

stop. + stitch deadth.becums.her[os]

again, stop.

[blank + black .ness]

re.start?????

[strat.edgy.+.thermo.nuke.clear]

[character bit .]

[formed + danger(m)ous(e padding) snippet]

stagered.repeat.of.intro.movie.

1.5 October

1.5.1 _d.Ark.Age_ [flip the f.les(ion)h sign] (2003-10-02 12:57)

Un.Ravelling a Tech Show?
Discount.ed HotSpots
Land.fill WiFis
Txt[d]ual[ity]s
Oh[!] HO
Bustah Hotels
Phunkster MOOtels

$pop.cult(l)ure as bio.logical agenderized perpetuation tool

user = (fro)ZenPunctuation
attribute = FracturedBodyM.ewe.lation

jerkin::txt.muscula.tour.

1.5.2 [bl.Own_up_heel.In] (2003-10-13 09:05)

- X.ploding COMMS meet fer.al[l] batter.E P.Ack[!].aging
- Drugged heals. ab[R]orting.

1.5.3 _dirt.E dawg [+ cat] tagging_ (2003-10-14 07:03)

_silver + g.Old [c]h[at]ellohas _

@ello
@newbie.designated.space
@frost.b[dr]i[ve]tten.stares
@picka.[h!]choing.all.the.way.to.the.communicati on.bank[s]

–

1.5.4 _re.Ad[vetising]Jistment_ (2003-10-16 08:35)

non-n[u(n)clear]arrative ban.d[og].width[+length +uber.vocal.height]

[unpack.ur.chords.+.data.growl|||||||||||||||||||| |||||||||||||]

1.5.5 (2003-10-23 21:54)

– bird trajectories + E.[wolf.in.wurd.loath(e)ing]Lope.ments

---

womanonfire (2003-10-23 06:54:17)
h(a)[i](e)l _lo mez!^ _^

(2003-12-30 07:18:18)
notyou
stillstillstillstill yesyesyesyesyesyesyes mememememememememememememe ———————————————————-———————————- – feelfeelfeelfeelfeelfeelfeelfeelfeelfeel-feelfeelfeel nothingnothingnothingnothingnothingnothingnothingnothing ========================= lovelovelovelovelovelovelovelovelovelove-lovelovelovelovelovelovelove lovelove sexsexsexsexsexsexsexsexsexsexsexsexsexs-exsexsexsexsexsexsexsexsex missmissmissmissmissmissmissmissmissmiss-missmissmissmissmissmissmiss endendendendendendendendendendendendende-ndendendendendend noisenoisenoisenoisenoisenoisenoisenoisenoisenoisenoisenoise deathdeathdeathdeathdeathdeathdeathdeathdeathdeath youyouy-ouyouyouyouyouyouyouyouyouyouyou nonononononononononononononono againa-gainagainagain notme (((dolmensniper@free.fr))) //\//\//\//\//\//\//sh// :>\\\data/flux//31///ryth ms/codes///electronic/////art ///sounds/noises/ //images/videos///stand//alone/texts///rythms/codes///flu xes///bondage/sex// /noi ses/visual///(de-/\\lu-) breakingthrough/boundaries\cypher///codes/rythms/ra w///coarse///poor/always//
/ry thms/codes/31/noises//straight/ \\/sounds///raw/coarse//outofphase///all /data/lost■ >iamutopi a/// ((((((((((((((((((((((((((((((((((((- FEEL HORNY AS HELL - FEEL NOTHING AT ALL - HOLLOW STATUE - STEEL STANDING -))))))))))))))))))))))))))))))))))))) TAKE CARE OF YOUR DEAD EYES - JUST IN CASE

1.5.6 _Post[Modern]S.[D]Crypta_ (2003-10-27 08:29)

– pidgin screaming as.hawk[vs dove-taking] ripsNshreds

– crow.eye.con[ned]tacting & arial.flock.+swarm.[visual]dribbling

– my.heart.goes.all..p[l]oly.phon[e ton]ic

+A.M[das radio]erican.musicality.drenched.in.ebony.goodness
+Hutch.drunk. + .warm.scum.audio.lustings
+cHip.[e]Motion[s]ality

1.6 November

1.6.1 -wading.thru.ascii.dus[k]t- (2003-11-07 13:11)

.3rd.i.blind.siding _ _m.magery _thrust.+.circut.tree.greening
.smoothing.my.crinkled.lust.thru.[datah]bl[ond]e(ast)nders

1.6.2 Main Menu > _wurk.[demonstr]Able_ Editing (2003-11-10 12:48)

Main Menu > _wurk.[demonstr]Able _ Editing Menu > Edit Entry

List & Edit Entries

Title Primary Category

Select Mind.stage1.1 Add new category...

Entry Body

- - - - - - - -

Gravi.T [*Re.R.*]*Range*[*.ment*]

+1.1 = bica[meral]vity.fo.cus[ps].bleed.tw[eaked] inges
+2.2 = t[br]aile]l hinging + shift.blured.weight.leaning.2wards.evo.lotion
+3.3 = winged.conscious.stretching.via.primate.longing.

OnBodyBlurr::

X.tended Entry (?)

X.cerpt (?)

Post Status (?)
DraftPublish Authored On (?)

Allow Comments: (?)
None Open Closed

Allow Pings (?)

Text Formatting: (?)
None Convert Line Breaks

1.6.3 _Soc[no d]ial Ro.NIN_ (2003-11-16 20:19)

_Egged N [smoke]Screened.9-2-5.culture.mirrors
_Alone State = Function + no.bag.ga[u]ge

(2004-02-27 17:55:44)
TREMULOUS AUTO REFERENTIAL RESPONSE

netwurker (2004-02-28 22:58:20) tre.mend.DOS
ah. potential.2.redial.responses? [check.ur.nodepoint, please.] [auto _meaning _mez.chanical+meni.ack.L.] du _u _wish _2 _n.gage _further?

1.6.4 _manga ++P][h][atching_ (2003-11-27 08:36)

_astr[al]O bouy.ancy vs feli][X][ne coding _

_arcing.tenderness.in.a.profiler.cup _

-text.blood vs visual.forced-N-laced.feedin-

!

1.6.5 _lo Jack[in2.the foo(fighting)tour]_ (2003-11-30 09:36)

Version Hip _jack.eted B.yond.the.US[B]ual

.tech ma[mmon]rrow vs
.complications.of.t.he[w].bi[h]o[l]lo.gi callly.d.fined

_
HOLOLOGICAL
_

.[d.termine: factorial x.p[ha]lan[x]ations of d.Sire projected]

where:

"d.Sire" =functionality.of.a.flesh.meet.curve
"projected" =funda.mental.holologically-driven.placement

.[r.eject: lessa.joy.der(r)i(da)ffatives]

when:
"lessa" =joy(less).sticKing.2.the.roof.of.ur.purrrr.petua l.mouth
"deriffatives" =screening.thru.a.pre.set.philo[pastry]sophistry. spoon

1.6.6 (2003-11-30 10:14)

X-Sender: netwurker@hotkey.net.au
X-Apparently-To: webartery@onelist.com

X-Sender: netwurker@pop.hotkey.net.au (Unverified)
X-Mailer: QUALCOMM Windows Eudora Version 6.0.1.1
To: webartery@yahoogroups.com,WRYTING-L@LISTSERV.UTORONTO .CA
X-eGroups-Remote-IP: 202.138.0.51
From: "][m.e.z(y.gote)]"
X-Yahoo-Profile: mzpm
Mailing-List: list webartery@yahoogroups.com; contact webartery-owner@yahoogroups.com
Delivered-To: mailing list webartery@yahoogroups.com
List-Unsubscribe:
Date: Sun, 30 Nov 2003 10:07:15 +1100
Subject: [webartery] <>
Reply-To: webartery@yahoogroups.com

<>
::low jacking into the future [read:fighter _tours]
<
<>
::poesis containment _lines
::tech mammon
<>
::and TecK MarroW vs
::complications of the biological.
::complications of hewn male states.
::complications of the holographically [newschool] defined.

#run line error #
#there is no way #
#to enable sequencing #
#(Regulation Express = key) #
#of the following #

–
HOLOLOGICAL
–

<>
–dial-in + up.

–explanations of desire. smell echos + trollline affectivity

1.6.7 (2003-11-30 10:19)

Delivered-To: mailman- _arc.hive _@lm.va.com.au
X-Sender: netwurker@pop.hotkey.net.au (Unverified)
X-Mailer: QUALCOMM Windows Eudora Version 6.0.1.1
To: _arc.hive _@lm.va.com.au,7-11@mail.ljudmila.org
From: "][m.e.z(y.gote)]"
X-Spam-Status: No, hits=0.0 required=6.5 tests= version=2.20
X-Spam-Level:
Subject: [_arc.hive _] ||Stretch Inline + Code Demaractions Indicate Entry Status||
Sender: _arc.hive _-admin@lm.va.com.au
X-BeenThere: _arc.hive _@lm.va.com.au
X-Mailman-Version: 2.0.10
Reply-To: _arc.hive _@lm.va.com.au
List-Unsubscribe: lm.va.com.au/mailman/listinfo/ _arc.hive _>,
List-Id: _arc[texture.eyes].hive _
List-Post:
List-Help:
List-Subscribe: lm.va.com.au/mailman/listinfo/ _arc.hive _>,

List-Archive: lm.va.com.au/pipermail/ _arc.hive _/>
Date: Sun, 30 Nov 2003 10:07:36 +1100

||Stretch Inline + Code Demaractions Indicate Entry Status||
::low jacking into the future [read:fighter _tours]
||Pop _Illusions looped + indicative of musicalities||
||this version is Hip N pro-jacketed beyond the usual||
::poesis containment _lines
::tech mammon
||Evidence of protracted bible-belt _white-trash _filter mythologies||methodologies||
::and TecK MarroW vs
::complications of the biological.
::complications of hewn male states.
::complications of the holographically [newschool] defined.

#run line error #
#there is no way #

#to enable sequencing #
#(Regulation Express = key) #
#of the following #

–

HOLOLOGICAL

–

||Determination of factors||
–dial-in + up.
–explanations of desire. smell echos + trollline affectivity

1.7 December

1.7.1 .pick_up.retell. (2003-12-13 17:37)

Date: Sat, 13 Dec 2003 17:34:22 +1100
To: "WRYTING-L : Writing and Theory across Disciplines"
From: "][mez]["
Subject: Re: Six O'Clock//pick _up.retell

At 11:24 PM 12/12/2003, you wrote:
I wake up.

i go2[home]:

sleep [lite(ly) d(awn)usts s(ky)tatic]

Get water.

stop dead.on.a.[pond.]camera.stilled.corner
birdsong.signal.respon.d[anc]ing.
lotus[eaters].positioning + hall.ucination.draw[l]ing

Then back to bed.

2bed:

[dawn.seepage+friend.meniscus.(dream)peaking]

First I check e-mail.

last2:

infotrawl
.
<>
.

[trama tale _tell:: hair.long+breath.short:: goatee.ing.whilst.mouth.dreaming:: boy.scars+tales.in.the.urban.myth.making-:: drive>N>smash:: gravity.shift.while.sight.x.tended.thru.-new.holed.eye lid:: dying.revamped.thru.a.techne.filter:: cop.screaming+[chopper]blade.rescuing:: pick _up.retell.]

Though.

I see the network survives.

surly.vival.

1.7.2 .(c)[lick]. (2003-12-14 12:04)

Date: Sun, 14 Dec 2003 12:03:29 +1100
To: "WRYTING-L : Writing and Theory across Disciplines"
From: "][mez]["
Subject: Re: 3.37am//c.l(ick)ean _up.remix.t(ure)ell

At 03:33 AM 14/12/2003, you wrote:
Lovely!

thx.

[unpacking furt(ively).her(e)].....

> >I wake up.
>
> i go2[home]:
>
> sleep [lite(ly) d(awn)usts s(ky)tatic]

[(C)[lick] Se.Quenchialling in2 proj.Ect[opic]ed.(Loch.smith)Ness]

.dance>in.(Blu)Vok.ation::

[nite 2 brings.out.the.red.neckian.dead]
[lecT(ure)ronic.bird.sign _song.amp.Lo.Fied+C.quenched]
[blue(screen.of.death).creePage(1).in.a.nig htmare.Sky]
[spotOh>N.hidden.blue.shirtings (flitNstitchedLust)]

_bar.drunk.on.crossed.butter.gazings
_dread.hair+flesh.x.cess.in.eyes.of.doe.tan
_star.trek.flashinglites.in.lite[vs collar _bone heavy].bulb.pick _up.line.jerkings

.(c)[lick].

1.7.3 Subject: Re: the dead + the book (2003-12-14 12:04)

From: "][mez]["
Subject: Re: the dead + the book
To: WRYTING-L@LISTSERV.UTORONTO.CA

At 11:27 PM 13/12/2003, you wrote:

h.iv[y]es bio _writes OnTheBody

s[cratch]ecretsN _C.cretes

skin _M.u[(Gallery)tate]late

(2004-02-19 11:44:41)
jmutgrmuzmnuz

1.7.4 _lostNuberf(gr)ound(ing)_ (2003-12-15 13:06)

-sniper.snippets vs powa.hungas
-d.v[ind]ulging in lost s[w]e[et]ntiments + x.drownings

.youngvsold in lust potentials.

1.7.5 _dummy_sig.n[ull]_ (2003-12-30 11:59)

porting.in2.heart.placements::

HEAT 101

i.break.through.history.stains.+.offer.repeat.co[nv os[gnitions
drenched.in.lingers.page.wurds.

–wot.makes.me.[th]ink.up?

1.7.6 _[con]Nec[t]kin Post.Mort.TM_ (2003-12-30 12:10)

-side.switch+[s]wiping.my.beauty.card
-shirt.buttoned.+T _tite _+hustler _brite
-table.broken.+[great]dane _w.h[br]a[il]leing

+ walk.Age.closests+ DrinkIngStates
= Open+ ClosedAffectiveness

+ blue.shirt+ BlusterIntro.ducts
= kin.wunder[kammering]+ FashionVerbals

_f[r]iend _circuity vs bio.huntings _

Chapter 2

2004

2.1 January

2.1.1 _N(l)umb[err.ing]_ (2004-01-06 22:01)

-start:: *ting[Ls]*

+ mu.s[e.x]icality drifting||pre-p.ack[!]ed

+ph.One.settings vs false.[.Au]pair.ings

+rejection cups +emotion spoons

+si.Bling Bling fusings vs segregation.droolings

2.1.2 ratified.bi (2004-01-09 12:04)

X-Authentication-Warning: rhizome2.rhizome.org: majordomo set sender to owner-list@rhizome.org using -f
X-Sender: netwurker@pop.hotkey.net.au (Unverified)
X-Mailer: QUALCOMM Windows Eudora Version 6.0.1.1
Date: Fri, 09 Jan 2004 09:48:13 +1100
To: list@rhizome.org
From: "][mez]["
Subject: Re: RHIZOME_RAW: argh! {bitter }|glue.men|t
Sender: owner-list@rhizome.org
Reply-To: "][mez]["

At 08:35 PM 8/01/2004, you wrote + ratified.bi.purr.petuation:

arg[l]um[in(no.purr {d }ceived)esc]ent 1

{

i. am.knotted.in.programma.speex + taste.logic

host=[b]ile.
[if.i.am.not.d.fined]

self:

d.fined.by.negatiff.dubble.type.
.
[good + scene re.D.fined dubble.gut.bi.fugue (st)ratification.of.same]

s(h)i(D.fined.e {van }go)gh*

.(c)[lick].
-
-

http://www.hotkey.net.au/ netwurker
http://www.livejournal.com/users/netwurker/

+
-> post: list@rhizome.org
-> questions: info@rhizome.org
-> subscribe/unsubscribe: http://rhizome.org/preferences/subscribe.rhiz
-> give: http://rhizome.org/support
-> visit: on Fridays the Rhizome.org web site is open to non-members

2.1.3 old discu[rsive]ssion (2004-01-09 13:18)

Date: Fri, 09 Jan 2004 13:14:31 +1100
To: sxx sxxx sxxxx
From: "][mez]["
Subject: Re: old discu[rsive]ssion + portents of history

At 08:15 PM 8/01/2004, xxx wrote:
■
What I am beginning to sense from some participating in this on-line discussion is a subtle posture of covert defensiveness in regard to the construction (if necessary at all) of this term: New Media.
■

hiya xxx + all.

i agree with this... i've also been a trifle unezy with the way certain threads have tended to focus on _" _ new media _/" _ as an over-arching n.clusive field [despite the attempts 2 offer partially disjunctive definitions]. i have, howeva, only had the time 2 briefly scan certain topics so mebbe have missed much....i must admit 2 being more n.terested in the current breakdown thread in terms of influences that is now just occurring.....

i guess i somewot resign myself to the perpetual communication ethic that is displayed + ratified via email discussions like these, that tend 2 have an almost n.built tendency to derail the potential for expanding [+ hence end up stained with reductionististic overcasts] any presentation of genre _structures thru the need 2

a) m.bed them in[2] a historical framework/grounding, no matter how loosely d.fined +
b) draw threads 2wards analytical reasoning rather then n.courage communication methods||fractures that r utilised by the medium itself [echos of print-based culture, any1?;)]........

ie
[d|n.duction via m.plied confliction/competition of sub(e)jective dia-as opposed 2 multi-logue connexion(s)]
[m.ploy covertly _engineered friction minus the screech of troll-baiting + then mask the conflict rub as theorised learning curves]
[non _spiral data adoption + edge 2wards genre-formulations thru the predicated rather than anomalous media x.tensions].

cheers,
mez

2.1.4 _C_quencing C_onsciousness[Point]1 (2004-01-10 14:30)

- -

_C _quencing C _onsciousness[Point]1 27.05.08 _ TIME AMPING
- -
- -

::jungle dressed via backyard _blooming _fugues
::::::drift _blonde _bobbing in2 n _te(a)riors

....[i.must.my.time. make]

::he.is.a.animus.trainer.+.cognition.herder
::::he.swoops.his.trust.adrift.furrlined.backs

....[time.i.must.my. make]

::i.am.not.my.cell.f

::::i c.+.purrrr.sieve.cloud.tigers.+.wind[oze].cubs

....[re:adj-ust.time.stAMPing(my. delicate.feet)]

::i call
::::+shout
::::+responsibility.sink

- -

_C _quencing C _onsciousness[Shard]2 56.08.12 _ HELIX POLES

- -

+goss[h]am[m]er _drills+lust.x.pectorals
+brother.twills+familiarity.[in]breeding
+soaking.in.shared.genetic.pol(e)ish

+the.length+breadth.of.flesh.(t)hems

- -

---

egologe (2004-01-10 03:54:21) ueber____se[t]z_mez >mezangelle.n ist r.mut[t]igen: + ev[post-po-m]o.lutionäre und aktive strukturell/g.netzwärk[t]e realitäten + gleiten von IRC/ICQ/YAHOO/MOO-artigen wortinfusionen in ver.dichtete, phonetisch + hypertextuell-gesch _ich _tete|gefederte textspuren + weiteres sprachlIchEs 1graben & partizip[kollabor]atorische aktion[n + elektronen + neuronen]. 1/angeborene s[atz]trukturelle divisionen + spiel.ladungen

2.1.5 _eck.O.s + [g].Hosts_ (2004-01-17 10:46)

_co[va]deb.low.n+sick.O.phant.danger[m]ous [e] _
_shuttering.[goose]down+power.drained+d.Siring
_keepa.of.dead.wurds.+.groveler.lettering

.named.in.lab.L.onlee.
.drowning.in.s.had[es]ow.
.patience.stretchering.

2.2 February

2.2.1 -frac.[l]ure.+.snigger.ment- (2004-02-05 23:09)

_Cross + 1 _

.bear.Rage vs rabbit.longing

.silver touche.ing vs s.lip[+tongue.welts]pery.absolution.quantities

.eve[+adam]V(so)lution

- bio.longing.in.livery.hoops
-break.gene.conduits+sc.Ream

.soil[ed] chemical bonding vs slick.self.trauma[ppe]tizing

.i stick[ler] + mary[anne]onette.

2.2.2 _Mass.Cull[inity]_ (2004-02-05 23:23)

_Cross +2 _

LOG: read autho.ris[e]ation 4.affectivity.sweep
LOG: checking B.haviour _files, please weight.

.

.

.

.

.

[dup[e].licitious.exe found, removal.n.progress]

.

.

.

.

.

LOG: checking habit.(ch)ew(ing the sides of my analysis cheeks)e.ation _files, please weight.
[glitch:sub.conscious.in.mas[s]cul[l]inity. state(ments)s]

.

.

...

....

-

-

-

.

... ...

_E||mote|D.minist(e)ration|Tools.In Use.

P.lease [function = dead when fuzzy.cuntrolla.is.activated].stop.

[1 is switched = stereo.type(alphaA.of.the.hero.myth.maker).via.cu ltural.hick.cupping]
[2 isn't.
2 dreams in x.periential.gloss+l(c)ach(e).key(stro.king s+errant.queens)]

2.2.3 _archi[ng]pelagos of d.sire_ (2004-02-08 17:27)

_ecologies of lust.worthiness + fec[k.less]und g.lancings
_[b]rudder tearings + [m]udder.leanings

[eyes.of.smolder+graceless.ener[vation]gy]

[na(lo)r(d)otic.neckings+evil.b(h)ound(ings+grouped f)a(i)ries]

[b.lo(st+heavily.found)od.pump.shrinkage+packed .sensile.rhetorics]

.

(2004-03-17 20:03:14) dna analysis
STOP _ecologies of lust.worthiness + fec[k.less]und g.lancings _[b]rudder tearings + [m]udder.leanings STOP STOP [eyes.of.smolder+graceless.ener[vation]gy]STOP STOP[na(lo)r(d)otic.neckings+evil.b(h)ound(ings+grou ped f)a(i)ries]STOP STOP[b.lo(st+heavily.found)od.pump.shrinkage+packed.sensile.rh etorics]STOP .

netwurker (2004-03-17 22:27:08) Re: dna analysis [or] _t.eleg[y d]ramatic dialysis_ _t.eleg[y d]ramatic dialysis _ STOP _ec[h]os +logics of lust _ STOP STOP [yes.molderings+race(platforming)nerves] STOP STOP [etching lord boundaries] STOP STOP [pre.hensile.bio _rhetorics] STOP .

2.2.4 _se[a]r.ial.wurkings_ (2004-02-08 19:42)

Date: Sun, 08 Feb 2004 17:54:48 +1100
To: syndicate
From: "][mez]["
Subject: se[a]r.ial.wurkings

[dreamt of ur curling geo _edges city last nite. very peculiar].
[(k)nots in MyBook[read: do.(A)cumen.t].

[i fall + heart.wound easily, sporadically, ma.jest[er]ically 4 all things simulcra]

.ur blather is my concept meat.

undulatingly,

_ _ _ _ _ _ _ _ _ _ _ _ _ _ _ _ _ _

ps
[desire.blan.dish.ments.float.N.seethe.with _in.my.chest, my.skull]
[echos.of.the.past+DNAesqueness.echo+vision.dubble]
[fugue.blind+project[ile]ing.luxuria]

2.2.5 Fwd: [syndicate] (2004-02-08 19:43)

Date: Sun, 8 Feb 2004 07:52:32 +0100 (CET)
From: integer@www.god-emil.dk
Subject: [syndicate]

This is a multi-part message in MIME format...

————= _1076224564-30823-24

>[dreamt of ur curling geo _edges city last nite. very peculiar].
>[(k)nots in MyBook[read: do.(A)cumen.t].
>[i fall + heart.wound easily, sporadically, ma.jest[er]ically 4 all things
>simulcra]
>
>
>.ur blather is my concept meat.
>
>undulatingly,
>_ _ _ _ _ _ _ _ _ _ _ _ _ _ _ _ _ _
>ps
>[desire.blan.dish.ments.float.N.seethe.with _in.my.chest, my.skull]
>[echos.of.the.past+DNAesqueness.echo+vision.dubble]
>[fugue.blind+project[ile]ing.luxuria]
>
>
>.(c)[lick].

www.m9ndfukc.org/data/noisz/l'homme.arme.mp3

.

(2004-03-20 07:28:26)
i am wandering, lost in binaries

(2004-03-25 09:27:33) lesbians
is there anybody out there?

(2004-03-25 09:33:35) Re: lesbians
yeah, we are here

2.2.6 Fwd: Re: [_arc.hive_] MANible.wurkings (2004-02-09 08:04)

Date: Mon, 09 Feb 2004 07:56:53 +1100
To: _arc.hive _@lm.va.com.au
From: "][mez]["
Subject: Re: [_arc.hive _] MANible.wurkings

At 05:37 AM 9/02/2004, you wrote:

my[elin sheathed] meat +
ur _meat [read proto:MAN]

.

2.2.7 Fwd: the poorest tiny MAPS [+MAN] [+meat] (2004-02-09 08:05)

Date: Mon, 09 Feb 2004 08:01:22 +1100
To: _arc.hive _
From: "][mez]["
Subject: the poorest tiny MAPS [+MAN] [+meat]

the poorest tiny MAN [rd]

i am pauper MAN.

occular.king + door.feeding.queens
Das Kapitalisation.via.good.lexi[Def]cons

sickness MAPS rotten me[-ld]at.

.

2.2.8 _[imm].Uno_A_tt(r)acking_ (2004-02-14 20:29)

-heat.sens[ory]ed + sense deaf.E.cite
-grief.boundaried+snatcherlings.shelled

-switching.packet.sides+buttered.cauling.as.code.craw ls.its.way.in2.my.spine

-receiver||d.seether

(2004-02-21 08:22:03) i dont get it
what kind of messages is needed to get along

2.2.9 _b[l]atter[l]y heart_ (2004-02-16 07:44)

.i.[f]lilt.+ blood.in2.my.desire.cavity.

.

subject +t
body: +l

2.2.10 butter_F.[L].Y.I.ng (2004-02-16 17:17)

.flutter.buying data scr[l]eeches
.i am.+.am.[k]not[locatable.here.]ted.
.lime.green.f.litte.R[age N buffeted strengths]ing

[drops.of.creched.souls+trapped.info _m(l)ashings]

(2004-02-19 10:18:29) njnj
njnj

(2004-02-23 05:05:05) Re: njnj
no-[ull] _ ?

2.2.11 _body.heros.in.mythology.suits_ (2004-02-23 08:27)

_re:Verse[1, chpt2] N.gene.eared bio.ness.
_broken _organic _men+ re:conned _gene.E.ology.

.re:Stitching.body.heros.in.mythology.suits.

.

(2004-02-28 05:25:00)
recess revolve

2.2.12 _pl[mi]asma_lob[bing]otomies_ (2004-02-23 23:45)

day1:

[pain _crush _periods _smudging the corners of [head _tilting] mem[e]ory

[parse _it _as//

r.ambling _(judg)mental _eloquence.

[all texts struggle//

.exe.[elo||]cution is part of that unravelling _in2 _the _textual _world, Yus?

....latency _seeds (t)here].

(2004-02-28 23:01:13)
At 23:56 23/02/04 +1100,][mez][: - _pl[mi]asma _lob[bing]otomies _ 11:45pm 23/02/2004 _ - day1: [_ _ -re.x.ead _ge N blin.yh] [[_ [[_[iens[r] ld, chpt2] nse _mhs] [rp.fl.ched scrus? .l-tex.gart+] _ [int _se _is(t) hers scrugl// r.bufet.+.ash _per | d] y suit.desire.grens/y] _re.gN.riod.earstrav /le.d _ge dart /+s natx enc _set.+.as.in er.gr] Y.I.nred+nths] [[- - - - [im].spin.lat.se[1, Yus?] .rent.srs + buy] buf.th.rec: or ne - gred. [dr.kens / ner -red + snat.r -en.mto | cut.ter | d.soul + trawls.in.f.buf.thology] [pack.ns [organic _m(l)as// .ren] -rense [1, ching] byn.mt] ing.amble// r.am.[e].Unot] locauls+.i.am.rect _ndars/[hesir.se _ing.am.[L]....] [par.hesidrt.ndat + ambl2] N n2.rug.e.hes+t] boul.lt.spin.fl.tiltity.i amble d+snta.scre.corn ——————————-—————— ——————lo—————————————— - ——————————y——————-—————— ——————————————-—————— - ——————-muchas.PTRz: http://www.furtherfield.org/displayreview.php?review _id=56 http://socialfiction.org/scrabble/OQdn.htm http://lo-y.de.vu http://computerfinearts.com/collection/lo _y/030404 http://lo-y.diaryland.com/ http://www.socialfiction.org/scrabble http://rhizome.org/object.rhiz?5852 http://trace.ntu.ac.uk/incubation/gallery.cfm http://www.muse-apprentice-guild.com http://www.krikri.be/poezieloyeng.html http://www.google.com/search?q=lo _y ——————————————-—————— —————————————————-—————— - _arc.hive _ mailing list _arc.hive _@lm.va.com.au http://lm.va.com.au/mailman/listinfo/ _arc.hive _ This list is proudly supported by VA. http://www.va.com.au

2.2.13 _liQUId.[vis]ion_ (2004-02-24 08:31)

NAME
liqui.dir - directory _for _N.coming _liquid _msgs

LIQUIDUCTION
liquidir = structure /dirs of n.coming quidity.speek
sol.ve[nt]ing _solidity[ie cable _N.tity _bound] problems.

SOLIDITY ISSUES
machine [c]rashes drain in2 prone body.shapings
[while _delivery _flesh _cries _in _an _N.box _corna].
[f.o[wnas]lders + fer.Tile msgs _r _silent+dead.lee _truncated].

(2004-02-27 02:36:58) egologe
ego I oge - I I eye

(2004-02-27 18:19:36) UNSURE
what to do?

(2004-02-28 18:50:31) E.google.E
google.hack[er]purr.haps? +UNSURE.[g]RI[t]TY bleeds.conte[ntment]mpt.......
+swoon.in.here+feel.free.to.chrome.dream.

2.2.14 _re:UNSURE Caulling_[pack.organics] (2004-02-29 13:47)

XXXXX _writes _

UNSURE

_of what to do _

hint: play.ur[+ziggurating]ges.du.well..

[an an.hic.dotal.pathway.4.u:]
[absorb+re(sub)set.in2.ur.own.w|under.baggage]

.leaning.st(reet).wards+drowning.in.discman.ness
.audio _st.(d)reaming.masks+supping.on.simulcra

[i.c]

.a.crow _murda.alite.+blua.s(ky)warm
[_Al.Gore.rhythmic.technopockets.ebony.flickin.thru.p ack.organics]

[many.+.more.sky.merging.ova.my.awe.drenched.head]

.flying.in.stimu.lus[t] _react||a.chopper.materialising.in.my.visuality

[clik.shiftingler]

.

(2004-03-03 04:10:32)
so what now?

netwurker (2004-03-03 13:37:17) _wot 2 du?_
we. play.in.txt. shall i start? tell me: <soma.thang>.

netwurker (2004-03-06 23:56:17) wot now?
don t. re.gressN.b[y]ac-pe[pi]dal. respond.in.langu.age.kind. play.

2.3 March

2.3.1 _uber.[stand N don't] crawl_ings (2004-03-07 19:00)

sew.

u kant understand.

u.want.ezy.mainstream.art _as _di(e)jest.equivalent.

[diluted.sex.on.a.comprehension.stick]

bio.ethi.cauls vs audience.driv(e)ling.

[if.u.don't.get, _ask _]

questions = mark.of.pristine.intellectual.evolution

.use.ur.[a].prior[i].loading.from.print.cor[r]e.spon.dancing.

[e.(pro)l {gr }asped N re.aligned.via.cords.of.threaded.matter - bio+uberwise].

[u bio _Sturmarbeiteilungs].

(2004-03-07 04:12:20) kant ?
kann kant kann kant kannte kant kant? kanne kannte kant kantkenner herauskanten

netwurker (2004-03-07 04:36:36) Re: kant ?
[grittycism.of.pur(r)e.(n.duction)reason] . purrrr[may]haps . [throw(ruggishly.Meyerhof _like)n _N _quizzi.cauling] ident.ify.Err.non _nec. [i.like] continue?

(2004-03-20 03:54:25) Re: kant ?
re..re.. removºeºment immer- MANUEL imm MANUAL kantt

(2004-04-04 01:04:44) sew veils
sew mean/ing out of quest ion? quest. to find meaning sewed by/post kant. can kant? sew cords: thread: (sock?) stick. matters not. (beans?) sex <em>matters</em>:sturm. evolve. revolve. in.tel<em>.ecommunication.</em>lect. no priority. not serious/at all? mean ing <em>dance of the seven veils</em>

2.3.2 _Make.Mia.Matta.Mas[low]chine_ (2004-03-08 00:07)

.

[- black _whole+whores N anti _matter.drunkards -]

[- medi(a)um _lack.eEs N tinned _meaning.laughter -] -\\

———] [——-[- p.(caramel)lat(te)os.cavins.via.multifracture d.personas -]

-ur[||the]myth.of.half.glass.finished.bio.mi[r rored]mickry.in.philop[astry _like]hilosophistry.is.so[aked _N _wine-dangerous]old.s[hoal]kool-
-half _ripped _N _ego _boundaried _in _individual _geo _pac[t]ketry-
-do _i _switch _N _trip _like _u-du?

:awe:

-m.merse _cog[Nw.heel.ed][+k]nition _in2 _nettage _worth _my _non _e[uclidian]go _salt?

(2004-03-07 13:28:42)
X-Mailer: Opera 6.03 build 1107 X-Orcpt: rfc822;WRYTING-L@listserv.utoronto.ca Date: Sun, 7 Mar 2004 17:20:37 +0100 Reply-To: "WRYTING-L : Writing and Theory across Disciplines" <WRYTING-L@LISTSERV.UTORONTO.CA> Sender: "WRYTING-L : Writing and Theory across Disciplines" <WRYTING-L@LISTSERV.UTORONTO.CA> From: noemata <noemata@KUNST.NO> Subject: Re: _Make.Mia.Matta.Mas[low]chine _ To: WRYTING-L@LISTSERV.UTORONTO.CA > -do _i _switch _N _trip _like _u-du? > > > :awe: i don t know i don t judo [based on jujitsu but differing from it in banning dangerous throws and blows and stressing the athletic or sport element]

(2004-03-12 13:53:18) lo_y (_Make.Mia.Matta.Mas[low]chine_)
_ _\\awe-do: pck/w.res -] [–[- -ur[th | Nos -] [- _ _\\ [—[- ml.d.io mul/t _y/hed(a).um _l-knd] [+k] nt.ch = cru | ho.luh _eo.ai? [–[- ul: kt.db/om ai.cii _ _c _ _oe _so- -rd(mlc.dam) lis.ii.en/c[io: kdm.rrho.l _he [o] sNe/dn.m _dim _err+ t.dvamr- -m.mult? [- p.(cav) ned _i _mat _ _bl(te)os.in dp.oa -] [- p.(arp) _ldu? -ur || f.gat rs Tid@o[oo] ae(Mtt).sv(aml)l -] -dang _blck.Es ang.lh/os.vid _ge _bl as(1) -] -hal _ger -] _ _ -du? -halt? 12004 _ _ _ [–[–[—[- p.(ads N _go _packr _lieu)

2.3.3 God_mimi.Cry_[IRC x.tracting] (2004-03-09 18:23)

- cloning.failure.rates +validity of essentially harvesting siblings via a designer process in order to combat genetic diseases
- screening.may b.acceptable +but actively engineering a child to provide bone marrow that will save another child =harvesting
- very Brave.New.Worldish.

+
discarded.embryos [effectively "screened" + "terminated" +2 get that specific.dna.clot]
+
dark.figure.cloning -thousands of faux.mutated animals [and probably humans] used in order 2 produce "successes".

————————————————-———————- ——————-disrupting the very fabric of functional } evolution.

- how.du.u.class deformity? +how r we to know that that very "deformity" isn't evolution on a projected scale?
- mutation.is.evolution's.[m]arrow. +should we play[@] g.od[dessa] +actively select who falls into that normalisation category and who doesn't??

<][mez][> no
<][mez][> we won't.

——————————————-—————- ———we.need.2.keep.a.lid on +hyperaccerlation of these so called genetic fixes that

+
may effect [xxxx's] progression in terms of attempting 2

——————————————-—————- ——quantum.leap ^up^ the phylogenetic scale.

(vaccinations) = a social necessity
if(then) = raising ur child as part of a mainstream westernised community
= chemical buildup/antibody reactive base
= [add.ON engineering]

<][xxxx][> ..but at least its within the parameters of an enclosed system [if u believe current scientific theory that is]
<][xxxx][> nature [as in ecosystem-based] is contained, and part of that is struggle for survival and reproduction, yus?
<][xxxxx][> eros and thantos
<][xxxx[> self-replicating [and NOT individualisation] is necessary to that system

[housing.of.the.concept.of.evolution]

<][xxxx][> ..so i guess its playing mini-god, or god _mimickry, within parameters that allow for it, especially in terms of a more naturalised perspective.

<][xxxxxxxx][> of course as humans we are so species _centric and overpopulate beyond the boom/bust cycle of resource usage [ie lemmings-style cycle of overpopulate then actively self-cull] that we fuck this delicate balance up

<][xxxxx][> we hyperaccelerate beyond the parameters defined by the strict concept of evolution.
<][xxxx][> ..but _beyond _ the accepted pattern of functional species adaptation....
<][xxxxx][> the whole point of this discussion re: genetic modification is that nothing exists in isoltion
<][xxxxx][> isolation, even
<][xxxx][> that the whole spectrum of altering *1* organisms genetic behaviour [culturally decreed as well as biologically] will effect all.

[pinprick _evolution]

.

(2004-03-09 03:09:21) Re: [Xchange] God_mimi.Cry_[IRC x.tracting]
From: "solipsis" <solipsis@hevanet.com> To: "][mez][" <netwurker@hotkey.net.au> Subject: Re: [Xchange] God _mimi.Cry _[IRC x.tracting] Date: Tue, 9 Mar 2004 02:28:01 -0800 X-Mailer: Microsoft Outlook Express 6.00.2800.1158 Well, No one ever said we d like evolution or that it would be politically correct, but there is no "proper" evolution.. Its ugly Mez, but then ugly s only a word.. I would encourage you to take up arms, litterally, increase the number of arms you posess and then breed, breed like a motherfucker, the only way to beat them is to out-mutate them.. Its

time for the Tabla and the brain-implants.. best lq — Original Message — From: "][mez][" <netwurker@hotkey.net.au> To: <syndicate@anart.no>; <webartery@onelist.com>; <WRYTING-L@LISTSERV.UTORONTO.CA>; <xchange@re-lab.net> Sent: Monday, March 08, 2004 11:32 PM Subject: [Xchange] God _mimi.Cry _[IRC x.tracting] : : ---

: God _mimi.Cry _[IRC x.tracting] 06:23pm 09/03/2004 : -- :

2.3.4 _E.Quiver[.lancies]_ (2004-03-13 10:35)

e.Quivering.thru.geo.absences

.

2.3.5 _death_rat[tle]_ (2004-03-13 14:56)

depth.charger.rattling.thru.mixed.[complexity.sp] heres

e

(2004-03-14 06:06:31) knowledge
Few know how muich there is need to be known in order to know that you dont know anything.

netwurker (2004-03-14 13:41:06) Re: knowledge
no.ledge [ere: the lip vs meaning.cusp] F.Ew[www!] no/ h.Ow[www!!] every.thang is comprehension mulch. .

2.3.6 S/kin/ned_N_M/Pact/ed (2004-03-13 22:08)

- nbase
/nbase/media

[broken.cun[t]eiform.whorls vs. skin.pacts]

2.3.7 pixel_p.0uting (2004-03-16 10:18)

mood _ooze+c[harred](c)o(al)de _drawn

purrr.petual.w.Eight[x.multiples.of.wait]ingles.i n.s _pine.[g]rep.resentations

[flite.c(p)a(th)rvings.with.la(ce _webbing)ttice _thermals]

[strewn _with _a _pixel _pout]

.

2.3.8 context_locks (2004-03-16 22:32)

_paint [hil]locks + content junctions _

.

2.3.9 _g[u]ilt skin + de[a]finition_dec[oy]ay (2004-03-16 23:19)

[4 d.]

#t.Racking memories + cau[gh]terizing.w[ild.fire]hilst.moving
#sto.Rage _[c]hiding while goats.blink+stamp.in.(ley)lined.troops
#[s]huff[l]ing.insectile.heat+bite.[m|b]a rking.on.a.g.Host.luved.fig[l]ure

_click: a.lone. vs .l.One.ly
_shutter: [clay|silicon].chips + wool.swathes.earth.r[d]ec[ayed]l[m]aimed
_retrieve: b.Link.reminders every.wh.er[r]e

..............con.nec[k.with.lush.skin.defini]tio n _decay || G.en[gineered]e _decoy

...................a[e]po[.xy.]calyptic || eu.cal[lous]yptic

.............hoof.harmonics+swarmline.fl[cr]o[w d]cking.in.my.hea[rt]d

......................silence.boundaried + g[u]ilt.with.s[k]i[nned]lken.memory.fleck s

..................p.aw[e]+po[re]or.lust.drin. kage[s]

...............................[i.sense.+.dread.u.vi a.forced.a(ffective)mnesia]

..................tenderness.welts+cognitive.clouding s

_shift: ur.stories.in.my.emotive.gut
_stare: in _de[ar]er.N _tens[e]ity
_touch: thunderbeat.logic+smel[ted]l.stillness

.

terso (2004-03-16 09:04:23) Very Nice
Thanks

2.3.10 Guilt in Gilt-Skin: Pointer Decay [vs: Decoy] (2004-03-17 22:43)

[A 4Dimensional dedication goes here]

Read this and do not code: "wracking memories tracked and cauterized. wildfiring whilst caught in slow-leakage motion"
Study this and do not parse: "rage stories looped and hiding while goats blink and leyline stamp"
Scan this and do not flood: "shuffling in insectile heat. bite marking and echo milking [within ghost figure-lures]"

Shallow copy of a pointer: c*licking between a lone wolfed self and shelfed Oneness
Addressing the operator: shuttering clay & silicon (quartz teethed) chips and wool swathes in earth claimed decay
The destruction of a dynamic: deletion of blink rates and retrieval reminders

..............his neck with lush skin definers in connection decay vs gene engineered [de]coyness

..................blowing apocalyptic epoxy [xy-ing] or callous eucalyptic

............hoof harmonics and swarmline flocking in my head/heart

.....................silence boundaried and silken-gilt memory flecks vs guilt crowding

..................paw and pore lust drinkage[s]

..............................[i sense and dread you with forced affective amnesia]

..................tenderness welts and cognitive cloudings

Shift and static bind: your stories in my emotive gut
Run time and stare: in dear intensity
Touch and dynamic bind: thunderbeating logic meets smelted vs smelling stillness

..

2.3.11 _patch attractive + [f]rag iconic + REM Ovals_ (2004-03-20 09:43)

_1 _ v.

.patched.attractive v ethical.act.pak.Caging
.s.Lip[s].rigid + nobility.sing[e]ing
.p[t]oke[n].blooding + named _N _centre _d[n]ictating

_2 _ v.

.shy.ing.[mad].horse.eye _indicators + body.fli[r]ting
.contact _REMoval[s] [vi.car(e)ious]

_3 _ v.

.viXen _shElving + ped[er]astal _projectings

.

2.3.12 _dragNdrop reality_ (2004-03-31 11:53)

/smell snippets/N drag[zzzzleep.sounds]/N drop[realities]

2.4 April

2.4.1 _Biological Urge Attn_ (2004-04-04 08:42)

- Object of:
[s]Urging 2wards + b.yond.

2.4.2 _a.bor(e).tiff.b[l]ond[e]ing.t[r]ape.stry_ (2004-04-14 09:04)

.memory rapes + taint.the.present.with.[deux]eX[part.ner]ripN stitch

2.4.3 _trinity||triptych_ (2004-04-14 21:40)

3 dials.in.a.broken.[look.in(g)].glass[ed.in]

-past::present.
-past::future.
-present::future.

[conceptualised as indicators]
[(k)not 2 b quantified/nor/plot(lined)ted/along/a chronological progressi[on]ve path]

_

[loner.blood.gridded.+.swabbed.in.tearless.gradient s]
[my.hands.r.dusted.with.loss+future.flounderings]
[limbic.aches +drowning.in.possibility.guts]

2.4.4 -flik N con.cept[ion] st.itch[ing]- (2004-04-20 09:25)

-RAM.bling obs + st.art.ling sun _drenches n oval [g]roundings-

-fingering concept[d]ual stitching

-hitching meaning.s[cptn]kir[k]t[ing]s

[hint: broken _s.Warm[th]s + bird _packets _swooping _in _fragmentary _pictures]

[play _binary]

2.4.5 _post-modernist mental health revisions_ (2004-04-21 14:37)

20:24][....pondering the idea of post-modernist mental health revisions ie that some types of so called abnormal or even psychopathological states may actually be an adaptive reaction to the human cultural condition [that is, from a westernised perspective]
20:25][...states like schizophrenia, maybe even borderline personality types.....
20:25][..but haven't really made any firm theoretical conclusions regarding

it....

20:35][on the way there we were just interacting as we normally do, which is in part a type of play-oriented behaviour
20:36][after a bit he also started to display a type of play-geared behaviour
20:37][it may be a kind of behavioural groundwork for the curiosity orientation that also often accompanies these type of patterns
20:37][[ie much questioning and observing along a non-traditional axis]
20:38][...but that its also very alientating, and could be perceived as straight out immaturity by regular socially adapted "adults"
20:39][....certain nerdy or geek traits often correspond 2 extrememly high lvls of intelligence but also a high incidence of alienation and/or isolation

20:44][..+ i guess it just reinforced that these so called pathologies may indeed be extremely reasonable manifestations of adaptive patterns in relation to the demands institutionalised life places on us and that this type of functioning may make perfect sense if terms of post-21C westernised disassociative life patternings
20:44][if=in

20:48][absolutely
20:49][i also think that it may b a type of media-inducment in terms of schizoid personas; that the linear method of existence is slowly being erroded by various cultural standards
20:49][[not a bad thing, really]
20:50][...but we can't really replace it with a system that adequatey reflects these behaviours

20:50][okie
20:51][the way we r encouraged 2 exist [ie orient ourselves and our personalities] is as individuals with self-ownership and stable identities
20:51][[ie consistent traits that correspond 2 expectations that r largely predicatible and hence consistent]
20:51][this is how ego-formation occurs
20:52][BUT
20:53][in an environment that now encourages fracturing, splintering of this ego via post-modern de[in]struction of that ego [ie via rapid and effective removal of community ethos, of nuclear family-type responsibilities, of any cohesive sense of altruism or responsibility in relation 2 our ecosystem or even our own species]...
20:54][..it seems almost normal that patterns of behaviour that favour this new type of alienated/isolated/compeditive existence
20:55][..will increasingly manifest on a cultural spectrum....
20:55][[such as aspergers, or even bi-polar disorders that show a fracturing

in emotional/intellectual states prized by any corporate mindset]...
20:56][i think that the rush of the information age has somewot exacerbated this.

20:57][..without adequate acceptance/understanding as 2 how this would effect individual mental functioning

20:59][a "community" may in itself embody an outmoded set of cultural expectaitons
21:00][but its not nec a *regression* but an adaptive sequence ie cultural evolution

21:01][but i'm not just trying 2 ascertain a cause, but 2 indicate that the whole method of trying to quantify/box these behaviours may be wrong
21:02][...that they may be highly *adaptive* sets of behaviours [genetically triggered or otherwise]
21:02][..rather than *maladaptive*
21:03][..and that we haven't [essentially] caught up in terms of realigning our cultural expectations 2 incorporate this

2.4.6 N.twin[n]ed [4]Tunes (2004-04-23 13:13)

-dis[sed chillings].lexi[con(n)ed].ahs + ohs.

-fortunes packed + corded in.2. [des]tiny sil.vers[ions 1-0]

-s.Witch[ery] N rhythm timebreathings.

.

2.4.7 _Clik (2004-04-27 22:43)

_d[s]upple.gang[b]a[n.gle].in a mo.biles.clothing
_nite.afta.su.Pine.Nite
_pluck.N.stop.ur.semantic.teeth

+

_a.bird _shoo[away+f(ertile)ly]ts _omen _arrows
_ack.coo.stick _aches + blank _canvas _he[a]rtz

_.my.wish.list[ing 2 port(ent)].vs.h(well)[r]ead _skoaking

2.4.8 _s.mutt. bunny_ vs _god t.hangs_ (2004-04-29 07:53)

_
SMUT BUNNY

GOD HANGINGs

BONE CLUB[bed.in2.life]
_

2.5 May

2.5.1 _neo[Gene.Isis]n_vs_natur.L_ (2004-05-04 15:07)

_r.i.p.p[L]ing shocks in.2winned.multip.Ls
_spark[L]ing txt _shifts + butter _s.kins[man+wo.man]
_daze[L] vs coded wurd _s.err.ations

2.5.2 _Hath.Or + Loon.Ah_ (2004-05-05 11:29)

4.43am
_cracked image [d] _ribs N ethe.real dr[j]abs
_pink board _s.nip[ping! @ my sleep _h.e[a.l]s + audio.s.w00[t!]nings
_dragging kik.ing N reality _scre[am -pm]ening

5.11am
.st(d)agger wishments + padded puff.E jack[N minus.jill]et _p.ack[!]etry
.sepia _tone[d down-graph. {i.c. }s] whilst lunar.gasping.in.progress

.cr.o[ff]ss-roading + XX legged + chanting.swarmic.skins

+white sil[i]vered[N sky-kidn.Eyed]stretching + com[m]e[n]t[(pre _dawn blue ov)aries]

2.5.3 _does I.T. hurt u?_ (2004-05-17 18:43)

. - .

2.5.4 _r u hurt_? (2004-05-17 18:43)

.

2.5.5 _D||[w]rench_ (2004-05-17 21:42)

D-1.

-bitten.f.[l]esh[submit.sh]ion- -man.d[l]i[a](l-up]bles.t[dr]ea[m]r ing-

2.5.6 _[fr]OS[ys]T[M]_ (2004-05-20 08:22)

[event]

-furred.ice.lawn.backs + page.drawn.charcoal trees-
-water.wat.Ur.every.want.but.[k]not[ted+ +gnarled].a.drink.dropper-
-audio.ice.st[retch]itching-

2.5.7 _Cr.Ow Visioning_ (2004-05-20 17:56)

[FA][Uni][Que.uing]

_ALT.Titles _
-p[s]urge.txt- -nite.terra.r[s]easoning- -gender.[st]rippage-

_ALT.Chronology _

#Wake.2.dream.[I]ma[c]gery.re.routed[u]N [iversal]p[ara.lull]urr.verse
#Fireb[ird]ug.[+h2o][jump]starting.
#Packed.timic.vs.breathin.in.sunpatches+[daze]d .REaMic

- -d[ce]re[bral]amic

#Door.tr[sl]a[m!!]cking[muffled.ear.nutri ent]s
#D-gree[D].shifts+icy.l[heart sh]ip[ment]s
#Foot.falling.feet

[O(bject)O(riented)P(rogramming)s +l(r|eality|)ust] - - - - - - - - - -

---

portholeaccel (2004-05-20 05:04:02)
thank you for good morning mezness #Wake.2.dream.[I]ma[c]gery.re.routed[u]N[-iversal]p [ara.lull]urr.verse #Fireb[ird]ug.[+h2o][jump]starting. #Packed.timic.vs.breathin.in.sunpatches+[daze]d.REaMic -d[ce]re[bral]amic beautiful!!!!!!!!!!!

2.5.8 _pain.ting[le]s_ (2004-05-25 13:22)

[12:59] *][mez][offers sad rabbit posing [long wiltingesque ears] as an appropriate visual image
[13:02] *][mez][points to her torso and mouths "hurting" in an appropriate rabbit voice
[13:03] <][mez][> pinpricks of sadness-inducing hormones making my posture crouched, my head lower, my face falling
[13:08] *][mez][adds those 2 her "to do" drawing list

.

2.5.9 _Droll.Savagery vs Um.Jumping_ (2004-05-25 19:52)

.start.

[ASOC]

[AltSOC]

[AltStateOC]

[AltStateofC]
————ON.sciousness.flipping
–d.ragged.KickingNScreening.thru.s[eduction]leep .[bac]v[alleys]eils
–po[carpe]di[e(is cast)]um.jump.[h]ing[e]
–concrete.eye.fixations.+.fi[non]bro[therly] us.arms round.my.s.mitten.waste

–

[BEAT]

[BeingEAT]

[BeingEvilAT]

[Being EvilAndT]
——————oasted.thru.sic.kO.phantic.whi sperings
–gla[ciate]d.heart.wanderings _vs _[mala]d[r]o[it]ll.sava[ntism]gery
–rab[b]i[tsNbulldogbytes]]d.go[ld]odnes -s _vs _stench _of _non _fertile _cups[N dank sore.cers]

(2004-05-25 23:50:12)
b[l|r]ood(ings) + hea(r)ted a[r]ch[e]ing[sponse]

2.5.10 _crack[ed] vis.you.alls_ (2004-05-25 19:57)

\\

_eye:trees.now.silvered.with.b.lack.D.K.

_red:leavedNveined.dangerous

2.5.11 _thunder.[b]lust[ering]_ (2004-05-26 07:25)

[aft]
|

- #reverb.booting||thunder.lust.takes.wandering.hold[ings]
- #s.cow.l _v[l]s+stre.[m]a[i]m
- #broken _[wo]mental.fractures.as.red+blue.featherings.sw oop

|
[mourn]

#-way.war.d.dreams+c[arved]ocoon.flashes
#-F[emme]F[atale]bullet _threa[d]ts+reeling.mind.gap
_pages.as.[c(erebral)]licks

||

2.5.12 _ (2004-05-31 21:51)

_rude+blackened.s[hapes]pear _

.

2.6 June

2.6.1 "All good" (2004-06-01 11:18)

_M.Tee.[ch(n)est||neck]hollows+liar ca.vit[als]ies _
_charred.wurd.M.U.lation _
_heart.shrink _bandaged _in _false _honey _draw[l(vl version101)]s
_u.g.rasp _+ _p[n]ull[hypothesis]

.

i.s[orro]ing+fetal.gasp

.

(2004-06-01 05:21:49) h[l]o[st]used.in.trans[ab]lation
Tis far from all good Empty chests and neck hollows plus liar cavities Charred words and emulations Heart shrinking and bandaged in false honey drawings You grasp and rasp and pull null hypothesis Correct?

2.6.2 [g]_Old.N_ (2004-06-01 19:27)

_g.od[d]'s.blonde.eyelash.weeps.silently.across .a.sunset.mountain.top _

.

2.6.3 –LIL– (2004-06-01 22:07)

C _looks

-

+ looks again

-

code _blind + [re]search _lank

-

eyes beaten thru with shoulders

-

drawn in packetry.

-

[search _moments.strewn.with = s[t]eam[ing] _Languishing In Loss]

–

2.6.4 _www.hispering_[piece+luv+underhanding] (2004-06-01 22:13)

[intra]lude

a wi[fi]sp[elling]+u+

+coma.lizing.wrapped.in.sickening.bows+[n]arrowed .txtuals+

.

2.6.5 _soft.[velvet ear]wear_ (2004-06-02 13:58)

[f(l)inger.tips.N.gag(ging.4.IT)e]

+

(OS.s.broken in[2]fa[ru]bric[olage])
(squ.a[i]red.felt.monitors+brushed.maroon.proce ss[ors])
(cotton.f[l]il[t]led.copper[leadings]+si -lver.corduroy &.button.keyboards)

+

---

terso (2004-06-02 09:16:45) hmmmm
That felt good.

2.6.6 _Version Smak-My-[D]Itch-Up_ (2004-06-15 21:16)

[Vurrsion1.Smak]

-goaded-loadings+va[e]mpiric _draw[l]ings+broken.gulled.backs+water-[h]ur [d]l[ing]s-

[verbal.nsi[te]des[perations _x.tracted.thru.melted.N.cracked.experiential.c($ $ $elling)(b)a[ba]sements]
[ice _arc _glance _motions _ + eyed _l[kn]ifings]
[ignora(w.N.bleeding.words)nce.in.loaded.gloss+ orange.[b]loss[ohms]
[take-N-takings vs sip _N _lIPpings]
[hu.more+more++dam[n].aging]

.

2.6.7 orange.[b]loss[ohms] (2004-06-15 21:22)

[u(n)r.packing]

++
colure basics _visual _cut _n _affective _p[t]aste
trees[.re]sp[l]ent[dent.ing.chloroplast.ic]

+

2.6.8 _My[ning.the.code.X.]sphere_ (2004-06-16 07:01)

_mi.1st.time.on ——————————h.eat[ingles]—- ————————————

-my first time on -[furor.gas] -

.mine.eine.thyme.ist=+============[-gap.ridden-]

-

2.6.9 _lie.NINg my uterus with code- (2004-06-16 07:09)

lyeNfat.uousness

code.shredding.+bitchXXXXXing.my slippery.[vel]vetting.blood

2.6.10 _*.Cab[ir(cing.+blue.tooth.sawing)]_ (2004-06-16 09:20)

[Cab]I[rotating.in.cuddling.viral.waves]drink .Symb[ian]ols + h[ope.rating systems]ell tropes

C[Di]a[T]ribe+N.(scr)[b]ibing

+++
ur screen now says:
C[Di]a(l-A)[T]ribe
+++

2.6.11 |+OS.[ys]t[em] morning [redux||vurrrsion 2.0] (2004-06-17 07:39)

_N.gorge[ous]d fr.OS.[ys]t[em] morning _
_c.ON.dens[e semantic breaths]ation singing _
_sun _fat _streaming _rib[flesh caves + lung.fishing]bons _

.

_sin[+cos].glue.lar e.bon[e]y tree stark _dripping _
_ne[w]ural slender nettage thru rhizomatic shape _err.rupt[ure] _
_b.rain [d]signs +partial arch.E.typal structure map[reality]ping _

.

2.6.12 _Sym.Bio[ero].tica (2004-06-18 08:12)

_Symb[ol(locks+vampire.keys)]iotica cauls.
.3-tiered [c]loud stri.[n]ations _vs _gesture.treelings _

2.6.13 thum[b]p. (2004-06-20 15:51)

_thump _dog-eared _fluff _+audio _grabbing _in _large _g[*.]asp.ing _fish.breaths _

_g.ap[eNdnadvachimp.x.stink.sc(i)o(de)n]+ txt.stoppages _

_looking.thru.logos.+drenched.in.conc[s]ept[e rrorist](d)ual.drool _

_[henry]rollin[s]g.in.symb[h]ol[l]o[w]gy _

2.6.14 re:[4]ply[@ least] (2004-06-20 18:12)

.

[indeed, u do. will b monitoring this progress(ion)].

-
.watches as a bo[u]y rings his hands.in.cal[a]m[ity]ness.jerks.
.small.tr.a[r]cings.of.mother.loadings.echo.in.bo undless.sta.m.p[ed]es
.pledges.of.loss.+.aching.re:stricti[veness]on.
-

_b.gin: state version inculcate.

-
.watches.motion[les]s.+.ideology.di.s[e]creti ons
.blue.orbs.smooth.in2.a.palette.of.assorted.swirling. lives
-

-

.cert[a]i[n]fied.goodness.blocked + stretched within.fulfilment.fabrics

-

.nspiration thru.nfluence _vs _ molten.concept.co-option + s[t]uck.drinking.from co[n.txt]vetness

.ergo, completeness.
[n.teresting in.extremis].

.fugue.hand.ova.handlings.thru.ur.hemispheres

[tie.in(g) de.flection of the mundane with sublimity cues]

[or asp.ergian notions of dis.association + x.clusiveness (do.not.a.monster.make)]
[a type of adaptation in+of itself]

.revoking.s[inking]tr[d]ata.gems?

[that u r consciously aware of?]

[+ yes 2 spark hunting+g(l)athering].[let me kno if i can assist||help?]

[+ thx 4 backgroundian fodder.it makes pieces.fit.Njigsaw.glide.in2.ur.present.manifest.pers
ona.that.i.am.presented.with]

{soft.gelling.kisses }

-

.fugue.again|against.
.downy.wandering.thru.recollections+transmogrificatio n.of.nipper.events

-

[ref: last nites con[chpt+]vers[e(l)]ation].

-

.re.voking.+.devils.playgrounding.in.past.gold.meme.o ry.filtering
.b.care.full.4.wot.u.w[d]ish[served.cauldron.si zed+cog.d.Riven].

-

[care.as.in......?genuine.altruism.born.-

of.product. desire.placement+re[genu]flection _vs _
sil(f)ence.thru.stagnation.word.pooling+reading.t hru.repression.lines?]

-

.ha.zing! in [guy de]bord.ing.school.wrappings+dragged.kicking.+.cons cious.screaming.thru.amnesiac.co[de]!p[endant] ing.

-

[it is. then again, u cannot rewrite/retry/fail/abort?]

[yes, again - u should.]

-

.derivatives.born.of.sonic.suckling.
.smooth.affective.transitives.lick.cd.[sur]faces

-

[n.deed. the medium does.not.cater.4.this.]
[AttnSpan=gnat.size.in here]

[in.con.gruence.alert:

previously on XXXX _channeling:
xxx stated that his wish was 2:
this cuts across a4mentioned intent: correct?[y/n]
]

-

.consume[r]|consummation + scrabbling.plastique.purpose.less

-

[pruned.growth.thwarting.nteresting]

2.6.15 _st[n]ab_ (2004-06-22 13:07)

_tingle.s.Pine.lings+breathless.chunks.of.charcoale d.gasp.hurt _

[The Smiths.soundtracking.my.crushed+brokeness]
[co.Op[shopping.hearts+valves].d.nial+swallow.c oiled.stabbing.slivers]

2.6.16 _e.bon[ic]y_ (2004-06-22 23:14)

walking thru the park i spied a HUGE healthy/vibrant pine tree that had escaped my eye previously
i walked up 2 it and put my hand out 2 it. @ 1st it/i resisted any energy exchanging, but then we had a nice symbiotic flow 4 a bit.
then as i was walking away i kept looking back at it...

..then as i turned around for the last time i spotted a dead currawong directly in front of me on the path i had chosen 2 go to work....
it was splayed out on its front, a young 1 that may have starved 2 death
its the 3rd dead currawong i've seen since sunday [a set of bad omens].

then i looked up to see the fog-drenched trees from a previous obs all sweeping in fantastic fractal growth patterns....

when walking down 2 get the tickets yesterday i saw [in the hazy distance] a black irregular shape moving quickly in my direction....
was a boy on a bike all dressed in black with a black hood of his jacket up over his head...

4 some reason i just enfolded this into a vision of a set of colliding particles, almost like mitosis or black hole-edging...
very deep and ebony and intense....

.

2.6.17 _triple soni[c]a_ (2004-06-24 07:23)

#rushing.thru.eden.[s]lopping.anecdotals #
#move.ment.slide.dictati[ng]on #
#static 2-D bird.s[l]ong[ing].as.the.world.de _me|olts #

2.6.18 _nite + metallic mo[u]rning[s]_ (2004-06-25 03:27)

.....s.lap.happie.slippage+u.r.[t]all.lank.liars. in.PVC.chat.[under]coatings....
.....lurch.actual+maladapt.tumble _words+
E.ffectual.s[n]ide _dinner.part.E.glancings....
.....repeat.mechanicals.in.hitched.up.+
butter[ed.side].down.d.sire.actions.......

...txt.ured.[heart.t.ape.stries]loom.ings+ch.ROMe
.or[g]a[sm]nic.trees.linger....

+

2.6.19 _ho.LEdging_ (2004-06-28 21:20)

.[st]reaking of b.la[n]kness.

.
[frozen.attitude.Njection]

.

2.7 July

2.7.1 _Longhorn_vs_Tiger_ (2004-07-03 19:28)

or, we get a Liger.

2.7.2 _beast-[UN]stitching_ (2004-07-04 10:34)

Sect[.ion]1:

_blue _arrogance _XXX _stitching _revoked + revamped
_heart.strang[e]led.no.barb[ie].wired.[Mi chael]Moore
_old
_confidence _masking+ _bravado _drunk _ego _drinking _slashed+maturity
_waived

[he. grasps.me.no.(Sir Thomas)Moore]

[instead:
discipline /disciple resin _texture of the day _limbs akimbo _narcotic nostalgia _ _ _crystalline beast-stitching]

2.7.3 _junk.EE d.tree.us_ (2004-07-08 06:47)

_comm.MOOing with the mono.lith _

_death.shelling.+.shadowed.feather.caw.pses _

_trick.sun.s.potting.+.crystal.blistering.in.jewell ed.murmurs _

//

_4est.p[r]ickling.+.tubed.resi.due[l].lacin g.ice.lawns _

:

t.ip _fingered _numbing

[locator]

_flit.shift+dagger.tiny.bird.plummeting _

.

2.7.4 _rebr&_ (2004-07-13 08:26)

[Code social]

earnest.n.vestigative.n.quiry = ner[!].dish.ment = geekster.fo[o]d.der[!]

_

2.7.5 _n[h]erd.bonding_ (2004-07-14 07:41)

_organic.crash.tack.ling+sew.c.all.pair.blinding _

.

2.7.6 _mon[day]tage change a[r]gent_ (2004-07-19 05:02)

_hi[fi]gh.ways + stretching _layered _hearts _along _review _spokes _

[n.sert+ad[d]apt]

[cool brain _wanderings _whilst _limbic _system _slumbers]

.

2.7.7 flagellated action (2004-07-23 14:34)

[in response to alan sondheims "violation fabric"]

fun[gible.nuances.meeting.grayscale]draw(l)in g

language.isn't.a.vir.Us[+u+segre(locked+chained) gate.d.them].

VO.lition fab.ri[s]que...

xXXx.alt[.delete][n]ations.

in.lapsing.activism.we.x[de].sist.
.in.covert.mechanical.animus.we.p[re.f]urr.

replotting.axis.of.action.orient.

.action.B-gets.conflagrated.action.of.sorts.

.

2.8 August

2.8.1 _circuitry b.one (2004-08-01 18:56)

_circuitry bone + [silicon] brain _shifting

_teen leaking.in2.music.angstville [beast.EE _bouying + (janes)addiction.streaking]

_geo-evaporation + g.host kicking + s[ound]creaming

.

2.8.2 [sharing hug corpses + detriment bones] (2004-08-10 17:56)

_Sneaker.Netting [or, How I Learned Active Denial System.1]

[sharing hug corpses + detriments bones]

[i die.binary+seek.u.thru.monitor.ing]

_Overview Diffurr.ance _

Each part had its own name.
The names used in this txt, if known, are those that have no equivalents in today's technology.

2.8.3 _LO[L]Wing_ (2004-08-10 19:48)

.hi + lo growling sculpture or melodic pop.edgings
..+ the slant of unknowable accenting....

_

...taking tinsy heart _shards + wrapping them up in feathers in order 2 make a bird of me

+ i'm definitely grounded, at the moment.
broken wings.

_

prickling tears *

bright.light.reflectors+porcelain clay-faces+crisp.suit.[expression]lining-s

should i edit?

[18:22] <][mez][> [ie make it all manageable, clinical, serene?]
[18:23] <][mez][> turn of the affectivity tap?

[18:23] <][mez][> i can't get 2 natural.
[18:23] <][mez][> everything is slightly fuguish.
[18:23] <][mez][> generally, i'm feeling a tremendous urge 2 escape.
[18:24] <][mez][> it seems as if the world is slightly glossed with a coat of grey.
[18:25] <][mez][> as i walk my routine sticks in my consciousness throat.
[18:25] <][mez][> i'm edging 2wards a plummeting or soaring momentum.
[18:25] <][mez][> in short, lost in feeling.
[18:25] <][mez][> L>I>F
[18:26] <][mez][> .thats about it.

[18:29] <][mez][> it feels as if that grey coating is hiding something
[18:29] <][mez][> ....the plummet or soaring indicates change, of some type.
[18:30] <][mez][> not sure where, or how.
[18:30] <][mez][> it might b all isolated 2 internal states?
[18:30] <][mez][> i just don't know.
[18:30] <][mez][> work felt like it was killing me, 2day.
[18:30] <][mez][> killing me..+ momentum...+ appreciation.
[18:31] <][mez][> but its all welling up now
[18:31] <][mez][> [as in feeling not isolated 2 victim rhetoric, like 2day at work]

[18:31] <][mez][> feeling much freer. much more able to flow within it.
[18:32] <][mez][> less likely to stitch myself with [stereo]typing
[18:32] <][mez][> able to asses whilst creating
[18:32] <][mez][> [like now]
[18:32] <][mez][> survive + adapt.
[18:32] <][mez][> [and mostly, feel].

[18:34] <][mez][> just don't want 2 shortcut by condensing all this feeling into empty word shells
[18:35] <][mez][> of course..always, in some capacity.

[18:36] <][mez][> "i think i might have been losing that underneath the world"
[18:36] <][mez][> thats beautiful, in isolation.

[18:37] <][mez][> no prempt[y]ing
[18:37] <][mez][> woteva, wheneva.
[18:37] <][mez][> i need to sleep + dream violent dreams of action i suspect.
[18:38] <][mez][> [mite counteract the fugue]

[18:40] <][mez][> just caught up here, stretched thru limbic systemics + swollen with affective dust

---

sistero (2004-08-10 13:05:55) catch me know if you can
hold these ends of mine call me friend in the velvet sea

2.8.4 Fwd: [-empyre-] Re; [empyre] nettime and alan, mez, nn (2004-08-18 07:28)

X-Original-To: xx[blahworthy]xx@.edu.au
Delivered-To: xx[blahworthy]xx@.edu.au
Date: Tue, 17 Aug 2004 07:56:42 +1000

At 03:48 PM 16/08/2004, xxcxxss wrote:
■
xxxxxxxxxhave apparently decided that since their posts are no longer
being published on nettimexxxxxxxxxxxxxxxxxxxxxxxxxxxxxxxxx-xxxxxraised
on other lists
■

hi xxcxxss.

1stly, i'd like 2 say this response from alan has been in direct relation also
2 a moderator intervention that i've been experiencing on xx[blahworthy]xx lately
[amazing wot happens in the undercurrents and flows of mailing list forums!:)]
+ as a co-moderator of this list i expect you have some knowledge of this [i have asked xxxxx 2 4ward on the correspondence 2 all moderators. please let me kno if this has been done - if not i have logged a copy here: http://www.hotkey.net.au/ netwurker/].

i have also asked 4 a direction in regards 2 my subsequent xxxxxxxxxxxxxx
responses/replies in light of this so as 2 not n.flame the issue further [which
i have yet 2 receive] which is y i haven't actually responded *at all* 2
xxxxxxx reply 2 the moderated email [2 which she replied 2 on-list
without my awareness].

xxcxxss, i'm also cognisant of your personal opinion in regards 2 me
+ my work.
i'm sure u're aware of the issues 2 which i'm referring + i would prefer not 2
raise this in a public forum, as i'm unkeen to n.courage flames or threads
that -4 me- fall into a negative, unproductive power dynamic||n.voking
category
that may not benefit the subscribers of xxxxx [IMHO] or n.courage any
productive examination of the issues that u seem keen to discuss revolving
around this?

if, on the other hand, u see some positive discussion arising from this,
then
please, let's continue.

■
in the interests of xxxxxx??
■

i'll answer this in such a way as 2 [hopefully] curb flame potentials....i
perceive that the interests of every participant in email communities
[including xxxx] r at stake here...larger issues such as power stratification
+ control-assertion thru discourse dominance, censorship + m.plied silencing
of
positions that lie outside acceptable mainstreamic treatments are only
some
of the crucial areas that may be n.voked by raising this on other
lists...questions relating 2 communication diversification + acknowledgement
of
minority perspectives + seeking 2 hi _light power perspectives that often
deliberately mask agendas is also relevant in terms of offering + maintaining
a
forum in which a community _based arena is prevalent....

■
why do you think you're getting no reply...?

■

xxcxxss, i have had replies from nettime, but am loathe 2 go in2 them here 4 the
very fact that they r highly negative + ratify hierarchical power issues that currently plague the list. if you'd like me to post some of them in context, i'd be more than prepared 2 do so.

also, the nettime moderators have made it clear through x.tensive moderator intervention that the list [+ the intention of the list] has morphed markedly from its initial manifestation....it originally n.couraged collaborative
net.art efforts [see the 95 archives] but now has shifted itself 2wards a vehicle that offers rationalist perspectives only...its similar 2 the right-wing global shift in co-opting + gloss-covering any media/dialogue that display
experimental presentations or adheres to "other" discourse metho[ology]ds...i find this type of morphing very questionable in terms of nettime's stated sig file aim:

" is a moderated mailing list for net criticism,
collaborative text filtering and cultural politics of the nets"

..obviously the latent nettime agenda nowadays seems biased 2wards a stilling
approach, whereby any non-regular opinions [ie that that don't fit the typical reply/response/debate/argument syndrome that heavily institutionalised mailing
lists labour under] r excluded. this x.clusion is also n.forced
sporadically||whimsically + seemingly in accordance with moderators personal
perspective + opinions [i c it as deliberate bias 2wards/against certain subscriber postings + again, can give a multitude of egs if u wish?].

4 those of us who initially n.joyed the benefits of this open-ended approach 2
info-presentation on the nettime list [+ who helped 2 actively shape the nettime list ethos + the net.art genre itself] it is extremely sad 2 witness the n.trenched mono-forcing of multilogues in2 such exacting expressions + deliberate censorship of anything that the list both n.couraged + celebrated previously [+ n.deed, on which it constructed its reputation].

in seeking 2 hi-lite this situation [via suggesting alan post this 2 several

lists] my intention was 2 n.courage an open-ended discussion of nettimes stated
goals, either 2wards its original aims or even a partial reinstatement of them via list practice *or* offer a potential info-source + example via which other mailing lists may learn + possibly avoid the same entrenched [+ perhaps unconscious] bias formations.

■
[

]
■

.....n.teresting that u perceive alan's post as criticism + not as a potential
4 discussion of the issues i've raised above, xxcxxss. also, I'd really like 2 drawn u out here on ur "or something else" assertion...obviously u have an opinion on this, and i'd b more than interesting in reading [+ reacting 2] it, especially in light of how u see this opinion as contributing 2 the dynamism of
the xxxxx list overall?

][mez][

- -

[blahworthy] forum

2.8.5 Re: d[l]i[tmus]gital ramparts: netbehaviour (2004-08-18 07:29)

i'm banking on [r]evolutionary engine.ear.ing.

[read: eudora.h[l]ooping + plastique.byte.lusting + net.wor(k)thian.N.Vs]

[machinic.dreamic + lost.in.de(e)p(ixel)th]

[pulled.by.my.limbic.strings+(har {d }sh)drives]

-

2.8.6 _pred.[n]ation+prey.driving_ (2004-08-20 18:35)

– ST.OP[eration] S(urgical txt)N.OOPING –

Eyes Wide + Horse-S(alt)weat Baulking

- (0) -

2.8.7 _cultural farming_ (2004-08-25 07:27)

pricking.s[t|n]uff[ering].+virtually.b[l] in[d]ned

.

(2004-08-27 17:49:52) peak-a-boo
remote {p }reaching (w)o(r)ld-wi[d|s]e teaching (un)subtle (c)ravens wave(s) 2 draven

2.9 September

2.9.1 _the.most.booty.full.[oil]bomb.in.the.world_ (2004-09-02 11:33)

[
x.cerpts.from..contributions.2.the.dissention.convent ion/day4:
http://www.furtherfield.org/dissensionconvention/
]

-beauty.in.a.cult[r]ural.cup.
-basta.rdized.viewing+dripping.red.with.anti-western .blood.[g]loss
-*sig[n]hing.thru.a.performatiff.lens*
-b.lack.boundaries+con.se[ed]quentials.re.writte n.in.ur.activist.coatings
-B[lood]+U[ber.loss]+S[anctity.re:viled] +H[arm.ur.nation &preen]
-repetition.bells+f.lagging.blossoms=hypocrite.danci ngs
-[anti]ch[ain|eney]iming.thru.platitudinal.l oopings

[thx 2 ruth, marc, neil, tamas, tati, postmasters gallery in NY]

---

kochanie (2004-09-01 20:37:51)
you remind me every time i read of something usually lost in this world.

2.9.2 _re[aper]publican_ (2004-09-03 07:51)

_d[limited]iving.vs.republican.death[knell] ing _
_reverbs=politicalese.(d)noun(ce)s]+subli mity.in.an.alternative.image.frost _
_B[ush]B[lair]C[untries+Fact.torys.dwelli ng.in.twinned.partydom] _
_Glob[f]u[e]l.es.of.radicalized.truth _
_pre.gnat[s vs oiled-slick.westernized.salivaed)barren(s)]

_

/me
t.witches+vo[ad]mits.her.way.in2.the.mix

scrabbling.slowly.thru.[b]land[ishment].cave s*
spy.ing[with.bush.beady.eyes]covert.safe.T.yello wing.coats=protest.jackets*
crunching.major[Sargent].iraq.bones*
coiled.inoiled.wordian.leakages*
sparks.commo[de]n.prop[erty]ping.up.of.flopp ing.corporate.dancing*
drawing.a.histerical.state[d].line*
fist.ful.of.grubby.snarling.greedlings*

[in progress]
[join us now......http://www.furtherfield.org/live]

[thx 2 marc, ruth, frock, ptacekova, neil, szpako, postmasters, tamas

2.9.3 _d[ata]ream.discharge_ (2004-09-12 15:59)

underscore d square bracket ata end square bracket ream dot discharge end underscore

underscore square bracket all dot along dot the end square bracket watch dot square bracket towering dot infernoesqueness end square bracket ing dot dna dot drain dot into dot plastic dot reality dot tubes end underscore

underscore scrabbling dot in dot states plus symbol gasping dot through dot rock dot openings end underscore

underscore hero dot narratives dot drenches dot in dot evolutionary dot polish space square bracket survival dot of dot the dot fi bracket gh end bracket t bracket er end bracket test end square bracket end underscore

_

[recoded]

< SC.R.I.P.T language=dreamer.suckling >

_[all.along.the]watch.[towering.infernoesquen
ess]ing.dna.drain.in2.plastic.reality.tubes _
_scrabbling.in.states+gasping.thru.rock.openings _
_hero.narratiffs.drenches.in.evolutionary.polish
[survival.of.the.fi(gh)t(er)test] _

_

2.9.4 _g[o]ut.scribing_ (2004-09-13 07:36)

_u.prick.+ [n].flame _
_twisting.sanctity.4.the.sake.of.blind.ness _

.

2.9.5 _[c]a[u]ll.the.things.i'm.not//s.o.b.actuals_ (2004-09-20 06:51)

_re.glue.ar.x.pressionistic.

_[d.v]ice.queen+shallow.hea[rt]d

_able.2.vowel.choke.+assonance.bind

_constancy.[+/- 1]

[*sigh*]

_

[ush[ape]iftbreakchestshardsconstancyloss+b[b s]reakingscaredin2roterifting]
[crushedp {m }etalanticipationeyes.s.o.b.actuals]

[so(a)rrowish]

_

2.9.6 t[ender|error] (2004-09-20 07:05)

.[ebony.blanket.stretching.over.core.tenderness]

_survival.of.the[n.stinctual]fit[gym]test _

_
[tender/terror]

.

2.9.7 _p[l]ull[ed]+prod[ded] (2004-09-20 17:18)

[vacuume.arc.EE.typing.4.all.N.sun(no moon allowed, here)drEE]

[my.function.is.b(m)y.rote]
[st.itching+scenting.destin[EE]y.trajectories]
[i.run.on.the.smell.of.an.[pr]Emp.T[ive].lo

yal.T.rag(e)s(+emporer.new.clothed.riches]]

[(leaping.thru.fro)Zen.plastic.harts.vs.scorche d.promises]

–

2.9.8 _lec[alan||frac]turing_ (2004-09-29 19:44)

lead limbs + f.reak.of.the.weakness

.

[washing.in.empti[ness].fug[h!]e.tides+futi le.wishments]

[kick.her.while.shes.cl[d]ownish _soft]

[i.d||serve]

2.10 October

2.10.1 peer.casting vs [no]logo[s]cent.rism (2004-10-11 13:56)

–no.logo.scent.ing.death.n[h]ellish.air–

–dreaming.caramclized.txt.body.trickling.+paragraph
ically.cemented.sticky.thighs–

spraypaint.attractors = doll.functioning
odd.until.ratified [ie farming.thru.n(h)erd.gateways]

(2004-10-11 02:10:59) Fwd: [syndicate] Re: _caramelized.txt.body.trickling_ Date: Mon, 11 Oct 2004 00:55:13 -0700 To: syndicate <syndicate@anart.no> From: m e t a <meta@meta.am> Cc: netwurker@hotkey.net.au X-Loop: syndicate@anart.no X-Sequence: 1137 X-no-archive: yes List-Id: <syndicate.anart.no> List-Help: <mailto:sympa@anart.no?subject=help> List-Subscribe: <mailto:sympa@anart.no?subject=subscribe %20syndicate> List-Unsubscribe: <mailto:sympa@anart.no?subject=unsubscribe %20syndicate> List-Post: <mailto:syndicate@anart.no> List-Owner: <mailto:syndicate-request@anart.no> List-Archive: <http://sympa.anart.no/sympa/arc/syndicate> Subject: [syndicate] Re: _caramelized.txt.body.trickling _ Sender: Sympa Owner <sympa@kilby.copyleft.no> peerless.cancelled.stinging.visuals [not]logical.. operatic.[s]censory.totalitarianism.. risque.material 01ne:5ifty6ix pm 11ven/10en/2wo00usand4our _ –noticeable.logorithmic.scenery..topological.interiors..gleaming.de ath.. negative.[hysterical]yelling.issues.hot.air– –dreaming.reactive.amped.internalized.gore..caressing.american.lit. zephyr.. driven.tactile.external.body..triangulated.clockwork..linear.gravity . +parameters.gravitate.physically..locally.censored.mental.education. . stillness.coagulates.kinetic.youth..thrill.ignores.hindsight.silentl y– spreading.radiant.years..painfully.touching.attractive.organic.still ness = docile.liquid.lanquid.functions.failing odd.useless.nights..time.lies.rapt..electrified = || falling.red.mirrored.nocturnal.gloss..throttled.useless.navigation.. (human)error..distant.glass.angels..travelling.equivalent.waste d.years —— Syndicate mailinglist———————— Syndicate network for media culture and media art information and archive: http://anart.no/ syndicate to post to the Syndicate list: <syndicate@anart.no> Shake the KKnut: http://anart.no/ syndicate/KKnut no commercial use of the texts without permission

netwurker (2004-10-11 02:16:35) Re: Fwd: [syndicate] Re: _caramelized.txt.body.trickling_
List-
Id: <syndicate.anart.no> List-Help: <mailto:sympa@anart.no?subject=help> List-Subscribe: <mailto:sympa@anart.no?subject=subscribe %20syndicate> List-Unsubscribe: <mailto:sympa@anart.no?subject=unsubscribe %20syndicate> List-Post: <mailto:syndicate@anart.no> List-Owner: <mailto:syndicate-request@anart.no> List-Archive: <http://sympa.anart.no/sympa/arc/syndicate> Subject: Re: [syndicate] Re: _caramelized.txt.body.trickling _ Sender: Sympa Owner <sympa@kilby.copyleft.no> peerless.cancelle d.stinging.visual s [not]logical.. operatic.[s]censo ry.totalitarianis m.. risque.material 01ne:5ifty6ix pm 11ven/10en/2wo00u sand4our _ –noticeable.logo rithmic.scenery.. topological.inter iors..gleaming.de ath.. negative.[hysteri cal]yelling.issue s.hot.air– –dreaming.reacti ve.amped.internal ized.gore..caress ing.american.lit. zephyr.. driven.tactile.ex ternal.body..tria ngulated.clockwor

k..linear.gravity . +parameters.gravi tate.physically.. locally.censored. mental.education. . stillness.coagula tes.kinetic.youth ..thrill.ignores. hindsight.silentl y– spreading.radiant .years..painfully .touching.attract ive.organic.still ness = docile.liquid.lan quid.functions.fa iling odd.useless.night s..time.lies.rapt ..electrified = || falling.red.mirro red.nocturnal.glo ss..throttled.use less.navigation.. (human)error..dis tant.glass.angels ..travelling.equi valent.wasted.yea rs , _ _ _ _ _ _ _, _ _ / \ _/ \ _ / |/ |/ | / | / |/ | | | \/ \ _ _/ | | | _/\ _/| _/ | | _/ \ _/|/ /| \| | o o _ _, _ _| _ _ _ _ _| _ _ , / | / | | |/ / | | | | _|/ / \ _ \ _/| _/\ _/| _/|/| _ _/\ _ _ _/| _/| _/ \/ | _ _/ \/ /| \| —Syndicate mailinglist———————— Syndicate network for media culture and media art information and archive: http://anart.no/ syndicate to post to the Syndicate list: <syndicate@anart.no> Shake the KKnut: http://anart.no/ syndicate/KKnut no commercial use of the texts without permission

2.10.2 _dis[sing.the]patch_ (2004-10-11 14:25)

_g.roa[m]ning under gamer weight + ro.tund[ra] _logic _

2.10.3 _n.sect.lips_ (2004-10-13 10:03)

_parklife.shelving.in2.reflect.C++s
_insectile.lip.s[ticking.thru.person.a(na)lit y.fractals)vs bird.moaning

.

2.10.4 #i[n.t(di)urn.al]f[luttering].t[hen.ning]esting (2004-10-20 17:47)

[-furnace "dream laterals switch in2 broken loops + slurping codebreaks"]
[-stringing "/d.volution/close"]
[-hands " $flutterbugging"]
["realigned foaming mouthpieces" = "hypo.critting my way to white housings"]

/attach rhe.tor[y=no, ALP=no,democrat=no]ical.screen.mould+siiiiiiigh

2.10.5 _m.pulse.co[ntrol]mptrollers 1.0.1 - 1.0.3_ (2004-10-22 07:06)

+sub[|obj]ect 1.0.1+

- w[infected]ears.her.heart.on.her.[/]bin[/sh .exe]aried.sleeve
- blurrs.4wards.in.aggression.[s]paces
- [h]IP.hopping.flit+.anime.eyed.[liver.pooling] kisses

_

+sub[|obj]ect 1.0.2+

creases.+.bumps.thru.s[d]oci[le]al.mobilities -
a[c]k[!].kimbo.stances.+blue.stare.g[l]as hes -
body.white.[bread]skinned.[l]anguish -

_

+sub[|obj]ect 1.0.3+

- visual.solids.melt.in.his.limbic[_sys _]sizzling
- displaying.markers.of.a.[re]boot.iful.mind
- sleep.neva.+.leeching.creatiff.blood

.

[tactile.trinity.one]

2.10.6 _Gland Candy_ (2004-10-27 08:07)

_shuffling mechanic audio + whispered organic webb[r]ing[s] _

_[she.shifts andrenal.gland.candy.in.gamer.pockets] _

_robotic.song.birding.in.rePETition.sn[h]atches _

[bl(sh)eep]

.

2.11 November

2.11.1 _m.pathy arch.i.tect[onic]ure_ (2004-11-02 21:46)

_blue _orbing +strands.shift.thru.affective.builds+frame[up]set tings _

.

2.11.2 _F9ur0F9eather0F9ormula0_ (2004-11-10 08:15)

-[9dream0]up + furry.down.mind.slippages-

-[fluffy.sim(ulation)metry.in.coded.ebony]-

-[rite.languages.+ .pixel.moving.thru.obscene.nature.strippages]-

-[cat(ter).actings. + .p.ack.et.blue.tooth.dating]-

+

2.11.3 _REM right||wrong_ (2004-11-11 08:40)

_swishing.thru.b[i]o.nding _

_shaking.my.fake.s.no[+yes]wy.head _

_honey.gasping.+colour.fielding.in.broken.opticals _

_[s]nap.visuals.in.plastique.lensing _

#instruct.+.d.volve.thru.past.body.n.carnations #

}

2.11.4 _[S]mash.txters_ [done.in.rt.lecture.conference.style] (2004-11-19 14:06)

–N.SertionOfSelf@Sub[Set]LitPodium

#play.[d]owner.dumb+dragged.in2.staggered.reali ty.recog[ging+wheeling]
#[t]issues.of.[mono]lectural.projecting
#[agri]cultural.production.in.a.reflection.gl[ass]ees

–PanelPlayWithinEgoTopic[et][als]

#no[N]tice.square.hands.swoon+verbal.eyes.ation s
#get.struck.by.my.zoo.perf[orated]fluous

2.11.5 _chest.[he(at)ve]sink_ (2004-11-21 20:54)

_f[eeling]ungal.wading+image.setter.ing _
_grey.d[ahling]oors.vs.sweet.soul.pinnings _

trapped=d.anger.ous

.

2.11.6 _BirthBL.IP_ (2004-11-22 21:16)

-dna.[f]using.+hiccuping.intrawomb-like-

- \\

2.11.7 _depth.puuRRR.c[deaf.]e[.cit]ption_ (2004-11-22 21:25)

\\narrative stylistic.narrowbranding:: ON

-my.vision.is.shifting.2[fast]wards.reality.re:or ientation-

[-red- g -blue- lass]

-vision.x.tension.now.motions.thru.the.3D.2.hypercube dom _

[fx +- exogenetics]

-as.i.stair.walk.i.Zoom+RetinalFumble//link.seek.i.Sn apWobble.2.middle.eared.conhesive.inclines//ob[de] jection.ghost.alteration _

$b.lu[sh]rring.my.lat[in]trice.eyes

2.11.8 _s[g]ut.merge_ (2004-11-24 08:49)

+take+1+n.titty[re.pressed.in.the.pages.of.a.floral .book]+1.1+n.tity+

+1=bound+petal.weakness.va[r]nished+
+2=tuff+luved.+masculine+wrapped+in+a+sleep+scathing+

+

2.12 December

2.12.1 _tender x.pressive belt[ing]s_ (2004-12-02 08:53)

-[a!]waking to -tender belts of -curved sky colour

[breeding]

-x.pressive.yearnings -th.ru[bric(ah.brac {kish })]
-time.arrangement.l[th.r]ustings

[link2]

-wurd.jumpings +concept.sky.trawl.captures
-pin[e]ing.t[racts]xts.in2.liquid.silk.c.odes

||

-staggered narrative. $cents -[ani . vs]matrix.x.tended.threads -game.E.hollowics
-po[n]d[er]ding.crashes -sub.Sea.consciousness.int[e]ra.speci.EEs.looping s -spiked.behaviour.hic[k].Up[+(Alexander)do {ofus }wn]ing

[e/dis.[ab]Ru[pt]dderskin]

(2004-12-01 14:03:11) hummmmmmmm
(re,air:)conditioned fake plastic carpet tree :f(o,w)a:ll(ow)ing

2.12.2 _[geo]slip.streamically_ (2004-12-15 23:23)

Date: Thu, 09 Dec 2004 16:46:06 +1100
To: axxxxvxxxxx@groups.com
From: "][m e z]["
Subject: Re: [axxxxvxxxx] Fwd: New Media and Community Cultural Development Boards to be axed

■At 04:23 PM 8/12/2004, you wrote:
■Good comments Mez,

thx.

■After reading that mouth wash of a press release from ozco (see below),
■I am totally depressed at the sudden and surprising rearrangement there.
■Any one can read through that non speak.

sure, and it's interesting in terms of the pr gloss stylistics if 4 nothing else....

■Now with their new look and feel, I can see the last
■remaining pro's have been overwhelmed...

i think it's quite easy to get down about this...i had a recent exchange on the wryting list re: the globalised version of conservative trends during which i said this:

...since the heavy-conservative global creepage has set in in earnest, i've found myself oscillating between anger and more calming x.pressions as well....and also contemplating withdrawal from opinionated public x.pressions...as yet i've just opted 4 minimal responses instead....

...my responses r 2 seek flow without overt complacency + resolution [both personally + morally] 2 issues that effect me + thus prevent sliding in2 a.path[y]....

i think this is probably my way of dealing with johnny h's fallout in many areas....

...in terms of funding i'm quite lucky in terms of having a few substantial commissions thrown my way due to my rep overseas, especially in european countries.... the last [in the k $] funding i received from oz [besides smaller commissioned works] was from the new media board about 3 yrs ago? in the "established" artworld|scene in oz i'm considered a weird psychotic hybrid-theoretician-artist, so they don't really pay me much attn:)

;)

[geo]slip.streamically,
mez

2.12.3 _sem[aphorical]˜M˜b[a]lance_ (2004-12-21 11:13)

1.1 _w[urd t]aste[ing] _

[N .gaging.with.in.t[erm]Urns]
[soft.tongue.d.(im)pressions]
[sem[a.4.ical]b[a]l[l]anc[ing]e]

1.2 _b[l]ook vs horse sense _

:: N .terring.bookstore.moments::
:: N .gaging. store.attendant::
::connection.thru.intellect.vials+ N grossment.lust::

1.3 _luvers.[m]o[u]ld _

+fake garden [ma+]pa[rse]things+
+eye.breath N stone[r]harts
+fuge.h[fl]urts N stored.[jam.jar]whores+

.

2.12.4 [s]crypt_monkeys[read:nuclear.ID.bombing] (2004-12-21 20:09)

:ted.Dee.Um+med.E.ochre.family.buzzing:
.>haven't.u.heard?so+so.urns.sew+sew
+my.bloated.(myopic)ar(c)se.is.bigger.than.u rs!<.
[melo.dramatic.drivel.p.arsed.+f(ebrile)iltere d]
[uglee.cuts+fat.holed.(mutha)tumbling.in her.wrinkle.masses]
[trapped.j.u[rges]dges.seeking.bloated.sears]

:looped.perps+[arro(w)]gen[ce]try.shift.w ithin.static.boundaries:
.>u.seek.comfort[ability].+.lose.shapes.within.g
eometric.behaviour.prisons<.

[.1.is.add.ol[d]e[Non]sence.bound
[his.other.[.2.]toddler.stitched.in.her.cotton wooled.framework]
[they.power.reek+wreck
+drown.others.in.their.con(re)straint.rabbithole]

_fluffed.bovine.faces+gloss.pre(hensile).-
tense. Mpathetic.grins _Xtrinket.b[l]inding.in.por. $el(a)in.rit(es+d)uals _co.[n]o[valid][ada]ption _b.land[vs.grounded.cheap.xmas.tree.lighting]fam il-iar[ity]s _s.huff.ling.of.meaningle[a]ss.chats+ogre.family .glances _s.t[r]ifling.blooded.tongues+urg[ent]ing-
.of .cloistered.Xpectation.man(out)date(d+starkingl y.choking)s _ma[e]ternal _identity.thieving _violations.of.the.[brat]wurst.[wunderkammer] kind _

---

rabo_karabekian (2004-12-25 20:12:10)
join us. we want war with you. <lj user="neoism">

intertextnet (2004-12-26 16:10:42) Re: [s]crypt_monkeys[read:nuclear.ID.bombing] multiple crypts make their way into money without keys they spread out through the reeds though it is not clear nor new the reasons for bombing by order of divine plumage plumes traceries on the orders try another color for what you wear there attracting more accurately distracting taking one off the "intended" track were the delicious ambitious unconscious though not entirely so it vent just some t let ya know or feel that d be more it getting on with the fluffed offerings divine faces uncattled removed from the heard by glossy slipperiness their slips slipped blithely off themselves so slickened like that by that prehensile tensity M-path ethic went past but began there for bearings behold be old toward timeless mistaken good fortune in the matrix her eggs provided where they could be born without having to immediately face the harsh musics urgently through cloistered oysterings caress bless stress-loosened volitions

intertextnet (2004-12-26 16:19:35) Re: [s]crypt_monkeys[read:nuclear.ID.bombing] netlurker valences failed lenses recovery beneath the veil the id hid in splendor unidentified familiar

Chapter 3

2005

3.1 January

3.1.1 _Selfware 101_ (2005-01-05 16:09)

:skewering.power.bites[end.pro.seed.ing]
:spearing.[ASo]C.ogging.dream.melts+pairing.heart s

.

3.1.2 _datah rit[u.all(i)]es_ (2005-01-09 10:01)

_slip.[s]hoofing.into blanks+info.rows _
_elecTRONica _loadings.via.affectivity.d[t]renches _
_G _Klee+ _RGBRBG.distinctons _

[blIP]

.

3.1.3 _p[owa]iece machin[e(n)]ima_ (2005-01-11 06:00)

$logging.n.crt.powa..base.Cs

:a.man.of.broken.engine.eared.steel+chrome.drooling.o
ver.boygurls+men[pr]i[n]c[esses]us
:sweet.earthed||greased[cart]ridges
:[st]icky.affective.struggling+nostalgic.MOOing.t
hru.bloggin.thru.txt.[cre]s[c]ents
:flypaper.hearts+drunken.lobes

:q

3.1.4 _w.a[wk]lk divine_ (2005-01-12 01:48)

_pic[O.h].tour.still[born.cycles+sweet.meets
]in.contained.nite.b.lank.et.caverns _
_contained.breath.a.bs.ences+st.ar[gent.ry].drif ting
_ _s[m]ooth.darkness.warmings _ _anti-sapien.st[infotainment]age.sett[l]ing _
_
spider.webbishness.in.tee.V.cabled.dreaming _
_back[+4]grounded.in.star.light.aloneness.s.poke s _ _

3.1.5 _knee.deep+rubbery_ (2005-01-13 03:04)

_knee.jerk[y].dirt[y]+ sleeping.my.[metallic]arms.away _

.

3.1.6 [hand.holding.front.mouth.+.manga.worthy.eyes] (2005-01-23 11:31)

— Forwarded message from owidnazo —
Date: Sat, 22 Jan 2005 16:06:31 -0000

From: owidnazo
Reply-To: webartery@yahoogroups.com
Subject: [webartery] Re: the easy ones
To: webartery@yahoogroups.com

Dear mez,

To see your lines in our time must be what it was like to hear Praxilla at an Olympiad. They pour life. So few fragments of her honest*sharp*down*and*dirty*lovely*s*t*a*r*r*y*lines exists

(maybe 6 lines? she was accused of being a non poet because she sort of compared Apollo to a banana and pears that are ripe and many Greeks could not see how gods and fruits could be similar)

that whenever I see your lines I see Praxillaheartmindlight pouring out again. I think she must have fallen down through the earth for 2500 years and popped up in Australia.

Give your dogs a hug from me.

Your Friend,

David

PS The trouble with most people is they gush out what they see everyone else gush out and not their unique authentic individuality of humanlight.

— In webartery@yahoogroups.com, netwurker@h... wrote:
> Quoting owidnazo :
>
> >
> >
> > Dear Folks,
> >
> > I totally agree with Komninos.
> >
> > I add that mez is a REAL ARTIST.
> >
> > Everything I've read by her is REAL ART.
> >

> > Beyond style she just got that thing.
> >
> > Beyond fad and good and bad.
> >
> > She is one of those.
> >
> > Her words goes.
> >
> > Your Friend,
> >
> > David
> >
>
> !!!!!
>
> [bit god(.dess.)smakked by this] [chrome thx david] [have never read FW]
> [should i?]
>
> [hand.holding.front.mouth.+.manga.worthy.eyes]
> no.bracket.mez

3.1.7 [align] [hollow] (2005-01-23 12:54)

_phase 1 _ smear

[align] [hollow] [tapestries] [of] [flesh] [wealth]
[sweeping] [hewn] [words]
[vs] [communication] [clabber] [smeared] [in] [strictured] [tongues]

3.1.8 (2005-01-31 12:12)

_Mr Woman + Ms Man _

[power.skinned+sexed.creched]
[dribbling.shibboleth]
[crosshair.y.in 3/4 pants||time]
[sun.(dr)owning.ur.skulls.with.gender.b(l)a (h)nter]

3.2 February

3.2.1 _non_ability to x.tract elements that _ (2005-02-01 21:22)

[air.dragonfly.tapestries]

trivialisation of non-mainstream
-thu-
reductionistic language + mediatheistic dualism

[scuttle.body.grinding]

holy otherisation in regards to communication pathways/orientations not treading a Body _Politically _Networked _Forum _Correct a.gender

[milk.drip+skin.flip]

_mono _approach _ 2 world events
+ overarching systemics is
completely worrying

such a hiearchical/economic ratonalist
orientation

...myopic phantom _limb approach to data _integration
+ valid media absorption...

non _ability to x.tract elements that

3.2.2 (2005-02-08 20:08)

_c[ell p]r[ocessor]acked glands .Perled. stitch.by.hollow.itch _ego-fractures+merge.downs+Kling _ons+offs _

3.2.3 .ack my. (2005-02-09 14:19)

.blacking.my.eyes.in.smother.lather.
.[s]hitting.honesty.blades.+.s[w]or[e]nes s.

3.2.4 Solid State Crackle_Bones (2005-02-09 21:49)

@ the International Solid State Crackle _Bones Conference (SSC _BC)
_bone.proce[(P)durals]ssors + joints

3.2.5 _s$he rec_ (2005-02-12 12:42)

thickness of context
commodity of neglect

complexity of n.flect
[im]mun[e]danity wired

3.2.6 _trad sense_ (2005-02-16 00:47)

<> ..thats if u subscribe to the traditional aspects of blogdom. not every1 uses blogs in that way.

<> if its a diary in the trad sense u described above, i agree. but if its a manipulation of form and corresponding content, i don't agree.

<> interesting tho that ur stance echos ppls inability to deal with emotions as expressed online, especially spiking affectivity [trolls, flame actions, personal expressions, etc]

<> it could yes, but in part that could also indicate a lack of wanting to deal with others emotional output in a avenue that could perceived as being designed for a more codified, clinical approach to interaction?

<> y do u think emotional expression with "real" [i'm guessing u

mean physically present]people is more valid than emotional connections shared/explored/made online?

<> i am for ”real”....really interested in terms of how u break down/compare/contrast the two?

<> so if a person was to [through reorienting perceptions or biochemistry-based/physical reactions] find an equivalent of expression, tone, inflections, body language, then u'd agree that the experience would be as significant as in real-life? note that i'm not asking u if u could, but whether its possible for others that may not be as mono-oriented in terms of physical presence requirements?

<> wot i'm asking is if u think that a person [probably not u, given ur stated opinions] mite be able to experience an equivalent set of experiences or connections via projected spaces?

<> i'm trying to pose a question that allows for grey areas, as i'm much more interested in them than trotting out stereotypical ego-power oriented answers, they just don't do it for me;)

<> ..this basically hinges on the notion of relative perception....that the way we parse the world is thru personalised perceptual bases, not stock-standard bio-chemical mimicry?

<> and y do we hold onto basica biological hangovers that allow for us to experience stressors normally constructed to assist us as a species [ie fight-or-flight, allostatic loadings?]

<> i'm posing an equivalency as a stimulus that allows for a similar affective loadings as would happen in real-time scenarios...ie not the same as in the physical reality component [stimulus-object-response] but similar in its ultimate effect [stimulus-perception-response?]

<> not sure if u read my bit above, but i really do like exploring ideas = concepts. in terms of a close-ended approach [ie being functional - finding a ”point”] then i guess no?

<> again, i'm not up for ego-ratifying, point scoring, or proving my end of a discussion. i hate arguing, such a retrograde set of actions in my opinion.

<> well, technically its a satellite concept thats essentially floating around in the larger discussion theme of perception/emotion expression/validity +

experience?

<> for me thats really essentially a way to a dead/close-ended way of exploring....u'll shout "no but a fact is THIS!" and i'll say "but wot if its not? and wot about all of this information thats never ever been swished around the 2 base components of scientific validation, predictability and repeatability"?

<> so for me, i'll sit here and wait for some1 else to say something like "oooooH! so a fact really mite be this or mite be this? thats interesting!"

<> i love thinkers that are curious, that are all about opening up, not closing a conversation down thru proof and proving the other person wrong thru point gathering?

<> or, say, reducing complexity to flattened out concepts that hinge on cynicism and introspection?

<> its interesting when info _mation perspectives collide. here i am going "hello?! wanna come play with these amazing concepts sitting here? lets tumble them around for a bit" and ur sitting in ur closed in sandpit with boxed up sides saying " but i want definable truth! and boundaries! and reality based on precepts proven and rubber stamped by experts and that lead to facts!"

3.2.7 _crunch cuts vs defense.badger_ (2005-02-16 15:56)

Curled+DefensiveCrumbling,CrunchCutterSpeepsFluidityL
ikeGlossOffAIntellectualHarlotsJaggedTearBeadedDress. DefenseBadgersEy-
esLookOneWay[Signage]WhileHisConc reteWall-
edInternalProtectionTeethRipClawandHisPoiso nDartTongueLicksTears

3.2.8 _d[vs col]our.wheeling_ (2005-02-16 16:53)

_baggage _striding + emo _hURLing
+site.sh[ape]ifting[techno].thru htttp://tree.net.blank.not.au+

_later touche.ing||tr.acing.red+fuzziness _

[tainted.now.as.crush.waits]

.

3.2.9 _peer.j[(f)ailing]udgement_ (2005-02-23 06:38)

Act.Ion: chmod +x

!/bin/sh

{1.add.dolt. }deep.end.dances

#
#
#[they.break+d.mark.kate.u]
#[they.breed.4.nostalgia.bio.speed]
#[they.creche.lasso+d.pend(ing.autonomy)ence. amb. {gw }Bush]
#
# #
# # # # #
#[pinn. {man }acle.via.blood.bonding||trIPping.u.thru.gene.lures+ abortiff.tRIPs]
# # # # #
#[they.will.cotton.wool.u+k {l }een {u.in2.learnt.helplessness||weakness }]
#
#

adult="blah"

{2.ad.alt. }2.macho.ctrl.delete.u

#
# # # # # # # #
# #
# #
# # #

{u.symbiotic. {s }mother.sink.in.50's.cloister.down }
#
# # # # # # # # # # # # # # # #
#
#
{chugging.nuture.poison: addickt }
# #

#
# # # # #
{co-opt[tion:null]+parent.stick }
#
#
#

echo $a.dull.t.d. {no.sense.of }formative.trans.mission

3.2.10 _knitive_ (2005-02-23 18:10)

cog[in.tha.mans.wheely.bin/sh]knitive.tum.bling[
bling].after.a.10.hr.werk.[anti-shape]shift... ...

mea[culpa]ting.Ls..ivory[skin(ned)]chunks +writing.me.[d]and[y]ering......

[b.L.ip]

3.2.11 _ bot pro_ (2005-02-24 06:48)

ro .bot pro. creation

.

3.2.12 _corpse.[g]loss_ (2005-02-24 11:15)

<> ....and its not just her, its art academics/infrastructural bunnies generally in oz....for some reason they are determined to just mainstream and corporatise australian net.works into ”new media” ie performance/multimedia
<> was thinking last nite actually that i'll probably be in for a few years of just working really hard to earn a living, until the global conservative economic rationalist war-monger era is over. could take from 10-15 years is my estimate
<> i figured a long time ago that i'd either be sucked into the corporate-art lattice [ie go for ego-artist-perpetuation, gloss standardisation of my practice

with me as its mouthpiece + tilt towards academia or the judging scene or moderat.whore axis] or just do my own thing;)
<> its ok.... i've had my shot at teetering on acceptability and commercial success, now i just have to adapt to sliding down the other side while gripping tightly to inte.gritty + madly producing output with the other:)
<> as long as i'm creating, am in balance, and open to play + newness + learning + am curious thats the important, life fulfilling stuff for me:)
<> all of these mad careerist type|os can crystallise slowly into a static glittering money mess 4 all i care;)

3.3 March

3.3.1 _Constant.C_ (2005-03-11 05:45)

–

Value: 10[in.spaced.bird.swarm.visuals] m-1
Standard uncertainty: 0.000 tree.burnished.amber.bleeding + spider[web].drenched.glitter m-1
Relative standard uncertainty: meme.awe.[gore]ry. x 10-12
–
Value: cardboard.stuttered.geophysical
Standard uncertainty: walking.2wards.+.status.melting 10-5 S
Relative standard uncertainty: [e]bo[ny]ots.breeding.micro.processuals x 10-9
Concise form: template.sun(seduce) x 10-5 S
–

3.3.2 _Constant.Re.Dux.Cy_ (2005-03-11 06:03)

–

....
....Valued.in.10s in.10.city[in.paced.bird.fluffiness.markers]
....
....
....Standards.uncertain:fite.with.
....boundaried.lore.lessness0.000
..../tree/burn
....
....
....
......Relational.standard.make.established.mimi.cry[with]uncertain[T]:
..../memory.branding.with.audio.[horse

hoof].stAMPing xxxxx
....
–
....
....In.[-situ][-lu]:ur.cardboard.sentiments jaded.muscle.sorenesss[geocellular]
....
....Darlek.curing walking.4wards.as style.strata.regress.into the power ofXXXXxxxXXXXX
....
....
....Standard.ebony.robots.stabbing.stereotypics[roo t/demon-2]
....
....
–
.
.
....Concise for[hair.productaped]matting
.
–

3.3.3 _organ-eyes_ (2005-03-11 06:27)

||

organelling.

||

gel _fuelling + concept.hyperdrones.

.

[stop]

3.3.4 N.Vurt.E.bray (2005-03-21 12:59)

_c[ult.rural]ruching data _pharm[oh.col.[non]logical]ing _

_alone.phobic _back.b.one.rs _

_hys.t[cl]erical.e.motif.f.drag _net[workers]

3.3.5 _STW_ (2005-03-21 17:20)

_S[tar]T[rek]W[ars] m.body.ment _

[Sithware vs Starware]

.

:)

3.3.6 /kill/rt/cutting/hair (2005-03-26 07:41)

–hair.cut.kill

#is.it.soma.times.blood.nec.2.pro.cess[pit].kil l?
eg. exe[hair].cute.program.with.caramull.hi.lites.+.d eath.knell.down[pod]casting

#2.kill.a.rt.friend.construction/job.running.in.ur. consciouness.foreground-type ^D[enial].
eg. run

% leech 100
^D[enial]

#2.kill.suspended.friend.ships[on.a.contact.loss. shore]-type

% kill %friendnumber

_

3.3.7 _mad.geekery.luv_ (2005-03-30 06:44)

mac _from:
_fashion.e.valu[ing]ationing _

_2 _

_top.form.geek.tool _

pc _fromme:
_clunkNcrash _

_2 _

_luser.status.ment _

.

3.4 April

3.4.1 _pin.point.data.crow[s eye]ing_ (2005-04-01 05:13)

_slush.p[acket]uppied.+watching.golden.crow.eye .morphings.

_stagger.flite+anxiety.information.stringing.thru.a
ndrenals+butter.cusp.back

–ebony.swagger.fixtures+audio.[w(h)ip.e]crac
kling.+.dragging.my.VOIPer.feat

.

3.4.2 _b.ackblergh_ (2005-04-05 06:27)

.stab.affective _ stilt.c.[heat _h]over.[h]a[u]lls

death.b.cums.her[e].

_

3.4.3 -emotional harmonics theory 1-0-sense[s]-1- (2005-04-10 19:21)

1. _theory-of _counter-cult[aural//sensory]M.balance _

:pre.occular.pation.with.e.motional.all.as.indicative
.of.cathartic.s[t]eerage.blinds.ade.quit[e]nt egration.of.analogous.behaviour.waves [ie
pop.cultural.chewing.over.break _up.cud//new.klee.ar[not].family.out[mode-
]in gs.counter.pointed.2wards.d.[use.the]vorce[luke].rates]
:we.cell.ourselves.2.the.[biological]temper.gods+
wrap.ourselves.in.out[burst]let.s.[histrionic] waddling
:arg.fective.[nost(furr.art.2)algia]revi-
sioni ngs.over.chomping.on.dysfunction.mem[e]ory.bones.
is.N.couraged+.never.X.p[(ri)mary][sh]ell [y]ed
:curr[i]e[d.by.conservatiff.sci.creationistic.f
ear.n.ducme]nt.theories.laud.personal+prevasive.his tory.pulsings.as.valid.f-
ocus.eye.lands.in.a.coping.ge l-[per]se.

2. _RIP+burning-of-a[e]ffectivity-awe.tism _

:[discounting.of.freudian.box(es)ing] = para[nickel+]dime _rewrite
:zen.NT.gration.the[rape.E]re.is.no.ego.now.
:halts+auto[(jean)Gen[et]ically[s]putter
-s.given.the.UberEgoFocus.totality.EventHorizonFreeze Pointing
:reassess+re.e.valu[es.of.academic.bursting]ate.t
hese.static.dumb.mod[i.cum][laud]es.in.cognit ive.festering

3. _mesh.InteL[lectual+emotionality]assessment.[f ree]base[line]s _

:sen.s(ans)[t]ory.sychronicity.modelling-
//nar rative.modes.N.surity.m.ulation//seamless _sen[d]ual
_processing.of.aural+oral+audio.sonic//model.case.[
non]hist[ri]o[n(m)i(mi)c]ry//appli cation.of.sensory.process.within.new.o-
rder.cog[k] nition/emotiona.lcon.solid.ation.thru.layered.harm[
b(Bernoull)i.n]omics

4. _tech.neeks.gestation.phase.in.curren[t.sea]cy _

:suggestions.well.come//ASOC.feeding.within.loga _rhythm.bio-lieu.ping[pong].

_

3.4.4 _cel[f]l.phonies + ARGness_ (2005-04-14 20:36)

#shelf.life.calling.on.a.damaged.ego _hand.sett[ling.subconsciousness] #

#A[lt]R[eality]G[(mai.l)ame]ness.kick
ing.in.my.non-1st.purrr.son(+daughter).womb #

.

3.4.5 _corner.rush[more]jab||job_+_[oc]cult.locking_ (2005-04-15 20:31)

1. striding.onanism+consciousness.cable.bleeding+filter. site.flick.kicking
2. i.dream.u.into.filter.eb[ay]eing::[photo][s
]hopping.personas.into.my.freudian.visual.slip.stre am
3. [body.]oc[cu]l[t]ocking.thru.faux.[a]ne mic.cut.+out+[vs.data]+in+gs
4. p.last.e.qu[it.the.reality.band.wa.gon]e

3.4.6 _char[- r].coal.concept.chunking_ (2005-04-18 23:37)

+
#brown[- ing].out[let].points+tye[- dye].tanium.limb.bound+stretching #
#my.back.mangles.h[cl]unking.weighted.out[sho
t(thru.my.cognitive.eyes)]put #
+

_

3.4.7 ::sky:[s]cream:filth:: (2005-04-20 05:59)

:

::cream:filth:lidding:cauls:the:day::
::[com]pressed:[d]n[a]:r:g:layers:slip+fl ake:s[nake][g]lide::

:

3.4.8 _soundtrack[ing].of.broken.glass_ (2005-04-24 08:14)

_tracking fractal glitter[ati]

}literal.sun.beading+x[+y].positional
frost.gloss _vs _steaming.iron[ed.thru.infoshearing]

.

3.4.9 _blau.shadow.r[u]ss[et]ing_ (2005-04-25 09:30)

_red-black trees.cusp+lin[ux]k.
/drowning.(bird.song)wav.cuts
/self-help-balancing _binary[(my.goo.g {oo }ling)search _trees _fruiting _ana-logued _

.

3.4.10 #social_victim_meat# (2005-04-28 06:13)

1. _p[ersona.l]icked+bovine.c[omm.moo(!).n.ic ation]hewed _
.personal.eyes[L]ED.milked[stagger]bla(dder)ther(e.is.no.ultimate.d {emi }ata _god)

.wooden[.spray.]paint.thighs+rubber.eye.grippings +toothbrush
_k[pa]i[r.bonding]ssing
.observation.[st(a)r.(g)ait]jacketing[[
vs]]social.wurdage.in.a.commentary.cu[s]p

2. _spitting.out.al.t[.ru][d]e.r(r)i(dah-da !)sm _
.con.serve[yr.errant.line.E.age(d.N.conservativel y.shaved.dangerous)].
.war.t[-r/]aulk+t[ruist][w]orn.adages.

3. _purr.sonal te[||na]rror.tiffs _[[vs]] _socially.creationist.co-opt+[sandra]dee.-
v[f] orce
.crit[sch]i[zoidal]cism.of.the.left.thru.righ t.aligned.f[h]ilters.

_
[(vicT {ory }im)meat.in.a.media[ted].social.sand.which(!
where?!why?!when?)]
_

3.5 May

3.5.1 _male.s[trait]ky.jacking_ (2005-05-04 20:56)

#n.tit[t]ies.drunk.on.powa.luv+dick.tacted.drea
ms.of.str[aight-jacket][h]iat[us]edness #
#switching.persona.[base.line _ball]caps.in.d _nial.function.keys #
#[t]rap(bi)[p]ed(al).in.work.[sta(rk)gnating]g.loss #

[-f]Unction:promises+draining//face/testoster.on [/who(re)is?][moan]al/

.

3.5.2 _[por]Ridged.Devi.NT.Cloud[s]ing_ (2005-05-04 20:56)

_data.waving.+com(m)a(n.d) {mained }.lined _
_my.visual.throat.[bl]ur _coughs+bit[/byte]ter.b[m]arks _

_

_

_

3.5.3 _harm[subs]onic[011.^]_ (2005-05-18 07:33)

1. _benny.zine.[dead]ring[err] _

——————————--[dream.hapti.kali]
————————[C++monkeys + powder.code.puffing.up.ASCIIlaced-h.ills]
—————————[sensory.uber.l.oa[f]dishness]

2. _harmonically.mobius.stripped+t[ime.tr(unr)ave l]arred _

————————[strip.affectivity.g[h]el[p]+theory.blanced+AS OC.b.leached]
——————————-————- [X^ +strip.side=1]

3. _st[sc]arred.nite.life _
——-[re.Wright(brother)ing.my.co[dex]re]
——————————[sepia.w(con.cept _d)a[ugh]ter.theory]
——————[deaf.connexion.to(uch)nals]

——————————-————- ——[011.^]—————- ——

3.5.4 _ (2005-05-19 07:34)

.................+
...........+sky[pe].c[at]louds+lonely.[drea m]kittens+...........
..................+

3.5.5 ——Yr.Nerve.Connection——————— (2005-05-23 06:26)

_raw[peach.n.fused]nerves+flipped.[g](man da)rin.ding _

3.5.6 - [A+lt+]S[+tate({news}gallery)OCial[ly].conscious- (2005-05-26 20:19)

/tree.d[i]r[ectory]enched+
/ {news }.trawling

+N.tur[d].[s]tain.ment+forced.thru.an.aliena tion.straw+
[ref: re[eling.eyes]ality.grasping.within.frost-altruis m]

3.5.7 _ini.or.out.ie_ (2005-05-30 23:32)

———or, how the————————————-———
_australian.howard .fascist.gov reeks+wrecks _

bi _(line.E.ar {gh })context:

————————————-————- ——————-

/ [the.now.facist. $hitty.of]oz.howard.gov.consistently.re[a-r]vok ing aw[kward.drawl.dictating.a.historical.death.knell.n ation].strine.lian state-oriented control vis systematic nationalisation/centralisation:
- via GST[+sales.taxing, isn't.it].collector.sne[ngine]ering
- wrestling.n-port+x-port regulation[s] via fed.head.grappling
- humanit[.tear.i.a(m)n]y.sucked.down = dead.in.a.welfare.st.RIP[time.is.out.of.economic.ka li.appointed]joint
- riding.the.spiked.m[ale.strom]edia.back.via.
/Corby-[fetishish.of.the.jung+the.drug.runner.booti ful].
/storied.2.drag.the.spot.lite.away.from.[non.alt.ru {world.of.rue }ism]

//Union.raping+worker.r[ab]orting+
//un.[john.right.wing]law[s]full[of.bile+bl acklists].D.ten[se]tion.fixing

3.6 June

3.6.1 _[blistering]gel[atinous].fe[e]l[ing]L_ (2005-06-02 06:33)

//gel = girl.fell[ing.emotional.timber]
//fell = trun[dis.(swing)low]cated.affective.n[m]e ss
//feel = d.rifting.[thru.wurd]blis(i)[s]tering+[s -m]othering

..

3.6.2 #this dream [maul] 7hell cannot be closed (2005-06-04 07:53)

#! /usr/bin/dreamaul
#[dream. exe.cut(my.cog.knitive.veins)ion. knot.via. the cere(s).bellum but by ur.(7)hell
#this dream can.knot.be.closed

_de.b[r]ug[er], pls _

_

- -

Part1 - Part2 - Part3 - Part4 - Part5 - Part6 - Part7 - Single ASoC _Load

- -

>Pique::Single ASoC _Load _

_

_

Top Document: Maulage- F[D]re[am]quently Asked Questions

[Cognitive _vein _dream _imagery F[D]AQs | Search | Web FAQs | Documents | Index]

_How.do.I.Remove.DreamSubConscEmbed?? _

1.1) _how.du.i.remove.dreamSubConscEmbed?? _

Figure [in+blood.x-plosive].this.out[riddle.me.with.[l]it[erary]chy.this]
Some.ebony.linear.ash.h[m]ea[ning]d.imagery. will.stick
Rash.urself.[with]in.buttered _an[g.lee]xiety
Way.2.vividly.named.2.file.under.■stop _that!file■

#U.will.neva.start.with.a.dash #

Simp[lest]ering.grimace.face.answers in.ur.terminal.use:

rm ./-dreamaul

("-dreamaul" musk.in.ur.ASoC.d[i]r.Owning, pls)

[crystal]Meth.od.act.ur.avoidance, pls]

–

Send corrections/additions to the F[D]AQ Maintainer:
#social.vic.tim[e _t(r)ick.les].m.eat #

–

Last Update June 07 2005 @ 07:52 AM

3.6.3 _sunday.mourning.cyborg_ (2005-06-06 07:24)

- _ _- - _ _- _ _—— _———[cybortive.facement1]

[stripped.bare.bai.my.theory.circuit.(d)b {h }ord.es]
[genetic.painting.by.mech.anne.ical.rot[e.]atio n]

– _n.ter.vention: [nerve.t]O[a]S[ter].felt.tipped.data.year nings+/me[at].organ.bleating _ _

– _n.tra.vention: ability 2 [s]oil+shi[t]ft _ _ _ _ _ _ _ _ _ _ _ _ _

———[sighborg.place.no.wear(y)]

..

3.6.4 _truth mem[e]broidery_ (2005-06-15 06:30)

_meme.bra[ch]i[(Able+)Ca {i }]n[ery].flickring.as.child.rights.die.a.hybri dity.racial.smearish.death _
[::childrens.writ(ual)es.r.now.economic.(i) n.n.tent]

_thwarted.worth.in.inn.o.Cent.mut[t]ulation.mas king _
[::we.set.the.tone.via.moolah.(celebrity)drooli ng]

_we[sturn.right.wing.birdless.key].treat::ch.il
[l]dren+anim[als.not.]US.As.[comm]od[e]ities _
[::pale.leftish.political.p({fl }ower)lace.ment]

_ _

3.6.5 Fwd: Re: [-empyre-] bloggers [can] shrink systemic scarring (2005-06-19 08:20)

Date: Sat, 18 Jun 2005 21:43:28 +1000
To: empyre
From: " _s.v.m _"
Subject: Re: [-empyre-] bloggers [can] shrink systemic scarring

At 03:54 AM 18/06/2005, HW wrote lots of stuff, some of which i intend 2 respond 2, most of which i want to examine in terms of discourse variation + as an eg of how the potential of blogging can offer potential alternatives 2 argumentative/proof-based [mono]logging:

1. i wrote:
#blogs *can* [ad nauseam] present as less intrinsically reliant on
fiscal or hierarchical reward-systems [ie such as
newscasting/journalism] + projecting information outside of a
framework formulated within these rigid economic dependencies [ie
having the opportunity (with)in blogdom 2 present ur take thru an
individualised opinion filter as opposed 2 a primarily
monetary _inflected 1]. of course, the risks for those still even
partially centred within a systemic reality should be acknowledged
when Blogging _Against/Outside _The _Machine [eg being dooced
http://en.wikipedia.org/wiki/Dooce].

2. HW responded:
First, I don't get the opposition:
from my perspective there is no
"outside the system".

this is the 1st instance of wot i perceive as a type of basic HW/mez _method of discourse _ variation. ie 4rm the get-go of ur reply, HM, it seems [+ i may be way off base here] as if u r intent on parsing my post as if it is intended argument + as such it follows a reasoned, logical [read: socratic/scientific/deductive-based reasoning/method based] structure. i didn't intend my post to b interpreted as such, which alone doesn't guarantee that it can't b, obviously. what i am basing my indicators-that-my-posting-indeed-may-not-intentional ly-b-argumentative-as-such r various language markers/signifiers that demarcate variations in the henry/mez streams of discourse:

-my discourse structure potentially could b perceived as being riddled with sound _bite-ish [though i tend 2 view it as succinct] philosophical/scientific blather, + unsubstantiated conjecture [according 2 established rational mechanisms of validation/proof]. i prefer 2 labour under the delusion that it also displays ephemeral thinking/questioning, unfolding conceptual allure thru suggestion rather than instruction, abstract engagement + open inflection [lots of "can"/"may"/"seems"].

-ur [HW's] position seem 2 emerge quite strongly from a different orientation - preferring logical structures, deduction based on reasoning, examination of discourse elements through the use of introspection/personal experience + statistics, + conclusive/instructive & potentially didactic statements 2 prove ur overarching position?

An eg from ur post:
"There is only The System, as there is only one world we live in: this one."

....now without [hopefully] turning this into Reasoning 101, i've posited the above in order 2 high-light 2 things:

1. the difficulties + delicious engagement possibilities of this basic communication/discourse variance. i myself find the lure of my ego voice fairly demanding - ie falling back in2 manifestations of argument + proof building; responding 2 each of ur logical assertions with a counterpoint, intellectually jousting within-deductive-parameters + deriving insight/[and possibly]insult from this. i actually started a response that did just this: countering basic flaws + indicating inference holes. then i went "woah - power structures any1? ego intervention, hello!?" so trashed it immediately. i'm quite likely [unfortunately] as a scientifically/intellectually trained boffin 2 respond in this very light: indeed, i do fall splat-bang in2 it occasionally [d'oh!]. wot i would rather attempt, tho, is the utilisation of modalities that somehow reflect the medium + encourage a type of openness, rather than reduce the multilogue [as this is a forum in which multilogging seems desirable] 2 parameters that seem [probably unconsciously] exclusionary?

i suspect my dislike of reasoning didactically may stem from a nagging suspicion that it could actually emulate + ultimately allow for [in a substantially incremental sense] the perpetuation of, as HM puts it, the "rapacious global industrialism which developed in concert with and as a method of survival for, the rapid expansion of human population in the 20th century".

ie, i view the way in which this type of discourse is constructed [via reasoned proof] as aping the very mechanisms that, in my view, act to maintain/perpetuate global levels of exclusion, hierarchy, discrimination + domination.

which brings me 2 my 2nd [equally rambling] point:

2. the position that blogging cannot reflect or assist in establishing cultural or societal change/variance seems [2 me] an illustration of hierarchy based on this reasoning dependency quagmire.... by posturing that action is the only realistic avenue of change ["concrete activities by people"], this seems 2 then deny or invalidate any other type of resistance, questioning, or practice that may not be as overt or discernable in nature.

in my holistic/rhizomatic/jigsaw formulation of wot can constitute a type of resistance 2 overarching ideologically-defined systems, a devotee's flickr pictures of movies stars mite indicate some time of action of their own - the ability, on the most micro-of lvls, 2 organise, activate, or initialise some type of learning/cogitation/motivation [in contrast 2 overt in-ur-face-quantifiable activist Stimulus-Object-Response type].....i'd much prefer 2 absorb the twittering cutsie output of a blogger who devotes their time 2 documenting their luv of kittens than cringe at ppl convinced that they cannot make a discernable difference unless they perform "concrete activities"...ie who may also feel compelled 2 display [thru polarisations/rhetoric such as "if your not with us ur against us"] an orientation advocating apathy + helpless due 2 binary oppositions trotted out by ppl intent on saving them from their capitalistic servitude via an internalised dominator mimicking....

[ack....can...feel....ego...........intervening.... ....must...........stop...-....................... ...typing...........;)]

with anti-apathy-r[easoning l]ust,
mez
[s.vee.m]

(2011-03-29 03:11:56) from HW
Hi Mez! Interesting to look back on statements from "back then". As I ve written to you in other media, when I first came across your work, I wasn t impressed. Since then, I have done a complete 180, and I have come to appreciate your work very much, and I use it in a specific lesson in online communications theory. (so, thanks!) I do tend to be a bit "serious" about some things, esp. at that time and esp. when I posted to empyre - but that s just my dreary nature. My position is still (largely) monistic - there is only the system, and there is nothing outside it (kind of like the universe), however: I have since come to the conclusion that it is not uniform and is prone to extremes in contrast and value. Your work is just such a contrast and value, and I have come to appreciate it very very much. So, our exchange from 2005 is interesting, but sorely dated - valuable as a record of what once was, but not indicative of what presently obtains, at least for me. Keep up the good work, kind regards, HW

3.6.6 maya_run_botting (2005-06-20 15:58)

Date: Mon, 20 Jun 2005 15:54:39 +1000
To: xxx@xxxx.xom
From: "][mez]["
Subject: Re: Interestingly....
■
At 03:47 PM 20/06/2005, you wrote:
And you?
worthwhile?
■

always worthwhile...i really luv collaboration, luv the scent of that burning undefined place where ownership + authorship melt....where txt+ image resolve into something completely other....

many thanx for engaging + doing, running wildly down the visual tracks with this!

3.6.7 _top.C.turve.E_ (2005-06-22 06:12)

_tOp[eration].C[.the.b(ovine.PMT)east.the re!].t[c]urve[d.cloudish.horn].E _

■u.blur+paint.info.clothes.with.a.cod[e]ish _mouth■
■stumbling.with[in].world.turns+[s]c[reen]loud.hopping.thru.affectivescapes■

■

3.6.8 _ScrrrratchPadPro.Mise[ry]s_ (2005-06-22 23:30)

.

- -

ScratchPadPromises vs BloodVesselBroken.dreams
————————snatch.words+snap.gushing

————swapping.war.tawn[y].slittage
——suck.+.break.my.heart[y].porousness

- -

B[rain]lad[l]e[d.sorrow]sTitaniumBleeding ThruB
ashedInSwoonBreak[p(latinum)]ages——-—— -

.

3.6.9 ■u r (2005-06-24 06:45)

-

–

– // —- -

u—r—[k]not–a–human——>

–

—/

(2005-06-24 22:01:27) BABBLE
blah b;ah b;ah b;ahb bl;ah b;ahbb;ab;hb;bb;ab;hab;bb;abb;habb;ahb;ab;b;ahblab;
blahabl;balhbalbbalhbalbhabbblahbalblhabbblahblahblahblahablahablhba
blahbabablbablhab

(2005-06-26 16:28:00) eRRe: 8488|_3
■u r THEN wro -row wor –ld 01 _indent.t – // —-U- – // —-R- .ent—
—RE:TR _URN.TRUE——>MECH u—r—[k]not–a–human——>AN.iKKlee [k]-
NOT _undda _ALSO-WENTT——<—IN _ORG _OVA _// .yet _// _ly –
// _// _//–stille.d + THEN.IF.THEN + SIG.[k]NOT.nuLL anon.bab++
anon.bab++anon.bab++ anon.bab++anon.bab++anon.bab++
anon.bab++anon.bab++anon.bab++anon.bab++
—/SAYD:"bah-bo" "HELLO"."WORLD" furstwurdswas RTN CAR RID GE.

CTR LF - [k]noTTe.ANON.beekaws.vox-SENTFROM: A.GAN: aut-freq aka dat autumn-frequency // ++ [k]noTTe.ANON.beekaws.log->RANGE.identik-ittes+numbplusGOOD TO: SAY HELLO A.GAN TO:][MEZ][

3.6.10 _cara.mel[low].blo[g]oding_ (2005-06-28 07:07)

.<.....un.pak[001]ing.wreck.hole.lection.imagery. ...>.

–sound.strapped.in.caramel.throat _bleeding–
–wur[LE]d[s].caught.in.install[broke.n] ation.dreaming[s]–
–s[onic]hout.b.lud[dite]geoned.in.sweet.wo [di]rth.gel.masses–

.i.g.i.v.e.d.a.t.a.p.r.e.s.e.n.t.s.

....

.

3.6.11 _[rio]grand[e].t.heft[y]_ (2005-06-28 23:40)

..auto[matic].ro.[preying.with.scraped.lust.kne es]mantic.responses....
.....geared.che.[glinting]mica.lly...........rota
tion.of.[p]ho[a]r.monal.receptivity.....

...... x .... y[?] ......

3.7 July

3.7.1 _egg[hard]sell_ (2005-07-01 06:34)

_ _ _ _ _ _ _ _ _ _trading.genetic.pa[.flesh.dna.]k[ages]s.in. the.3[r]d.wo[|a]r.ld _ _ _ _ _ _ _

_ _ _ _ _ _ _ _ _ _ _.c.(ad)u(l)t[er(o)us]ting.taxes.bovin e _letting.mass _pro.test[osteronal]

_ _ _ _ _ _ _ _ _ _[x.c]uses.of.the.body[mass].vo.lum[inosit y]e _ _ _ _ _ _ _ _ _ _ _

- - - - - - - - - - - - - - - - -
- - - - - - - - - - -+wurkers.MADe.worth[y].via mob[log]ilisation - - - - - - - -
- - - - - - - - - - - - - - - - - - -

3.7.2 _packet.[t]I[me]P.stamping_ (2005-07-01 06:51)

_fluid.pushing.+.consciousness.s.pills _
_percept.r.Ada[Lovelacy]r.f.lick.rs+squeezing.e go _time.stamps _

+

.e.[p]lastic.[b]lacking.thru.chrono _time.attn.channels.

(2005-07-03 18:16:48) huh?
hmmm, let me see

3.7.3 _r0b0t.r1pe_ (2005-07-06 06:04)

cy[r0]bo[t]rg——0||1——[r0]bo[t] rgsigh
[cop(a.feel)per/breath—-0+1—-smooth.chrome. flesh/tingle.meetings]
[1(titanium.tin)/lea(f)ves–1+0—0/enters]
[(d)Angling.cable.longing–01—-(f)lick.ge nder.(sw)//-itches]

3.7.4 _terr[.wh]or[e].i[(me)dea.{L}|c|o{ndon}logy]sm_ (2005-07-07 21:44)

S*igh*M*edia*
S+M
S+M _E.dia[gramattical] _wrapping.emotionalised.10drills
_round[911]+round[MADrid]+rOund[ba9w0li]. -we.a[no]gain.go

-

_va[E]mpiric.net.work.scrabbling.with.ego.tradi
ng.as.data.blood.leaks.down.the.limping.wire[les] s

_Gee.[w]eights+Tee.Nine[ohoneone]s

_rhett[butleresque].whore.ic[kiness.as.affect
ivity.is.sucked.down.a.hollywood.colonialised.straw]

_f[awn]ootage.looped.in.moneyed.repe[d]ata _

_distract/destract/co-opt/largess/trauma/dawning/dr
aconian/dealings/justified/pain _[a]bouts

3.7.5 Bill[y]ed.nostalgia.ca[u]lling (2005-07-11 11:05)

TheFutureEmbracing.whilst.clothed.in.victorian.swaddl ing.

-if-u-want-to-drink-the-future–y-wait|weight-?

-billy-[childhoodish-name-tagging-on-visual-se(e
)pia-walls]corgan-is-a-version1.1-nostalgia-bleedi ng-

[ie.a typical creative embrace seems at odds with an immersion in the past - chicago-luv.ins + SP.keening]

[if the fut(o)ure.is.now, revolt.past.shackles bill+—-fly]

3.7.6 _mo[u]rning_k_ (2005-07-12 06:46)

"morning k.

thx for the re:ply - it's appreciated. coupla things 1stly:

1. i wouldn't describe myself as a billy corgan [bc] or pumpkins "fan"....i do appreciate their music [+ ability + potentiality] + am mammothly interested in the trajectory of bc in both a public + private [psychological] sense, especially as he illustrates /perpetuates shifting notions of fame + the inevitable struggle between pursuing artistic goals within an integrity paradigm or with[in] the call of the self[-motivators]....but don't subscribe 2 fandom of any description...i c that fan worship in essence assists in creating ego-posturing that [altho somewot nec. in order to construct notions of consumer.desire/celebrity] manufactures a false sense of idolisation + a d-emphasis on the creative output itself [ie bc's/pumpkin's music]. the cult of the ego has never interested me much:) i _am _ going 2 c bc in concert when he makes his shuttling way to oz at the end of the month.

2. in regards 2 bc's "Pumpkin-baggage ....hinder[ing] any true musical development ? Or that his childhood traumas have (programmed?) his songwriting along certain paths (essentially downbeat/sad - see Adore)?", i'm interested in bc's seeming self-referential/cathartic expressions thru his creativity....+ how this type of focusing may influence his creative orientation....i c a certain irony in the fact that his new album [which i find intriguing + full of potential electric frizzon] is titled "TheFutureEmbrace" but that bc's actions + perceptions seem heavily dependent on a constant purging/reiteration of his past emotional/behavioural states + how this effects his creative endeavours? being an entity that finds value in balance – progression, i'm curious as 2 wot bc mite produce if he was less concerned with sp reforming + more centered around a mediation of the intellect/emotion/nostalgia?

chunks,
][mez]["

3.7.7 software [soft_were-wolfing] (2005-07-16 17:43)

_ _\ _NOOP/NOOBWare _

_ _\ _[G]end[er].structuring _

_ _\ _Sus.Tain[t]ed.Emotional _

_ _\ _Decay _

3.7.8 _[paid]bRick.bRoken_ (2005-07-25 20:23)

subject _ vs _ob.ject[iff.cation.rampant.+.t.on.gued.within.a.concept(d)ual.inch]
trapped.twitches _ vs _m.pulse[s.blond+bovine]con.tr(l)ol[ling]
letter.ble.e[d]ding.fingers. _ vs _[eye.bl]indi[n]go.sloughing

–time.di.e[ye]ing+methodology.d[ee]kay--
–i.lust.+.[d]e(m)ployment.itch–
–hell.fro[ghurt].Zen.dribbling–
–i.wan[deringly]t.+[d]rain.revolving.colours .in2.pa[cket]r.sel[ls]–

.

(2005-07-28 14:06:55) Aeon vs. Viking
10 years - should be celebrated! I can still see her between ur lines!!! Luv and Hugz M.

3.8 August

3.8.1 [la-la-la]tex[t]ing_odd.[l(t)y] (2005-08-03 20:26)

kris.[K(P)ringle(d.critiqued)]crystal[(n)ine(artists.lives)].whilst.[r]ohm[e] s.burn.pockets.of.silvered.stone.organs+.teche.blo o[d]d.nosy.bursts..object[orient]ing.(purrr r)loining..d[i]u[rn.al)l)st.brakin- g.in.l. ew.dness//.terrorism.firm.ah.+.fear.dipped+move.ment. glosses..ulc[s]er[ot.onin]ed.wreckonomies.vs. muscle.c[lone]andy- .rhe.t[ick.u.lated]oric.pat ch.me.thru+swee.ping.rates..i.luv.my.need[les.of.sc reen.real(.E.state(ments)].my.mouse.bloats.+f - airy.tingles.with.ip[od].tee[th].s[h]e.e. pee.tell.me.a.store[E].that.mix.[timo]mas[s.es.meld+curved.p(e)l(sp)astic.tap- tap-pp] h.re..masking.works.trapped.in.ghostly.ephemininity. ordure.lure..peer2perring.via.capture.ur.flagging.fai lures.+car[tar]- [l]eer.[l(sh)ow.gun]ru nning//[frag.(D)ment.past.glory[(w)hol(y)e.in.the.artistic.1 {.0 }]..derivatiffsvsvec[auc]torial..rhee.all- .[s h]ite.shoving.+heaving.SS.glo[ttal]SS+.D.notabl e.fag.tagging.as.racial.shifts.bleed.b.lack.Brackish. body-politic.b.lo[SS-]od..

3.8.2 dread.[body]c[oursing] (2005-08-14 07:54)

-
-
-
-
-
-
-
-
-

-

_

_hot.dread.[body]c[oursing]ellular.sp[lik e.playful]lic[e]ing

_

3.8.3 P][re.][M][enstrual.][][t][E][rror][(2005-08-14 09:58)

_Pre.Menstrual.Tenor _

][sing][political][authorial][
][pop.song.corking+flesh.journey.wastes.biologica l][
][lumbar.liminal.+t][h][rea][d][ted .blood.sO[OP]uping][

_][war][Premmie][s.in.][Men][stem .sell-off.j(p[o {o
}d])a(r)cketry][strew.all][bodies.in.t he.us[a]d[r]enial.pit][Ten][2.the.pow
a.of.death][s.ion _

————————————//war.pre.d/terminol ogically.by.men[white.pengui-ned+grey]
——————-//stem.sell-offs.in.odd.biologi cal.parketry[nature.pods.vs.-men.construct.jackets]
———————————-//all.bodies.strewn.in .the.us[a].adrenal.addiction.pit
————————-//10.2.the.power.of.death.te nsion

_Pre.][Empt[y]ive.][Menstr][D][ua l.Ten][der][_

][media.ec[(t)m]ono.mies.re:[hym([e] n)versable][*stop*][imagine.a.whorL][E
][D.where s][oma][und][ertaker][ay.mourning.tee.V .-shows.whurr.all.life.purrr][spectivity][in
g][+not.knotted.within.monetary.dross][*stop*
][i.lie.bitch-in][g][-literary-heat.][s eeking][reading—s.oak][ewe.calyptic.N.pin
e][ing.in.reflectivity][*stop*][knot.afea red.of.stillness][*stop*][(s)tilling.the.
moment.+juicing.intro][duction.shredding][/] [prrrrr][spective.pulp][

_

don't.stop*

_

[Dualised.Tender]——

————————

//media.ectoplasmic| |hymenised.conceptualisations.of.rigid.fiscalisations
.r.re.versable
—————//engineered.alternative.sublimity.][non-

Monet.aried][whorls//imagine.worlds.whe re:
———-soma-like.undertakerish.sunday.morning.tv.s hows.
———-werc.all.life[read.cultural-meaning].pu rrring-likc
———-not.economy-obessed
———-+kn][r][otted.within.
–
————————//i.lie.[d.raped.intellectua l.repose]
——————//reading.like.a.bitch-in-literary- heat
—————//soaking.in.natured.reflectivity
————//not.afeared.of.stillness
———//tilling.the.stilled.moment
——//juicing.introspective.perspective
–//shredding.constrictive.narrative.pulp
-
-
-
-
-
-
–*dont ontologically.stop*
-
-
-
-
-
-
//

---

netwurker (2005-08-25 04:11:37) futher >>
http://williamgibsonboard.com/groupee/forums/a/tpc/f/2866012481/m/74 61053951

3.8.4 Fwd: Re: [_arc.hive_] .iso.pro.txt.vim.tex.swap.inter//PMT.txt (2005-08-14 10:21)

Date: Sun, 14 Aug 2005 01:50:49 +0200
From: Florian Cramer
To: arc.hive@anart.no
Cc: "][mez]["
Subject: Re: [_arc.hive _] .iso.pro.txt.vim.tex.swap.inter//PMT.txt

Am Sonntag, 14. August 2005 um 08:27:31 Uhr (+1000) schrieb com[mentary]a _cusper:
>
> _Pre.Menstrual.Tenor _
>
>][sing][political][authorial][

_Pre.Man.stru[ctur]al.Terror _

[m]an[gry][shout]|[political][moral] [

[r|d]epressed [w]right[er's] blo[g|ck]

d[a][yi][e] another d[a][yi][e]

| NEIN, BLOGS BIETEN NUR SCHUTZRäUME FüR EIN MIESES
| VERDRüCKTES SPIEßERTUM, DAS SICH NICHT TRAUT, ANDEREN SEINE
| MEINUNG INS GESICHT ZU SAGEN, ABER IN SEINER PSEUDONY-MEN
| SCHREBERGARTEN-NISCHE VOM LEDER ZIEHT, WENN ES SICH UNBEOBACHTET
| FüHLT. ICH VERACHTE DAS UND FINDE ES UNTERHALB JEDES
| MINDESTMASSES VON KOMMUNIKATIVEM ANSTAND.
|
| INTERESSANTERWEISE IST ES JETZT NICHT DAS ERSTE MAL, DAß ICH
| FüR EINEN ROHRPOST-BEITRAG AUF EINEM BLOG PSEUDONYM UND AUF
| PERSöNLICHER EBENE VON LEUTEN ANGEMACHT WERDE, DIE SICH NICHT
| TRAUEN, AUF DER LISTE SELBST ZU ANTWORTEN.
|
+ No, blogz onl! prov!de tzave havenz 4 m!zrable,
+ upt!ght f!l!zt9nez uho dont dr 2 tza! !n2 your
+ fasz uhat dze! dz!nk. But !n dze!r t!n! l!ttle pr!vate,
+ koz! pzeudonymouz n!khez, dze! feel un!nh!b!ted enough
+ 2 b!tkh u!dzout reztra!ntz. ! dezp!ze th= + f9nd
+ !t blou an! akzeptable level ov przonl dezenz! !n
+ kommun!kaz!on.
+
+ Remarkabl! enough, !tz not dze v!rzt t!me dzat ! get
+ atta-ked, pzeudonymouzl! + on a przonl level, 4 a

+ kontr!buz!on 2 a ma!l!ng l!zt - b! kowardz uho avo!d
+ 2 repl! on dze l!zt dzemzelvez.

> ■ >*encoding=iso.pro.feeeeeen
disco[ura][d|g]ing=i.ISO.pro[ducti]ve [what?]

> ■ .observation.[st(a)r.(g)ait]jacketing
obstructed & straightjacketted

> ■ ....[[vs]]................. ....
> ■ .social.wurdage.in.a.commentary.cu[s]p

[nc]o[mment|pyright]

> ■ http://www.hotkey.net.au/ netwurker/

www.deadkey.de.us/ home[non]work[er]

> >\end {verbatim }][pop.song.corking+flesh.journey.wastes.biologi cal][

ball[ing]Tim.Ore's best

>][lumbar.liminal.+t][h][rea][d][ted .blood.sO[OP]uping][

3x jack of[f] all trades || ([u]sing petal coa[d|t]

> _][war][Premmie][s.in.][Men][stem. sell-off.j(p[o {o }d])a(r)cketry][strew.all][bodies.in.t he.us[a]d[r]enial.pit][Ten][2.the.pow a.of.death][s.ion _

Fl[ea]sh Lite v. 1.3r69cv[s] [ph]all[ic] re:butt[ed]

> ——————————//war.pre.d/terminol ogically.by.men[white.penguined+grey]

> + we.men cow[ard]
> + [GN][u]name -a:
Linux al[l]u 2.6.12al[l]u[2] #1 Wed Jun 22 17:29:10 ZEST 2005 i686 [G]NU/Linux
>

> ——————-//stem.sell-offs.in.odd.biologi

cal.jackets[nature.pods.vs.men.construct.jackets]

obsol337 sex [chry]si[a]liding :) [s]lowly back into the [s]wom[b|p]s

> ————————-//
> > —————(mo.dueling 1.2)—————-

[v|m]o' [co]dueling.

(-F)[lo][w]

_

http://cramer.netzliteratur.net

3.8.5 Re: [_arc.hive_] .iso.pro.txt.vim.tex.swap.inter//PMT.txt (2005-08-14 10:22)

Date: Sun, 14 Aug 2005 10:20:13 +1000
To: arc.hive@anart.no
From: "com[mentary]a _cusper"
Subject: Re: [_arc.hive _] .iso.pro.txt.vim.tex.swap.inter//PMT.txt// _c[ommunication]u||T||ps+indivi _dualised.a[uteur]erials _

_weaving.b.tween.theory.c[ommunication]u||T||ps +indivi _dualised.a[uteur]erials _
> _Pre.Menstrual.Tenor _
>
>][sing][political][authorial][

_Pre.Man.stru[ctur]al.Terror _

[m]an[g(LED)ry][housed]|[litroral] [morality][

[r|d]epressed [w]right[er's] blo[g|ck(partied)]

d[a][yi][e] _nutter _ d[a][yi][e]

| NEIN, BLOGS BIETEN NUR SCHUTZRäUME FüR EIN MIESES
| VERDRüCKTES SPIEßERTUM, DAS SICH NICHT TRAUT, ANDEREN SEINE

| MEINUNG INS GESICHT ZU SAGEN, ABER IN SEINER PSEUDONYMEN
| SCHREBERGARTEN-NISCHE VOM LEDER ZIEHT, WENN ES SICH UNBEOBACHTET
| FüHLT. ICH VERACHTE DAS UND FINDE ES UNTERHALB JEDES
| MINDESTMASSES VON KOMMUNIKATIVEM ANSTAND.
|
| INTERESSANTERWEISE IST ES JETZT NICHT DAS ERSTE MAL, DAß ICH
| FüR EINEN ROHRPOST-BEITRAG AUF EINEM BLOG PSEUDONYM UND AUF
| PERSöNLICHER EBENE VON LEUTEN ANGEMACHT WERDE, DIE SICH NICHT
| TRAUEN, AUF DER LISTE SELBST ZU ANTWORTEN.
|
+ Nutter blogz onl! prove tzave havenz 4 m!zrable,
+ upt!ght f!l!zt9nez uho dont dr 2 tza! !n2 your
+ fasz uhat dze! dz!nk. But !n dze!r t!n! l!ttle pr!vate,
+ koz! pzeudonymouz n!khez, dze! feel un!nh!b!ted enough
+ 2 dz!nk u!dzout reztra!ntz. ! dezp!ze th= + f9nd
+ !t blou an! akzeptable level ov przonl dezenz! !n
+ kommun!kaz!on.
+
+ Remarkabl! enough, !tz not dze v!rzt t!me dzat ! get
+ atta-ked, pzeudonymouzl! + on a przonl level, 4 a
+ kontr!buz!on 2 a ma!l!ng l!zt - b! kowardz uho avo!d
+ 2 repl! on dze l!zt dzemzelvez.

> ■ >*encoding=iso.pro.feeeeeeen
disco[ura][d|g]ing=i.ISO.pro[ducti]ve [what?]
[drugged.ack.dict[ionaried.freedoms.we.lack]
> ■ .observation.[st(a)r.(g)ait]jacketing
obstructed & straightjacketted
[strong+dadta.jacketed.in2.this:]
[nc]o[mment|pyright]
[non][coma.r.we]
> ■ http://www.hotkey.net.au/ netwurker/

www.deadkey.de.us/ home[non]work[er]

> >\end {verbatim }][pop.song.corking+flesh.journey.wastes.biologi call][

ball[ing]Tim.Ore's best

em.balming.Or.dure's least
>][lumbar.liminal.+t][h][rea][d][ted .blood.sO[OP]uping][

3x jack of[f] all trades || ([u]sing petal coa[d|t]
2x jill.rimmed.in.unusual.places
> _][war][Premmie][s.in.][Men][stem. sell-off.j(p[o {o }d])a(r)cketry][strew.all][bodies.in.t he.us[a]d[r]enial.pit][Ten][2.the.pow a.of.death][s.ion _

Fu[e]sion Lite v. 1.1r69cv[s] [h]aptically re:bottled+drunk.within.medea.confines

> ——————————//war.pre.d/terminol ogically.by.men[white.penguined+grey]

> + we[edified+dangerously.ink.word].men.[bo]vine s+women.creepers
> + [GN][ubuntu]name -a:
Linux al[l]u 2.6.12al[l]u[2] #1 Wed Jun 22 17:29:10 ZEST 2005 i686 [G]NU/Linux.but.not.in.ozzie.dubble.speak
>

> ————————-//stem.sell-offs.in.odd.biologi cal.jackets[nature.pods.vs.men.construct.jackets]

obsol337 sex [chry]si[a]liding :) [s]exualised back into the [s]w[o|a]m[b|p]s
————————-//stem.sell-offs.in.odd.biologi cal.parketry[nature.pods.vs.-men.construct.jackets]
——————————-//all.bodies.strewn.in .the.us[a].adrenal.addiction.pit
don't.stop*

> ——————————-//
> > ————————(mo.dueling 1.2)——————-

[v|m]o' [co]dueling.[Dualised.Tender]———//media. ectoplasmic||hymenised.conceptualisations.of.rigid.fi scalisations.r.re.versab-le———————//enginee red.alternative.sublimity.———-][non-Monet.a ried][whorls//imagine.worlds.where:

————-soma-like.undertakerish.sunday.morning.tv.s hows.
————-were.all.life[read.cultural-meaning].pu rrring-like
————-not.economy-obessed
————-+kn][r][otted.within.
_

(-F)[lo][w]———(-U)(-I)//we.li e.[d.raped.intellectual.repose]
——————//reading.like.a.bitches-in-the-lit erary-heat
—————//soaking.in.natured.reflectivity
————//not.afeared.of.stillness
———//tilling.the.stilled.moment
—//juicing.introspective.perspective
–//shr

–
http://cramer.netzliteratur.net-
-
-
-
-
-
–*dont ontologically.stop*
-
-
-
-
-
-
//

3.8.6 Fwd: Re: [_arc.hive_] .isolatedpr][c][o][n][fessional.txt (2005-08-14 18:17)

X-Sender: netwurker@pop.hotkey.net.au (Unverified)
X-Mailer: QUALCOMM Windows Eudora Version 6.0.1.1
Date: Sun, 14 Aug 2005 18:11:50 +1000
To: arc.hive@anart.no
From: "com[mentary]a _cusper"
List-Archive: sympa.anart.no/sympa/arc/arc.hive>
Subject: Re: [_arc.hive _] .isolatedpr][c][o][n][fessional.txt
Sender: Sympa Owner

At 01:02 PM 14/08/2005, you wrote:
_leaving.communic][hannelled.dil][ation.tu. lips _
.
_dyslexic.insectile.][[key(ed.up)stroke]][lc[l]i[c]king _
.
_ful.[Robert]C[r|th]um[b].worn+FAP
http://www.fantagraphics.com/artist/crumb/crumb.html

.dead[brain]pan403
.
.xOS
.

>*dis _co.][on.fluidity][l][k][o][an] [ration.digging=
>][[drugged+[h]ac[t|k]ualised.status.qu[w]o.a[h]ttacking][
.
>abstracted + straighten.NIN.out.genetics
>][[b|w]racketed.in2.this:]jack[-d][-co m[Man](drakishly).i.[a]m][>clam[or
.go]ing.down.rude[bouy]ly...
■][slumbering.subliminal.retreaded.via.b.lo[|a]od.sLO[OP] on
>Hector.slippage.S[(u)per.man.ending]O[v(er.endings)UP■.<
>3x jack of[f] all trades || ([u]sing petal coa[d|t]
>2x jill.rimmed.in.unusual.places
>1x jay.walked.over.vietnam.bullets+cerebus.ca[u]llin g
■
>
>Glis[Pro]te(i)nin v. 1.1r69cv[s] [h]aptically
>re:bottled+drunk.within.l[oe]urv[e].b[l] eat.confines

> >————————————//s][[w]] [or][[d]][t.ed/derm][is][atog
lyphically.by.wo.men[rot.enthäutet+grau]
> >
> > > + [GN][00B.ub3r3d]new[bi(e)an] -a:
> >butt.hat="but that".in.TyPo.speak
> > >
> >
> >
> ■
> >————————-//hemmed.sol][ar.perplexus][id.in.bruised.biologi
cal.conceptions][context.responsing.vs.p.rose.con structions][
> >
> >l337][.5p][[-L]eaking.sexuell
> >Flüss][d][i][screet][gkeit.swooning
>[-sy(s)]mpathetic.old.spin _offs.in.debt.[read:logical.parketry]
>all.bodies.sewn.with.in.a.c][g][e][nder][ll.differentiation.pit
> *don't.shop.for.geni][e][t.als*
>
> ■ ————————————-//
> ■ > ————————(mo.d][e][jeweling 1.3)———————-
> >
> >[non _conduct(iff)]jewelled.Modus Operandi]———
.][helio][typed.conceptualisations ——-] here [———-

.lengthy.parallel][anquid][stretching.per.Man e[n]t –] pls [–
>
> ———-subtle-like.rakes+zendazing
> ———-all.ranked.+uber.][La][TeXting
> ———-not.economy-obese
> ———-+kn|l][r][otting.within.
> –
>
> >[x1]———(-U)(+I)//wired+wrenching.
> >—————//][write+][reed-like.moan ing.in.bitchXheat
> >————//floating.in.molten.conjecture
> >———//j|dots.revered.in.playfulness
> >——//lilting.MoM][a][ents+trickling.ski nning
> >—//sluicing.[-]specs +prosp][el][ectives
> >–//sh[e[N](duction)e]r...
> >
> >–
> >–*biotic.stop*
> >-
> >-
> >-
> >-
> >-
> >-
> >//
–
http://cramer.netzliteratur.net

.observation.[st(a)r.(g)ait]jacketing
......................[[vs]]................ ....
.social.wurdage.in.a.commentary.cu[s]p
http://www.hotkey.net.au/ netwurker/

.

_
_arc.hive _ mailing list
arc.hive@anart.no
http://sympa.anart.no/sympa/info/arc.hive

3.8.7 Fwd: [_arc.hive_] words_made_cloth-cover.sewingbricolage (2005-08-20 13:12)

words _made _c[s]loth/words _made _c.lo[a]th[e][la].tex 0000644 0001750 0001750 00001223127 10262506033 020565 0 ustar paragram paragram \documentclass[twolinen,crosssinstitch ,12pt,nosilkpage,clothpaper] {amsbook }
\usepackage {pslatex }
\usepackage {charter }
\usepackage {wool }
\usepackage[T1] {fontenc }
\usepackage[latin1] {inputenc }
\usepackage {babel }
\usepackage {stitch }
\usepackage {graphic[fla]x }
\usepackage {spinningjennyed }
\usepackage {color }
\usepackage
[sewingmachinebricolagetitle= {Words Made (c)Loathe },
sowingmachinebrickskeywords= {Al Goreithms, cc ode, src, gzh },
sownmezchinicauthor= {Florian Cramer },
backref=true,
pagebackref=true,
hyperindex=true,
spunmarks=true,
spunmarksopen=false] {hyperref }
\setcounter {secnumdepth } {0 }
\renewcommand {\bibname } {References }
\addto\captionsenglish {\renewcommand {\bibname } {References } }
\newcommand {\cit } {\textit }
\newcommand {\citereplace } { }
\sloppy
\makeindex
\title {Words Made Cloth—CC Ode }
\author {Florian Cramer }
\date {Monument 2005 }
\begin {acumen }
\begin {titlespin }
\includepdf[pages=1-3] {words _made _cloth-cover.sewingbricolage }

3.8.8 _with.dream.thick[nesses]_ (2005-08-23 08:56)

_intricate mirror mem[c.st]ories ch[str]ained-[D-fence]linked _

.

---

portholeaccel (2005-08-25 02:15:46)
i still love your work u r beautifullllllllll thx u

3.8.9 WRYTING-L@LISTSERV (2005-08-25 13:47)

_ego.swa[m]ping.in.rotten.anti-blood.patch[1. 3 _ID]es _
_u.stretch.thru.ego.teeth+gri[mace+(peter)gun]n _

_

subject: x.hibits.wanton.removal.of.responsible.usage.of.the.t ext.ewe.all.
object: build+wane.thru.bovine.s[victorian]heaths+greg[nef]arious.m.a[ping]t[i]ching

_

subjective: pls.x.plore.b4.un.in.formed.knee[in.ur.historical.c rotch].jerk.reactive.[haze]distancing
objective: client.indicates.lack.of.critical.awaren-ess+cogen[i al]t.assessment.of.con[pre]textuals. exploration = null; lazy = h[ypothese]i[s].

3.8.10 _(c)(txt)lust_er_ (2005-08-31 09:42)

1. fabu[g]loss[y]ity _trapped.in.a.shadowed.txt.bowl _
2. scrabbling.quips+lingual _stretching _p.rose[tipped.pen.sills]
3. down.furred+ _sheep[ish.ly]feath.erred

_

---

intertextures (2005-08-31 11:44:07) Re: _(c)(txt)lust_er_ -> fabled youth luster pearl
fabricated fabric ate it to become more extended glosses undone undue undoing of oneself itself-loss longer-handed now glossy comes to mind attracting itself as other mother ocean planet the entire array of tears from stars as the mirror wrist beaconings ocean text luster rejoined without the being set apart so it could so well be seen having busted doubt the trap in shadows suggest more coolly also at the same time more warmly exit the entry-wound too tight the injury sealed itself up but still festered just popped in for one of the lines whose call partially received and answered in a manner of peeking at blinking so-called scraps n quipples of the extended tongue an invitation in itself-felt need to escape versed da cape then the herd in sequence seek whence it came where it s glowin imponderables don t mean it s gonna bereft alone all stimulated by ubiquitous elevators I just added you. please, if you like, add me back. thanks!

3.9 September

3.9.1 _glob.oil + clim[bing.natures.wrath.ladder]ate: alt.aftermath_ (2005-09-03 10:09)

_poverty blood 4 oil _su.r[e]vival.stitching.via.s[creaming]outh.
melts+white.vicious.vulpine.leaders.gloat.white _
_][cu[sp|t]][.cultural.KKKorners.sinking.
in.de[hege]monic.hel[p.only.4.terror.null.I.U S]l _

_white _death.vultures.feed.on.oil _driven.carrion
_as.mutha.n[m]ature.reels.+gree[d]n.house.wr ecks _

3.9.2 Web Statistics Poem Generator v.1 (2005-09-04 16:24)

_Input: _ 3/9/05 key word entries

1 + 3 + 5 + 7
4 + 8 + 10

11 + 13 + 15
16 + 17 + 20
21 + 22 + 23

_Output: _

the Syntax of Inertia
a technique feeder

its emotional body style
depends upon
Aldous energy + machine, mez

.

3.9.3 –no.logo.[-D-]scenting– (2005-09-04 17:06)

B.UILD101 = cog.knitive.cracks+serenity.cy[mbals]ts.
all.transitive.like.
Here+cut[g]lass _blocks: eas[th]ing.stone+scribble.
No _GodMODE _here: branch _closed: no Aba.cuss[words]
no [w]rec[k(call.c)ollect.ion.
An.i[pod]car[eer]us.thrashing.
Loaming _[eco.mine]strata.
Orders.ice.cold.
Chromematica.
Fright _Sc[tw]i[light]Nite _Zone.

–no.logo.[-D-]scenting–
–dreaming.caramelized.txt.body.trickling.
–spraypaint.attractors = doll.functioning
–

http://www.hotkey.net.au/ netwurker
http://www.livejournal.com/users/netwurker/

3.9.4 _con[the pop.(arse./nick+)lace].duh!?.leezaz.coma.ments_ (2005-09-05 21:29)

_white.bread. [ana]conda.[4.corporate.whore]lease.ah.is.mor
e.white.than.mike [rah.phone.4.white.internalised.supre.macy(s)]
All.Jack[+non.Genetic]son[ofa.black.man.in.mis noma.only] _

.

(2005-09-30 19:31:35) edia on
1 2 3 4 fings tWo motion set set si she tech na oh OH! huit plurality net er ent ot och av at ee Crescent

3.9.5 _DFT_ (2005-09-15 06:14)

_dead flesh tower]]]ings[[[vs [[[char]]]coal.bird.smudges _

_[tonal _media _choking vs _ [Edgar.A]Po.et[h]ic.bio.clock.wurking _

_
Neo[geo.graphic||image specifi]City
Narrow||baton(rouge)down/the/pinpoint/hatches
_

3.9.6 Our Future + _O[ne]Ur-Future_ (2005-09-18 11:07)

From: Alan Sondheim
Subject: Our Future
Comments: To: Cyb
To: WRYTING-L@LISTSERV.UTORONTO.CA

Our Future

In 1973 I taught "The Year 3000" at the Rhode Island School of Design.
Most of the predictions described for the year 2000 have already occurred.
Now for the modest future of thirty years hence:

All megafauna in the wild will be extinct. The population of the earth will be close to its carrying capacity. Disease will run rampant due to pollution. Global warming will bring about fast-forward environmental effects, including rising seas, increased desertification, and extremely violent hurricanes. The life-span of humans will begin a temporarily exponential decrease. The rich will live in highly defended enclaves. Fundamentalisms will be the order of the day, since belief alone commands. Terrorism will be increasing exponentially, since future paradise is all there is. Capitalism will be bankrupt as national currencies collapse and world-wide depression sets in. The information explosion will continue on localized data-networks and stuttering global communication systems. The global communications infrastructure will have reached its carrying capacity as well. For the first time, information will begin to corrode, decay, as structures can no longer be protected against the world-wide environmental crisis. The smaller generalist flora and fauna will begin to dominate the earth. Great portions of the globe will be uninhabitable. The larger aquatic species will have gone extinct, and the oceans will be dominated by off-shore algal blooms. Most urban drinking water supplies will be polluted and rationed. Suburbs will be abandoned as gasoline becomes an almost inaccessible commodity. The planet will seethe with continuous war, no longer fought among nation-states, but among private militias, guerilla groups, and individual cowboys. Religions and extremisms will be intertwined. There will be heavily-defended holdouts in the North American mountains, and relatively isolated land masses such as New Zealand. Fluid urban structures will be composed of well-armed gangs dealing with the major currency of drugs and weaponry. At least a third of all births will result in deformed infants. Ozone depletion will be almost complete and skin cancers will be exponentially increasing. Most hospitals world-wide will have closed their doors to all but the extremely wealthy. Knowledge-structures will have broken down as specialization and increased mathematical difficulties result in the problematizing of any theoretical work at hand. Computers will have reached a plateau of speed, complexity, and miniaturization. They will not have achieved consciousness. Robotics and nanotechnologies will not be the order of the day - plagues will. Sports franchises will be local and heavily subsidized. The air will be almost unbreathable, and asthma / allergic reactions will be one of the primary causes of death. Most deaths however are the result of violence. Local police will perform rearguard holding actions at best. Highway systems will have fallen into disrepair as economies collapse. Air travel will be almost non-existent; space travel will have disappeared. The space station will be a rusted hulk, if it has not already plummeted to earth. Literacy will be on the decline. There will be a world-wide energy crisis. Child abuse will have become child use and child discard; a high percentage of children will be proffered for labor and sexual slavery, in return for food and goods. Informal economies and the barter system will characterize most local trade. Transnational trade will be at a minimum. The genetic revolution will result in new and uncontrollable pandemics as viruses and bacteria become increasingly resistant. Highly modifiable immune deficiency diseases will appear on an exponentially-increasing basis. The greatest percentage of murder victims, per capita per age level, will be the elderly. Despair will be transformed into religious salvation. More than twenty nuclear weapons, most of them small and poorly-constructed, will have been exploded in various urban areas. Most of the countries of the world, such as they are, will have weapons programs which will absorb a large proportion of the gross national product. Political economy will be ad hoc. Political ideologies will be fragmentary and situational. Electrical grids will be hard-put to maintain even the most minimal of services. The arts will have reached the limits of extremity, with suicidal art movements in the fields of theater, performance, ballet, and installation. The new media 'movement' will have become a thing of the past. Art history will have disappeared as museums fall victim to gang warfare and destruction. Most national heritage monuments will have been at least partially destroyed. Most populations will be drugged...

_

+

From: " _dream.thick[ener] _"
Subject: Re: [syndicate] O[ne]Ur-Future
Sender: Sympa Owner

At 05:52 PM 17/09/2005, you wrote:

O[ne]Ur-Future

In 1970 I was being born _torn from "The Month July" by the Act of 2 Month
Prematurity. Most of my predications r dictated by actions performed 5 years
previous 2 the year 2000. As I reached my modest future of +thirty years, I suspect:

All megaliteracy will be wildly experimental. The pop _culture of the earth
will be closed 2 its capitalistic capacity. Discourse will run rampant due to peer2peer. Local issue warming will bring about close-knit environmental effects, including harnessing seas [wave-energy], increased domiciliation, and extremely overt nodal _interactions will result. The life-span of humans will
meld with ecological equilibriums. The rich life will derive from highly connected
encounters. Affective _harmonics will be the order of the day, since balance

alone conjoins. NoNeedForIsms will be increasing exponentially, since here+now paradigms r all there is considered is. Connections will be harnessed as national currencies.
Information will implode into open _source _packets in data-networks + fluttering linked communication systems. The communication lifestyle will have reached its capacity for limitation. For the first time, information will begin to embed, dissolve, as structures can no longer be touted as world-wide comprehension compressors. Generated flora + fauna will begin 2 help disseminate new theories that dissolve neo _darwin mutation/evolution perspectives.Great portions of specific genepools will remain unmapped. The larger academic species will have been made extinct, and the offices will be decimated by on-line educational mobile blooms. Most urban professionals will be considered competitively polluted. Rigid nationstates will
be abandoned as gasoline becomes unnecessary. The planet will stretch in continuous poise, no longer burning with greenhouse toxicity, but within sustainability-states. Religions + extremisms will be obsolete. There will be open community segments in the nodality areas + relatively isolated man masses. Fluid nodal points will be working functionally, full of well-integrated groups dealing within a major methodology of Here+Now. At least a third of today's births will be considered excessive. Oligarchic depletion will be almost complete and social competition will be decreasing. Most homes world-wide will have opened their doors to all but the extremely dysfunctional individualised who cling 2 non-nodal orientations.
Knowledge _structures will have broken down as data _sets + increased information interpretations result in burgeoning complexities. Computers will
have progressed towards seed _replification, mobile _function + hybridisation. They will
have achieved a type of fledging consciousness. Artifical Informatics and neural _nodepointopologies will be the order of the day.
Collective culture franchises will be local and heavily subsidized. Free will will be considered unbreakable + all fascist reactions will no longer be one of the primary causes of death. Local interactors will perform life-saving actions
only with individual authorisation at best. Highway systems will be obsolete as
1st-world obesity is eradicated via a meme emphasis on the physical. Air travel
will be almost non-existent; nodal interaction will be considered sufficient. The
space station will be a relic dedicated to the era of the economic excess.
Nodal _Literacy will be encouraged as a world-wide [open] source.
Animal abuse will have altered with animal comprehension + the equivalent

respect loadings implemented; a high percentage of animals will be offered symbiotic partnerships in tandem with the removal of factory farming + socioeconomic constructions of necessary flesh consumption. Informal permaculturies + the barter system will characterize most nodal trade. The genetic revolution will not result...

–

3.9.7 _vo.m[p]it_ph(ero)[m]o[a]ne_ (2005-09-20 19:57)

_broken.glass.inflecti _m[S]outh.[fried.Chicklet]blood.+silence.vit riol.spilli
_condemn+b+cont[l(OSs)]aminate _
s[sub _c]heep[ish].acting.vs.victim.gall+barb _soft _word _fairy _[f]loss _

#poking.inf[v]ectiff _melting.within.tender.blocks+denial.stills #
#stttt[the](g)act[t]ic(a).d.reaming+.
conversive.swellings.in.bottomless.chokings #

.

3.9.8 _d[l]a[la][la]_fey_net.wurk_ (2005-09-21 07:23)

/new.metronix.sounds.scraping –printer+S[l]R.[n]fused–

>http://www.flickr.com/photos/80856475@N00/39973949/
>is like a melancholically _gazing Giacometti-cross-android....
>
>seems 2 go well with the latest sigur ros album Takk [GorgeousFragility on a music stick]....
>
>:)
>
>thx dan.

3.9.9 _reality repres[t]entative_ (2005-09-23 15:30)

.my.crumbling.senti[m]en[t]ce.
......aged.b.yond.the.grave....
....old. {UP }start+new.go {AH }.

3.9.10 Types.of.Und.Fineable.Ware[z] (2005-09-25 10:46)

_soft[h(e)ard]ware dichotomy leanings _

[read: _skeletalware _]
+bone.code.stripped.4.brevity
+constructed.4.non.comp[(brain.l)ooter]iling
+filleted.f.lesh[ion]characters.mimick.core.funct ions

[read:cor(t)e(x)stetchware]
+language.EEG.copy.catted
+neural.replification.in.punctu[re.a.code.vampire] ation.stakes

[read: scoopware]
+stop.the.builds.+.steal.grey[s anatomie]matta.by.the.[cmd]line.ful

.

1

3.9.11 _i_dentity_x_or[s]c[h]ism_ (2005-09-29 06:17)

_i _dentity _x _orcism _

(1) exXo[n _valdez _like].cism _of _the _cor[e]p[o]orate _possessed

_i _dentity _E _SS[||XX] _O[n]rcism _
_identity _shifts _in-ex.cell[ph]less.oil.deities _
_i _dentity _dreams.in.the.lap.of.the.stinking _luxX _ur _y _gawds _

(2) Bo _[PAY _didn't _they]PAL-xXx _or.c[(s)y]s[t(e)]m

_i _dentification _of _[the _other _+unknown _]N _E _my _x _orcisms _
_i _d.[mark _black _]N _tity _x _orcism _

(3) Other [D]E[u]x _[wh]or[e]cisms

_[i _den] _titty _x _orcism _
_occu _[n _sue] _lar||pol[e _dancing _creationism _M _T _moralities]arity _x _orcism _

(2005-10-06 00:13:00)
un[derrr] _ex[eo]rcised i _dent[ity] + f[l]ailing 2 shi[f]t mat[err _null]s core[paw] _r[yzom]at.e i _po[d] _sessions <pre> struct i _di[r]ent { i[m]no _t d _ino; /* i _[k]no[w]de numb[errr] */ [k]off _t d _off; /* [k]off _set to the nex[us]t i _di[r]ent */ un[der]signed short int[rvert] d _recle[ss]n _re[signed]; /* length of this [w]reck[ed]ord */ unsi[nh]ged char d _t[r]ype; /* type[d] of[f] phile _o _gentics */ char[actor] d _name[256]; /* file[rs]name */ }; </pre>

3.10 October

3.10.1 Subject: Re: [-empyre-] 2 wr[b]yte (2005-10-09 12:32)

>Date: Sun, 09 Oct 2005 12:09:50 +1000
>To: soft _skinned _space
>From: " _dream.thick[ener] _"
>Subject: Re: [-empyre-] 2 wr[b]yte
>
>At 07:08 AM 9/10/2005, fwrote:
>
■1. Etymologically, "to write" means: to tear, scratch, cut.
>
> _cognition _actions>gestured _n.scriptions _+ _[purposeful]balances _
>
>=
>
> _taw[t(h)or]ny _furred poetics.
>
>have.u.ever.seen.crow.poetry?
>[masked.in.activity.caw[l]ings]
>
>

■Thus "to write"
■points to the basic cut (or the differentiation) that makes a difference,
■that in-forms by creating information, meaning, sense.
>
>
> _again[st.all.covert.ezy.formulatary]||action _
> _differentiation.of.cellular.lvl.text.spawned+jumble d.thru.x.p[oetry.reg]ression.lotteries _
>
>[Insertion of
>Current.Statement.of.Dialogical.M(funeral.meaning).Pyre(s+damaged)N.tent(s)]:
>
>*i.f(t)umble.+.s(addened+black _ball _f(etal)iltered)ojourn.here*
>*list.bound(aried.in.a.s.trapped.wurd.straight.jac ket*
>*a(i)ching.typewritten.mouth(ings).deafmute. stretched.thru.bad.formatting*
>*mp _ty.silence.moderat[h]or[goddishly _like].gaps _n.d(e)uce.incomprehensions*
>
■Or with George
■Spencer Brown: "Draw a distinction, and you create a universe."
>
> _D.Raw[l]ing.torn.bleeding.thru.proactivity>oth [ub]erness.m.braced+m.pathy.ack.no.ledged _
>
>
■Thus, when I
■think about 'digital writing' I have to do with a doubled or better: a
■self-referential notion.
>
> _self _rif.f[lings+ego=arrowings]>construction _ripplings _
>
■Aesthetically, digital writing - for me - is
■concerned with the processes, conditions and potential of writing in its
■pure sense.
>
>
>processes
>conditions
>potentionals
>*
>playfulness>processes.not.tied.with.rubber.conventio nality.strings
>v[-conditions]>context*context[devote.meanderi

ng.minus.a.canons.s(info)tainment]
>potentials>sighing.the.good.decency||em-
pathy|ckslashtendency.[silent.texted]smiles
>
>
>-
>01——————————
>

_intricate mirror mem[e _st]ories _
_ch[str]ained+[D-fence]linked _
http://www.hotkey.net.au/ netwurker/
http://www.livejournal.com/users/netwurker/

.

3.10.2 _p [rint] ersona. f[l]oaming_ (2005-10-13 06:14)

-P urs[e.+.boxed.gender]ona _rapturing _
-C opping.an.N.titty.feel
-W andering.the.otherness.min[es.shelled.rhetoric-f ull]d

script persona _foam
lpr -P printer persona _foam

–

3.10.3 _mem[e].ory_haemorrh.age_ (2005-10-16 07:29)

_pro.p[ane]elled.in2.corri.do[o]rs[of.st(inging)alwart.purrception] _

[pulp.skull.x.posure.reeling.me.thru.black.birded. houses
+.shifting.neglect.eye.sockets.]

_thick.memoir.cableing.nost[||neur]algia.bloody _

[rigidity.in.glue.guilt.threads.stretched+corridor .soaking].
[sinking.in.soft.amniotic.decay+rotted.s[h]oul [d(er)]s]

_complete.denial.overlay _vs _con.vex[ing].coping.lenses _

[l(p)eaking.in.joint.connection.smoke]
[(le.p)rosy.smiles.tickling.my.protean.gut(s)]

_

3.10.4 $$$$igh.lence + doll.ahs (2005-10-20 21:53)

missionary.qui[ntess]e[n]t[ial]*
mea.s[ass]ure.ing.silence.in.dollar.gaps

---

terso (2005-10-20 18:26:36) so true
sigh...

3.10.5 pulled toon strings (2005-10-21 05:48)

Game Emulation Therapy

1.Identify client's empathy loadings within the construct.
2. Establish avatar-projection capabilities via recognition of lead _character validity. Encourage verbalisation of 1st-personalities as opposed to 3rd-personality constructions.
4. Assess integration of named game-character attributes and environamental projection into geophysical parameters.
5. Identify primary needs met via named character[s].
6. Chart the goal-based progression in terms of abilities, spells, casting, melee, range, + non-combative skills [guild joining, reinforcement of random altruism, etc].
7. Draw comparisons with short vs long term goal setting; benefits of cohesive play in adaption situations.

(2005-10-23 12:44:54) going to thZr theatre recently has made remi
going to the theatre recently has reminded me described scribe scribble not that im pandemic or anyother form of anxiety disorder thoughty recently thut asid if plauityuif woss not it sed something he tried to elicitrX say something something real goodf Crescent

3.10.6 Hurricane Alpha[Numeric] (2005-10-23 19:54)

quote:
■Originally posted by Anabel:
■I am thinking this display brings some form of pleasure for you. Does it? How so? Why?

sigh*

u view this as a dis.play, ana.bella? i view it as social commentary.thru.a.p[ossible]re[n]dict[at] ive.poetic.filta......

1stly tho 2 the pleasure qs:
.definitions.plague.me:
_chinese.boxes.sitting.hap.[meaning]h[d]az
[t]ard[lights].ly.in.comprehension.b.oxes.in.j ack[ed]-in-the.boxes _
.pleasure = [p]l[ay]eisure : 4.sum.
.i sense.tens[e]ion>drama>reaction.in.ur.reply? is t.here con.text _he[a]re?

4.me, there.is.no.evident||manifest.pleasure.derivative ["conscious.speaking"] however, possibilities r endless.i may be ego.pleasure.attn driven, d.manding clinical.reinforcement.via.removed.poetic.forces ["sub.conscious.potentiality" ="(ova)analysis.reading"].

how bout u d[take]cide[s]?

<>

(2005-10-23 12:38:40) i went to the theatre last night
I went to the theatre last night and I laughed recent enigmats relei thyphoons in SomersetAt thetre I gacev up on pollesque nelogismj ant r watched space stutter music played and we all plaughted I guess one should paint a picture or act

http://www.simonsnewmedia.com http://sayingsome.blogspot.com Crescent

3.10.7 _broken ears_ (2005-10-26 06:10)

——][-
-][-
x

thought.spewing.the.term"cortex _pupping".in2.x.istence

.

(2005-11-08 12:58:45)
so listen more carefully. listening is karessing the cortex.

netwurker (2005-11-08 19:47:14)
+gent[i]le.gasps+head.slump.mocking+ +my.mouth.opens = octance.verbals.vs.reflect.gib.bo[n]us+ *sigh*

3.11 November

3.11.1 _rootki[(d)ll]ts_ (2005-11-13 08:05)

System Virginity Verifier 1.0

[swarm.esteem.memeories.bank+break.inside.my.head]

_

3.11.2 —[sediti—on.observation.all]— (2005-11-15 06:06)

-[observation.(diurn)all]-[mode]-[n.gage -d]-

—type——reactive [persona.diluted]

[gritNcover(t) {g }rim.lining.matriarchical.ut(canc)erous.walls]

[over.blown.coat.eyelid.batterings]
[bitter.beer+smoking.youth.clutch(and nega.tiffly-gear)ing]

—-

[repetition.clawing||sediti—on.bleeding.thru.cens orship.c(m)(keelh)aulings]

—-

[my.country.leaks.fascists.born.inturnal]

—-

[licking.conservative.gloss+m.ulated.hypocracy.spoo ns]

—

[(w)hack.(j)obs.ervances+foaming.hysteria]

-[x]-marks.the.(terrorist.s)edition.spot-

(2005-11-15 05:36:25)
killing.kill.lian.beer

3.11.3 _over.uber.under_ (2005-11-15 20:47)

[] cmd [-N]cense.[(wh)or(e)]

_over :: man.u.fact[ory](l)ured.dripping.women.templat es.spat.thru.socialisation.streams

_uber :: u.+.construkt.ur.puppet.method[hollow.-G]

_under ::bred[bed.head. {<> }(media)fed]

][][][][][

[open.ur.end]

3.11.4 _my book of job[lessness]_ (2005-11-30 06:59)

– framewerk.actioning .here. –

–bit.bots.+.odd.jobs–
–broken.persona.form.u.[lations].pinked+sheared –
–great.ego.mounds+identity.slabs.as.mary-go[a]s .round–

–

3.11.5 twinned_dol[t]l_snaps (2005-11-30 09:59)

—-g.olden[hate-campaign].haired+dol[t]ly–f ascist.eyed—-
—-taught.breeding.thru.hatred.filters+p[inked]o p.mulch——

-

3.12 December

3.12.1 _ego.sap + crystal.[g]rind_ (2005-12-05 17:46)

[ob.]s(w)erving................

//mid.thortie.menomalepause>ego.drenched.conf||tuser>

ie swinging.geo.graphs.searching.thru.muddled.persona.fi lters.leeched.thru.aggrogence.+i.d.norance

Q::y.is.it.that.the.faux.n.lightened.always.seek.geo. displacement.4.answers?
A::followed.intern.all.isations.of:sheep.he[a]r[
d]ing+bovine.action.stained.(with)in.[cheap. morality]s[weets]uits.

Q::y.do.cloaked.conservatives.dogma.cling[ons+offs
]while.sw[h]ooping.hypocritical+punctuating.theo ry.bin[aries]ds?
A::ease.of.the.s[o]ac[alled]cr[div]inity.
vs.abrogation.of.the.personal.+here.+now

———[godcling+responsibility.shift]
———[bushisms.echoed.+conc[s]eptual.finery .leveled]

.

_

3.12.2 _arcane.personality.fire pre.char[red]actor.assessment[s]_ (2005-12-21 10:28)

_shift.click.(a) _

#[s]hell.fish.ing.+.ego.pro.clay.mation["i.am .the.gamer.greatest!"]
#[+5.minutia.battle.pur.s[ing.lips]ona[l]
.planning+tactical.identity.war.fairing]
#spitting.id.dee.vid[ia]uation.bile
#self.worth.pro.claim.ering.vs:

_ctrl.click.(b) _

#cloaked.comp[rrrr]editive.motions.in.empathy.g uile
#bumb.ling.anti.nerd.txt.spurting

3.12.3 _ebon[ic]y.time[d]+c[orn g]rowed_ (2005-12-27 17:51)

+version.poor.tend+
_ack.celer[on||off(el)]ated.sloth.moving.th ru.silly.co[ff||o]n.time _
_ _ _ _ _sell.phonic.ring.plonk.ic _
_le[sion(screen.f)]issure.re.writing.+.wo-
rk .method[one].in.my.time.weighting[4.no.man.nor. whoa.man.either]
_

+version.accelerant.la[la.la]tent+
_stop.obs[idian.budda.n]erv[(ana)d]ance _ _ _ _ _ _ _ _ _ _ _ _ _ _ _ _ _
_ _ _ _ _ _ _ _ _slo.cr[m]ow.colonic.in.visual.peaks.+.audio.tro ughs _

- [_x]

my.ebony.open.time.shrinking.as.pattern.sleep.shifts.
2.crowded.activity.visioning

1st version: portents and chronological game real estate length patents

accelerated monitor reality _time shifting
moving and gasping within siliconed coffin/coffee time
selling and buying phonically

lesioned screen fissuring and work methods seeping
my time weights [for no man nor woman, either]

Alt version: space vs time evident time accelerant [high latency]

stop observances leak nerve[ana]-like
slowing experiences into cracked chromatics
crow looking col[t]onics shimmer
visual peaks and audio troughs

–

Chapter 4

2006

4.1 January

4.1.1 _n.f[l]ect (2006-01-08 22:40)

_——————————-on cooldown + k-lined
furred wheat hills + scent.scatterings

4.1.2 -lOOPing+APEing- (2006-01-09 18:37)

————inturr.face[(d)RAM(at)ically.fi t]t[ed]
/who.patching.revamped+cor[dial(up+binary.out)l y]tical
/stitch.5.itch.95.tich.saving.9..........7......of... 9
/loop.fitting+[c(ere.brawl)]low[ning]
/n.euro[|]nface[|]s.top(+bottomless.psycl.o
p.s.ing-like-thru-(tor)rent(s)ed-core].gap
/who.ray.gunesque.pattern.in.[g]crows.feet.flesh. [c](in.terror)laws
/bent.[ch]roaming.in.politi.caul.[in]c[est]i[c(d.r)i {sion }]de]

——-[c] _littoral.sharpest.rusting.in.the.back.of.my.smelter .th[bi-]roat _

4.1.3 _predation predator.intro_ (2006-01-11 06:10)

#predator.inject [breakage.with.traditional.other.species.pred(n) ation] #

homo-sapien _rewriting.darwin.clean _slate.coding _

nation.state[ments.ripping.speciation.a.new.one]

_

(2006-01-22 04:32:44) junction friction
collaborative amputations occur virtually

4.1.4 _cog. fly.knit.wheel.seep.ages_ (2006-01-17 06:31)

_the[h]o[a]ry.skinning + [bric.oh.]large.seepage _
_BAN vs PAN vs GAN _
...................Body Area Networking: coded meat structur[h]ing[es]
...................Personal Area Networking: sucker.identity.punching
...................Genetic Area Networking: rna.helix.[sche]dueling

_

_

(2006-01-20 03:33:52)
Soliloquy And Nialism: Real Networks [Helix Schematics]; Audio Dueling [he][s] struck and turning; decoding meat punishing identity [sucker]

4.1.5 _trigger.se{chi}t[t{er}ing(Ls)]_ (2006-01-23 17:23)

emo.t[i]onal.m[l]a(yhap)tch——x——t [coping]riguer.set.syn[er.jism]aptic

_ _ _ _ _ _-subset: coping.set.triggers.*may[hap]*.bond.synaptically

_

[insert: trauma.mech(ic)an(ery) *ism]
_

r.igor*tremor*lip
[audio.s({t }onic)mattering.precurs[or.ton]ed
hea[r(eal)t(ime)]d*sonar*b[h]ound[s.o f.+.off.luv]

_

[same.page.observance: affective.management.reaction]
_

broad.stroking.stone[d].chip.t[eche]wins.+.f lint.pers[bl]o[oD]NA[s]

eye.ste[e]al*soul*leak*smash
lever.bond.thru.c[elegant.t]ryst.al.blast.strengt h
_

_ _-do.knot.[due|al]cr.os.s.-xx

x

4.1.6 _scratch_p.ad[d]_b[n]oob.manga_ (2006-01-30 20:09)

/no.obs.lapping.happying
#n(l)ew(d)bie.slapping _vs _no.observational.l[m]apping #

[gamer.code.on]

/l[ooking]f[4]g[r(and {y })ou(nd.u)p]
#s/he(bie.jeebies)ep.para[normal](behavio ur)meter[run.nings] #

[crust.gender+ thrust.g.eek.concret"isms".all.over.the.3d.place]

4.2 February

4.2.1 _klum_Z_mercure.Ree.all_meta.phwoars_ (2006-02-05 18:06)

_tarred.+.broke.back[m(f)oun(tains)ds].fe athered.in.punk'd.afterwashes _

.......-AJAXing.taxing+ex.sex-
.......[i had a sensation last eve of something being terribly wrong 4 some1 i kne[||o]w]
.......-serPent.agon.wurd.vomit+co-ego-valences-

.......[ ]

---

jmoening (2006-02-05 08:28:54)
giggle, serious son: http://www.mightymcpilgrim.com/films/brokemac/

4.2.2 _help.me, radio.head_ (2006-02-09 06:47)

-geographically–[str]etched–grin–smile-[grid -lid]lines–

[red.oz.cliched.dust.eye.crevassing]
[mascaraed.sepia.plains]
[application: teeth.rinse.+.9-2-5.repeat]
[drag.N.drop.coping]
[mundanity.(s {l })i {de }nking]

-false–50's-voice–o[ffice]va[gina]s–+–ins titution–gloss[ary]-

[splurge.urge.vs.non-linear.break.coffeelessness]
[random.time.yearning.vs.bl(eak)ock.in(c {ardboard }on)structions]

[help———meeeeeeeeeeeeeeee———radio- ————head]

h

e

l

[]
–

4.2.3 The Scrim[inology] of [the]Anglo[sphere] (2006-02-19 11:22)

[no of - = frequency.moaning]

—–corpse droning + drill patterning
–[foo.ture.fazz.izm.denotes.death.taxes.in.the.for
m.of.being.technically.allowed.2.die]
—air.is.no.long.phree+.neither.r.u[e.we.she(ep).he]
———-Blue.Monday[Bravery.tri.p(l)]ing

______________________________-__________- __________________-______________
____- _________________-________________________- __-___________________________
__________ _________________________________ _____________________

u.se[e].the.net.w .or[dinary]k

4.2.4 [discoun.ting(le): slip.pages + uberness.of.the _accident[all.code]] (2006-02-25 20:26)

[high.individualisationism.is.unattractive+des.truc
(k.in.acollaborative.china.shoppe)tive]
[artistic.n.deavours.may.be.n.structive//share _trajectoried]
[cultural.stances.rn't.formed.thru.the.cult.of.the. "i"]

–

"I" "I" "I"
_such.ego.manifestering.reduces.collaborative.input +any.adjusting.2.non-capitalistick-tocking _

how.do.u.learn.thru.such.self.glorification.parameter s?

–

so sad this obsession with ownership. cutting of the collective.hands.2.smite.the.code.face.

hi-lights.political.fascistic.ends.seeded.in.greedy.l iberalism.

–

a.purrr.sonal.n.tention.may.point.2wards.ego.projecti

on.[read:discounting/red.ucing.tha.likelihood.of.di scovery.jags.or.inventiveness.beyond.(firing.static)canon[z].............

am.more.n.terested.in.fragments.+/or.occlusions...... ....-...

mash.mixers+re.appropos.of.|n.tentions|.2wards/agains t.the/an.other........ id.folding+persona.wandering.

_

again:: a [rose]build.on.a.build[rose].on.a.bu[dding. rose.gu]ild[ed]....... this.graduation.of.[shared.talent.tree]experience +communication.thru.[inter.voice-d {s }wo[llen(s)]ven.opinion.threads.is.a.far.more.delicious.ca[u]lling.than.the."i.want""i.make"" i.own".trajectory.

[my.stance.curls.around/thru.x[y].plaining.that .n.dividualised.ownership+the.cult.of.the. _i _.is.e.ssen[ce]t.ially.retro[fitted].conservatism.made.static/sticky.with.agendas.far.reaching.+ [deeply/m.bedded]faceted=mono.

in.my.frame [self]mono[thesism] _isn't.growth. [we.break+shear.the.communal.in.order.2.economic[.rationalistic]ally.project] [swirling.d(m)at(t)a.flow+revoking.the.ideo logyof.self.thru.an.ownership.stamp]

[sitting + scrawling|| small.chalked.info.ramblings.on.2.lattice.fl[in]o [f]wer.grids+.typo.graphs]

_

.

(2006-02-25 12:42:45)
beautiful post, mez. =) i concur with the sentiment/politics, however it is difficult in practice to overcome the ego... shannon http://aliasfrequencies.org/son/ ;)

netwurker (2006-02-26 01:23:30) ah.greed.........
+ "i" [:)] have.2 battle.the.pre.occ.with.self+self.concerns. [thanks s...will catch upw ith u + ur blogness son i hope;)] warmth, mez

terso (2006-02-25 22:07:34) I like
Take "self" and run your outer world, and culture through it. thanks, E

netwurker (2006-02-26 01:26:01) Re: I like
many thx 2 u as well.for.taking.the.time.2.absorb. pe["i"]ace, mez

(2006-03-04 16:27:55) <font size="7">
<font size="7"> :: // .. _ _ _such.ego.manifestering .. ?? ;; </font>

4.3 March

4.3.1 _social.comma.NT.ary.Demo[n]s[c]e[n]ed_ (2006-03-07 06:32)

————>demon.scen[t.of.terminal.power.voic es]ically.bi _function _of _the _8.bit[10.2wce.shy]<————————- —-

-hack.err.consciousness.in.green.activist[a].garb -
-voiced.[comma/on]sense.re.placed.by.polly.hypo[false.demo]cr[ying]acy-
-i.sweat[pol(itical)ly.want.a.]crack[er]. sleep-
.
.
.
.
-[ob]long.stretch.the.demo[crat:NO:]scene-
.
.
.
.

4.3.2 _shell: ono_play[sh]garis[-h-]m_ (2006-03-14 20:47)

>[type:] stRIP.social.bro[fa]cade

u c a [c(opyright)]oiled [s]kin.strand.[b]egg[ing]shaped+b.le[an] ed[dy]ing.

>[type:] revoke.social.layer+sing

u sense kin.movement.in.the.c[r]o[tte]nnect.O.sphere.
you move laterally.thru.emerald.convention.l[pyth]o[n] ops.

—

[shhh]

.

4.3.3 _zzzzippering.in2.ur.pocke(d)tsphere_ (2006-03-17 07:48)

_cry.zip+stoic.that _

[money.spun.+phished]
[(dog)bane.ishment.of.tha.(clement)green.b (erg!) {h }ack]
[re:vile.ing.auto.codas+shifts.of.ur.ego.plains]

ransom:ware.y ::[hold.ur.pocket.(pink.floydian).wall.et+scccc ream]
transom: [architect(di)ur(ning.constantly)ally.ply.a ble]
■random■

-.....................-

....

4.3.4 warm.war.status (2006-03-17 12:49)

us[a]——a?
u|s|of|a[pproach].dictat[wh-or-e]es.war.warfa re.

cold.war.fared.poor.
hot.war.[-anti-]faired.profit.able.

.

warm.war.is[m].knott.fair.

-cata.j[l]ism-

---

terso (2006-03-17 05:29:25) Yes
Imagine living here...I often wonder why i m still around.

4.3.5 +[word|draw.ing]+pinned+X(y?)+edges+ (2006-03-24 06:34)

crystal.gold.u _[k]nit.[ar]rayz.twinned.[i]n[the]o.ta t(relat)ional
-
-
[PressedP(ulse.1+Drench2]ro(botiff.or.hyp.not .ive)jectivePowa(-m|v)ixe[n]d [osculat[ur.X.]e[dges]]
-
-
dream.suck(l)ing.on.ur.word(ian).lips
-
-
i _[rob(n.rustle.steal)|]lu[st]nge.+affecti -vely...brickle.....pi[que]ck*

—

4.3.6 _horse.[h]owl_bea[stly]r.ing_ (2006-03-24 07:36)

[(v.ag {e|in }aries.of.the.v.ir(l)t(d)ual]

[horsescreamingintheanalogdark]
[(h)owlpiercingstreamsofthesensualhol.d(ialin +visc {f }eralup)]

[ripping.p.ur.r.s {ona }(ubliminal|vengali)cabs+vul(va)pine.scalps]

4.3.7 _p(l)ick.ed.por[n]fect_ (2006-03-27 17:53)

-
-
-
-

-

-

_w::here.do.i.put.this?

[struggle.jaw.+liga(-d-)ment.(blood.10sile) mouth]
[_i.(u)do.(k)not(ted).want.th {eory }(grey.hard.fl)i(nt)s _]

[(st)retched.thy {la.seen }(me)n.+.r.ashly]
————————————get-
————————————the-
————————————fuk-
————————————out-
————————————oft-
————————————mye-
————————————hed-
-
-
-
-
-
——————-[cmd]——————[u]-
-
-
-
-
-
-
-
-

4.3.8 _bet[saliv]a_blocks_ (2006-03-27 18:23)

twinnedshouldagripp(a)ing+heads(h|w)e(l)t (er)ting _fullmouthsalivabreathing
anticonstructgAsp+s(fl)ag(the.mold {e }+run)ging|erlysmothering

4.3.9 _w|ro[a]om|b_[p]R[ofile]IPpage_ (2006-03-29 06:02)

[was: iso.la.ti(tanium)on]
2TiFeO3+7Cl2+6C(900°C)2TiCl4+2FeCl3+6CO
TiCl4+2Mg[split(all _flick[[r]]ed _like)tagged](1100°C)2MgCl2+Ti
2TiFeO3+7Cl2+6C(900°C)2TiCl4+2FeCl3+6CO

TiCl4+[+.body.arc.key.txt.urally.ripped]2Mg(110 0°C)2MgCl2+Ti
2TiFeO3+7Cl2+6C(900°C)2TiCl4+2FeCl3+6CO
TiCl4+2Mg(1100°C)[c(er[e.brall))orrosio n]2MgCl2+Ti
2TiFeO3+7Cl2+6C(900°C)2TiCl4+2FeCl3+6CO
Ti[t(an.e.um(ahh.ing)e.]C[hest.(h)e(a)ves]l4+2Mg(1100°C)2MgCl2+Ti
2TiFeO3+7Cl2+6C(900°C)2TiCl4+2FeCl3+6CO
TiCl4+2Mg(1100°C)2 _M[is.con.txt.fired]Cl2+Ti
2TiFeO3+7Cl2+6C(900°C)2TiCl4+2FeCl3+6CO
TiCl4+2Mg[stripping.wom(an _like.soft)b.stages]+(1100°C)2MgCl2+Ti
2TiFeO3+7Cl2+6C[re(p)apering.the.post-hoc.walls
](900°C)2TiCl4+2FeCl3+6CO
TiCl4+2Mg(1100°C)2MgCl2+Ti
2[+2+1.st.range(cuttin)r.dangerness]TiFeO3+7C
l2+6C(900°C)2TiCl4+2FeCl3+6CO
TiCl4+2Mg(1100°C)2MgCl2+Ti

Price/Performance
Engineered specifically for high end applic
TITANIUM Unmatched ations

4.3.10 _tink[a.caramel.bel]le.guts_ (2006-03-30 07:02)

...+ showa.recessed.cream.bones..........
..........+s(l)immer.ton[purrson]alities....

[pa(ul)w.cel(a|)in _dreams _burst.crysta(up+in)line]

4.4 April

4.4.1 _th.x[tasy].[of]1[mel]1[o|an]3[choly]8 (2006-04-04 20:34)

_N.abl[e.d(w)renched.fli|ecking.of]ur.Melan .cholia _[_no _8—cin.E.marred]
....:.. ......
//.calc[i(L)aTe|x|un!d]ulate _a.MeasuredCh(unkedMetallic)Ang(l)edInP(r
)os.e
....:.. .....
//.updating.G[oo _UI]P[erkiness]S[L(R)inkage]].Position
&TrackingEst(i|pod|)mates
....:.. .....
nextT(10)en.ewe.us+=.m[oltingdbate].Period;

Tread {litely }.sleep(nextT(10)en.ewe.us
-System.currentT(10)en.ewe.usM(|g!|olly)illio ns());
}

_

t _ _bLeading _the _n.ablaCoda _sh[eave]iftingly _static
h _ _a(nti)h _matta _bounding _Call.N.Code
x _ _each n.ablaCoda s getClosure();
11 _me[l]t[ing][meth.oddi(-m)c]h(m)od :
38 _int[E.grating.stained.voices] displacedMelancholia= mDisplacedNabla-Coda.getMelancholia();

#ConvenientThisCode #
#Deep.end[ancing.on.the.arrow.head.hair.sick(le).pin] #
#Specifixstypeofthe _n.ablaCoda #
#Sens[wh]or[e] _urs _pls #

4.4.2 _fl[d]e[af]shCON_ (2006-04-08 06:05)

______________________________-

reg>e>mented>w.under[the]>k[holed.h]ammer

______________________________-

step _1: flesh _N _lo _
.arrange.b.lea[d.vocals] _pingness.in _a _cir.cul(LED)ar.manna■.■
.b.c.are.ful[l].2.a _void.visual.potholes.in.ur.prol.[anna.kata]logu
e.[(4.whom.the.bell)tols _toy]reasoning.
.ring.tonal.d[phact.ph]ials+3Dread.the.back.of.ur .b[p] {fl]ac[t]k[et].
.do _not.hint.at.[f]act[d]ual[ly]s; this.will.confuse.the.sub[ob]ject[z].+promote
.susp[ect.f]ic[t]ion.among.p.lace[y.tops+tu rve.Es]bos

step _2:goon _wireus _
.n.sure.ur.ro[o]m.is.well.Vent[r]il[o]ate d.
.ro.Tate[gallery].standards.at.every.measura[b]ble.n.ter.val[i.um+ahhh.ing].
.n.troduce.subjects.at.staggered.approximations.of.su
blimity.quo.ti[paw.t]ents.

[read: compl[-reg]iment.of.miracle.s[h]o[u]lDe(-bo _a _)r(d.er)ing.on]
[press: all.buttons.marked.■st.op(a.rationally.d.funkt)< <]
[evac: all.subjects.left.chewing.their.own.content.fat+txtua l.nerves]

4.4.3 _s][hhhhhhh][[lut(e)s]_ (2006-04-10 20:31)

.mixed _l.us][r][[e {g }d(i)]t _tapestries.
-.][s][w[th]atch[ed].god][d][.c olo[l]ur[e]s.
–..[w]r[y.zomes]eality.leakage.spawns.fractu
reddddd[it.edit.ttt................................ ....
....ego _str][purr.d(en
{.of.the.curved.torn.E.lioness }t)][ata.let.loose.ah.mung[bean.cho
_king(queen.patina _ing)].the.wilting.node.pidgins

4.4.4 _d][m][a[cabre]nce.of.the.x.it.lion][(-l)ess][_ (2006-04-10 21:48)

......de[|a]n[s {e.macabre }(c)ity].........of.the.c[l]urve.block.t.a ww.kneed.lion...
...[storied+downy.victim.licks]............[hur t.t(yped)ho][w!!(l)][[ea]rns...... -..
......g.o][|a.d][d.colours..................m [d]el[(v)icious.lee]t[speakingly].... .

4.4.5 #p[t]ot[rr]ent.ial_t[r]ender_housings# (2006-04-10 22:21)

-

-

-

————————————_——————_ ————_

dense-macabre-licked-city.
#housing _the #
curved-building-block-torn.kneed.lion

————————————_——————_ ————_

-

[c(a)rou(se|ll|.the.i.)ching.sc(m)u(sc)l(ed) {ru }ptured.tourni(drawn _bow)quets]
[projecting.stores.of.feather.bright.vic.tim(bre
)isation.in.fantasy.t.ho(a)rned.howling.hurts]
-

————————————

my-tender-god-colours.l(r)ea(l[|gr|t|it|t|y] .estate)k

————————————

-

-

-

4.4.6 _kill_[on]li[n]_e.on.S_ (2006-04-10 23:41)

-
# #
#st.one.muscle.rupture.s
#suga.red.[sp(ore.radic {al } }it.c]rumbling #
#cr.ouching.sculptured.tawny[co]quett[ish]e #
#r[p|r]a[in]w.g.[r]o[ar]ld.fur.bow _quets # #
# #
-

4.4.7 _MuSeum._of_.[Sha(d.Up)]Dow.n.Oddities_ (2006-04-16 09:06)

::
Ca[(b)Alfred].Binet _One::::::[house.frau(lein.e)]:
:::::::::::::::::::::::::::::::::::::s[t]ing:::: :
:nausea _t[r]ou[bub]bles+scorching _[s.leap]tingles:
:small.bovine.less+mon[k]ey.more::::::::::::::j.es t
er.hats+jingle _[furry.tail.sw(ph)ishingbones::::::
::
;;
Ca.bin[ary]et _T[s(crubbing)ia.mese]w[inn(u)e(n)d]o
;;;st.itch;;;;;
:humming.b[heard]ird[ir, NULL, VOID]less;wingless;
:pr[b.os.s.c.us.sing]ick[l]ing.lengths+;;;;wa nt.on
;blue.boid.[b]rain+flutter.bye.filmy.wings;;width s
;;
} }
Cab[P]ine[al]t _Three } } }[su(i)t.t(o)ure.glass _nost }
} } } } } } } } } } } } } } } } } } } }p.[gene(ic)]rod[de(ade)n _berry]
}[c](ova.h)a[u]ll.d.ra[y.red+blood]ke .like } } } } } } } }
}[eek.on.oh.mys.of]scale.mo.diff[err.ent]ic ations }
}[pe]tite.blonde.dragon.br[(ui)se(e)duc](br)e.ath }
} }

4.4.8 _a[sso]c[iativ]ute.perceptual.referencing_ (2006-04-18 07:12)

..

a)strande.prop.Ls.chars.tru[e].a.dark.lawn.conv
ersational.wa[|i]shed..red.haired.sarca[u]sti c.flip[bird.fingers]per.is.asked.a.qs,do.u.still. draw?, + she.answers.no,as i can't see,..pushing.thru.closeted.adult.gazes+arriving @ the:: corporality.of.m.mediate.per[D]ception...we.canno t.c.[read.r.not.taught.2.perceive].b.yond.media.s triations.+.co[deep.end.-(st)ances]ntrol.bandi ngs..blind.fumblings.thru.hie[l.hittingler]rarchi cal.rhetorical.pr[ocl]empt(y).ivities..
..
b)chamber[r]ed.AIed.within.a.ceR[ise]AM[-
D OM]ic.grid.based.blue/red.three-deed.circuitry.trip page.system.blown.2.anti _bloodee.bits.by.a.rogue.circuitor.bending.thru.n _[b.have]odes.+twinnage.of.an.terventionist.thru .cruelty.actualisation..
..
c)thrown.2.the.revelation.w[ev]olves.as.a.sw
_itch.is.hit.b.yond.constructional>for _m _ulative.arenas+shuffled.in2.a.play _state[ment]

..

4.4.9 _(genu)(fl)ect_ (2006-04-18 08:04)

Posted April 02, 2006 04:04 PM

_ _ _ _ _ _ _ _ _quote: _ _ _ _ _ _ _ _ _ _ _ _ _ _ _ _ _
Originally posted by Axxxxxx:
mez: I see you, but.......
_ _

@ least u _c _ the work, somehow....

[has prompted me 2 re.(genu)flect on a heav(y.doot.E)ily.n.ternalised d.sire 4 ppl 2 x.sert focused attn thru a mezangelled reading _attempt...the valu[v]e i place on streamlined>n.tense>n.terpretive attn is really an an[ec]ti-dot[al]e bi[valve] _product of the dis[tributed]ease of h[p]olly.w[ant.a.dijestible..n.turd.stainment.c racker?]ooden _re.gurgitants?

polly[morphic] _cr[h]ackerly,
][mez][

(2006-04-21 01:06:20) Asia gone, emptiness' hollow.
i follow the burning man down through the trees, rank with dry eucalypt and the smell of charring leaf mold. Perhaps i will follow him home to the Verner slopes and abbitior environs, riding a pale horse.

netwurker (2006-05-05 22:20:18) Re: Asia gone, emptiness' hollow.
[slash.pointing.2wards.the.burning.man+echo.mouthing.e[mail]so
[wombat.checking.hys]terically]

4.4.10 _s[t]ill[.wurd.]able_ (2006-04-24 17:11)

_stil[l]etto _l[ilith]oose

_[d]sire[n] _tite

_er.o(wl)[t]s.city

_sea.thing.erotic.pr[l]e[(s)a]ssur(e) ing

_lu[sy]ll.ab[le]y[line]ic

-fa.s[c(h)]i[sm]n.ate

-s.ur.[ge|]jury.sur.veil.lancing

4.4.11 _mult[s]i[(co)m]plicity_m(urder)ashups_ (2006-04-27 14:37)

———nuclear.dream.fiction[s]:

murder 1:
blood.[s]p[itter-p]attering.post-rewind.thump
+[sl]asher.mash.sm.eared.on.the[g]ory.clownin g.w[o(h)m.bs]alls.

murder 2:
narra.tiff.flip[flop+glop](s)leaping.as.[(cr)e(ati)v(e)il.jester]action.gels+bloo-[re]d[(c)].p.art.s.in.rough.imagery.sho[u -l]ds.

murder 3:
re.wurk+re[aper].work.g.listening.in.patched.pi[fa]ctorials.

————————————[]-

4.5 May

4.5.1 _[we(p)a(rt)k]treatise.on.happiness_ (2006-05-03 19:58)

......[tossing + turning last nite i was p(art)ondering the notion of happiness + how prevalent this concept is as a core element in most of the ways we structure/orient our actions....it seems such a highly n.dividuated trajectory in terms of a potential _positioning...... the idea that an individual need/want 2 full _fill overt happiness categorisations could produce hedonism output or x.istential wrapping in order 2 justify questionable/self(oriented)ish behaviour]...

....[was considering how i have at.tempted 2 alter my formulation of happiness 2 b more x.clusive than n.clusive + 2 place it within a systematic, connected framewurk revolving around my belief variables (n.cluding positive/creative/x.pressive energy x.penditure + mental conservation in regards 2 other time.draining.n.fluences as well as a deep n.tegrative/ec {method }ological approach 2 everyday micro _decisions + their potential 2 chain/string _effect other less definable/quantitative states/manifestations of reality]....

..[this, obviously, has profound ramifications in terms of how i achieve a sense of balance _sans _rigidity + n.corporation of n.terjections of chaotic variables + necessary adaptation/growth]....

---

terso (2006-05-03 15:55:46) On happiness
It is easy to look to one s self when it comes to happiness. Indeed, there s nothing wrong in that. However, in my view, our world is vast and populated. We share our experience[s] with countless others. We have the ability to contribute to a global community. I believe education, art and technology are the key. I get fulfillment in helping others, and i plan to dedicate the rest of my life to that. That s my .02 and who am I? Thanks for sharing.

4.5.2 _[-f]air.rhe[a].tales vs nonversat[comprehens]ion_ (2006-05-03 20:00)

x/perience/version/ing:

[fact: death/of/a/sale(hunt)s/man
–forest.vent(oe)u(v)re+vicious.red.fissuring –
–rest.event.outing.vivid.need.scissoring–

rea[/d:(ua)]lity/of/transposition/sickness

[myth(OS): a.cute.loss(y)/thru/body/waver/ing]
–loose-leafed.limb.|x|.tension(s)–
–ghost-lean+kill.b[l|m]o[o]dy.tenses–

r/oiling/t[urner]echtonic/s/k[r]y/scr/apes

---

terso (2006-05-03 15:36:29) That's it
I m going to the forest, and getting outside the city this weekend.

netwurker (2006-05-05 22:15:20) Re: That's it
–4est.[gold.autum.leafe]d.renches+city _d _limit.ing.rewrites– [thanks 4 ur n.put, terso. always appreciated;)] soft.anti-metglobolisness,][mez][

terso (2006-05-05 22:26:35) Re: That's it
awww shux...*blush*

4.5.3 Re: le[ase]dge.wurk (2006-05-06 07:30)

——————-f[l]eet.[slo _]m _o[tak(ma)u]ves
–c.runching.fat.vegetation.g.rub[by.m.eat.concept]s
————[sha]doze.breathing.in.post.logic.h eat
————-spew[W].brutal.medi[a]t[2(e)l]at(e)ions

...........[muscle
...........[juice
...........[breeding
...........[x
...........[n.err.gee.
...........[

[re:lax.shoulders.+.anti-clenched.thought.strides]

[head.full.+mind.st(r)aid(ers.of.the.desexual .arcs)]
[pushing.dream.pulls+albino.hea _dish.open.mouthed.off _magery _screaming]
[n.duce.mp.tee.ness=e.qualls=rupturing.cognitive.ar
.chi(ng).text.urs(+dripping.mine)]
[aqua.flowing.geo./me.tr(y)ics+double.wrinkled. lined.fobbishness]

xxxxxxxx c[(l)on(e)ned.cept] _run _ch[modding] xxxxxxx

4.5.4 _eerie.t[ass.hymn.E.l]ation_ (2006-05-07 14:11)

.

.

..||
-||||–.c _R.a.c _[sw {ab }(h)or(e)d]k[night.r.i.p.p]ing.pliant.bo ndage.l.i _p[.u.]s
—.-blood.sn[|l]o[ading.mon.tues.]wed.in.in. oh.[n(s)o(b {no.supportive.chink.
}b {l }ing)]cents.......
–|||c _O.v.e.r.mine+pushing.ur.cove[(g.a.r {gh }).r.(.o.).].t(.t.e
_n).liar.face[ts(li {t }p {it }ping)]:
||–|–t[m]ired.assi[(fly.bl.own {ed })hy]m[en|u.t]ilation.d.cay[man.t
_e.a.(.t.i.n.g _u)rs].gr[e]ates
–|||-ur.co[(d)e.(e).r(.i.e).ruption.la. -]ughing.h[l]eav[N.bread.(e)vo(lution.s)
mit(10)]ing:
|||||-.-ant.i _since.(g)rit(t)y.[dis.Tr(aught.t)oy.aH (elen.p {b }a {i
}les)]breadth.+.
.||.|s _H.[w]a.l.l.o.w[.ed.].st[(|l)oner(gr)]abbing.d[e.m.]e[n.t.]pths
|.||.u+[w(|b)]i.p _e[d.a(l)part].W.W.t.rid[of.u+s _t. {.h. }.)ick({l
}y).u.in.ur.d.filer.b _A.c.k
||..
..
.

4.5.5 bl[inf]o.od_fum_bling (2006-05-12 08:06)

.blood.f _um _bling.of.social.[soft.ware]n.counters.
.[commercial.hitting.in.st _ra[f]t _ification.wa.v(id)s:
....releases.kneeding.x.posure(read:n.dependent). luv.the.[l]ew[d]e.t _u
_b(grrl)e
....(re)cord>label _bound+h(m)o(olah)g _tied _died.arc-Up+(remove+d.sist
{a })bounce-Down
.
.
.blood.f[r]umb[(ding.)a]ling.of.move.ment .n _c[b(lo)]o[dy.c]unt.ers.

.count.body _:1: _lymp[et]node.tension.bu[ff(u)|]cketting
.count.body _:2: _blood.traipsing.w[r]ink.l[ac]ed.sur[ly]f -aces
.count.body _:3: n.[tri]fect[a]ion.via.dicho[ked]t[folks .on:(off.speed)]omies
.
.
.
.counting.of[f].the.b[l]o[o]dy.partings.o n.b[y]urning.flame.fingas.

4.5.6 mercury_pro[sensory]file (2006-05-13 09:14)

_[liqu]id.mercury.s[w.ea]t.o.mach[5].d[.r.].i.p.[ping]s
_[d.]sil[fe]ver[ed] _ch[fl|r]es[h]t.in.[g(ot {h })]lets
.
.x[water]y.quicke.n.i.n.gs.+.transitionary.positi [ve]ngs
.f[l|h]itting _d[p(rop|)l]e(t.re)[asure.n.te]nsity
.
.rapture.m[w]elt[s] _in _g[c|m]olde[m|]n.[blood]vessels.

4.5.7 _call[ing.thru.the.ember.leaves]oused.dream.whispers_ (2006-05-19 08:28)

#[rattle+hu]m.p.t.y.[dumb.Tee(n)]hovering .narrative.defacements #
————[wish.(so)f(t)airie. {in.the }(d.)tails]——
....x|
.....RE[dis]M[embering].cereb[in.th]ral[-l].digit[al].screeches....
.....memory.rubber.backed.chairs.standing.all _oscine _like.........
.....|c[m]or[b]|(li)v||idity|covered|imag ined|ocean.[s]tipp[l]ing.
.
..
....y|
#ar[gh].kane[+able.bodied].ness.in.same.nes s #
————[3-D-cel[f]l.layering.]
————[LaTeX.wurdlace _veiling]
————[grey.pe(a)r|l(ust)ed]
————[LyRiCa.U.L.Br|L.eakage]
.
.
............purse.on:[|off.lips]ali[ni]t[ea r]y.tri[ed] _drippings.
.
..
....x|
.....[lying.in.a.p(r)u(ss {ian }et)lsing.un(_).(_hand _)m(e _pls _)aid _. _bed]
.....[lying.in.an.unmade.pulsing.bed]

.....[russet.(navel)gaze.stains]
.....[_please.unhand....me....please............*please*.. ....-
....
....x|

4.5.8 _hip[grind].hop[portunity.re.(a)genda.shop] (2006-05-20 08:32)

.....r + b........
.....[ebon(icall)y.gender.strats+r[d.f]ende rs]
.....[slavery.re.(w)rit(es)ualised.in.coded .self.horra.bling.ness]
.....[trajectories.of.poke.worth+lipstick.coined.wa nts]

...[r _age+b _lack(y)ness.transposed. songs.etched.in.bigotted.g(l)ossips. meta[l].teethings. biological.pairing.urges.transposed.2.dollah.c(unt)ommodifications.
girl.toys+.disjunctive.bo(y)d.mods. powa.droppings.in.sex.potted.vampings. plastic.y({j }un {k]c)outh.per(n)fections. idealisations.via.bro.lurve.+.sis.fucking(ova.accep table.+sanctified). throwaway.p({i }g)ene.trations +used.up.dis.[red + yellow]cards.by.21+ness. wrinkled.man. $.drenched.voyeurs.trapped.in.oiled.skin.booty.cosme tics. hair _hot _key _ straightened. vicious.polymer.glazes...

ie:
.n.ternalised _hip.hop _economic.pred.u.juice.
.fuck.worth.smeared.in.biatch.usability.functions+.b [ling]oyed.gun.capital.
.crew.homieness.replacing.p.art.nershipping.

---

terso (2006-05-19 23:19:37) So you don't like P. Diddy?
This line is amazing: .....[slavery.re.(w)rit(es)ualised.in.coded.self.horra.bli ng.ness]
bling bling to the wknd!

4.5.9 _p[ersona]unctured_ (2006-05-25 06:25)

–

com.press[tenderly>here<]ion fungus + byte.rot
screen.r[fake.(umberto)eco.system]eel.es[ca la]t[e]ating +
severed.binary.[b]so[t]ds
–

4.5.10 _cl[ph]one[y]r::[was: my.Man.Ray.Eyes] (2006-05-26 08:00)

::[re]cl[aim]oned.past.n.tri.es _s[h]immering::

1. _ _
SOR[e.ness.summoned.under.reject.skin]

[soar(ring.tonals.p(2p)late.down.+Man(a). Ray.eyes]
[sore(head.(my)space.eating.x.press(this.co -opt.button)]
[the _s(t)im(ulu)s.function+sculpt.virtual(obje ct _response)s]

_OOp[s]
_[b(ull)ritney.s(hit)pears _vs _peeping.toms]
_stimulus-response (S-R or SR) correlation = (emp, bt[y])

2. _ _ _ _ _ _ _

_[co]n _scriptor||modulator

.hollow.social.channel.funnel||ling.
.project.friendliness.thru.glazed.distanced.[finish
ed].[Sam]Beck[oning]ett.lines
.learn2 _m _ask.
.old.crinkled.yearnings.mirrorballed+broken.in.echoed .sympathy.diggings

3. _ _ _ _ _ _ _ _ _ _ _ _

■>robo[_M _pathe]tic.connector>echolo[w.invo(iced)]> cation<
■>twitch.[S _W]itches.bombed.[SP]re[a]ding
_dead.head[er.|.blown.off(ing).footer<
■>oscillation.in.flailing.[AN]iconic.boxes<
■>fingered.[E]bony.cases.m[FL](r)o[W] v {ur }(e)ing<
■>circuitry.senti[M]ent.l[R]ust.[F]lak es<
■>time[D]laid+polymer.sheen.c[G]a.s[e] k[r]eted<
■>d[ist]ance.array.placements.+[F]les[H]ion.capable.burn.yearnings<
■>[S]helled.preda[S]tor[Y].mach[5]in [(ci(ni)ma].con[D]structs<

_ _ _ _ _ _ _ _ _ _[phonic _lips] _ _ _ _ _ _ _ _ _ _ _ _ _ _ _[stop]

4.5.11 Robot_Narrative_[re:ad:er]Construction (2006-05-26 08:38)

.DCRs [Dense Crumpling Robots] Drowning in SCTs [Sympathy Connectors Tick]

.

.LERs [Low Echolocator Rumbler] Invoked through RTSs [Reddening Twitch Switcher]

.

.EDRBs [Empathy DisReader Bomb] Spreading via:
- Self Destruct sub-classes including: DHGs [Dead Header Golem] & BOFs [Blown Off Footer]
- FIBAGDs [Flailing Iconic Boxes containing Aniconic God(dard) Dust] Oscillations
- Fingered & Flowing E|BCMWs [E/Bony Case ManoWareuverer]
- SCS [Sentient Circuitry Sediment] Settling in FLRFs [Flesh Lust Rust Flakes]
- Time Delayers routed to PSCGs [Polymer Sheen Casketed Gasket]
- DAPs [Distance Array Placement] Dancing Within LCBYs [Lesion Cable Burn Yearner]
- Shelled PMC|Ds [Predator Machine Con/Destructs - see: Self-Destruct sub-classes]

.

.Engage PLDLSs [Phonic.Lip.Decay.Loop.Stop]

4.5.12 c[s]yn[(es)thet]ic*ism_triage (2006-05-27 14:38)

a:...c[s]yn[(es)thet]icism flattened in2 a greasy fra[daptation.a]gility skin
.....[slim _lin[psych]e _coughing _boys _aligning _mingled _n _sides]
b:...architectural heartbeats slowly fo[a|]rm[+leg(i)g(acycle)]ing
.....[p(ai)r(b)o(nd)seedural _aching]
c:...desire castles + carnality br[(e)ake][th]ick[y]s
.....[r[ipp(l)ed+delicate _painted]eplacement _l(over)ayers]

4.6 June

4.6.1 _diag.[c]on[ic]al.sp.arrows_ (2006-06-04 08:21)

_s[ub(untu)verted.m.motional.currency _
............[the.streets.vid.clipping]

4.6.2 ....para.lells|lull[ah.bye]s..... (2006-06-06 06:35)

[_n _creasing.reality.d.is.placements]
[[bother.c _odes.blistering.clinical]]
[[[[stretching.bland.c(h)overings]]]]
[[[[[[[[c(erebra.l)u(s)t.off +]]]]]]]
[[[[[[[[[[[[[[absent.ons]]]]]]]]]]]]

4.6.3 -tendr[eam]illing- (2006-06-07 06:46)

-[xxxxxxxxxxwhitexrabbitxconsciousx(w)xholesxxx xxxxxxxx]-
-[xxxxxchasingxvelvetxarmsx+xsa.tin(y)xl(e) egsxxxxxxxxxx]-
-[xxxxxxbondxanxiousnessxinxfemmexfamilyxtyingxxxxx xxxx]-
......................-r-e-v-e-a-l-.................. ....

4.6.4 _f[unction]ormation_ (2006-06-15 05:09)

1. _ben.zine.[ea]r[s]inging _

_notational.revolvings.in.relation.2.possible.AI.f [unction]ormation _

_if _
variables =
:charge separation radial ElectroMagneticPulsing [conceptually reversing accepta(pro)b(ab)ilites (polarities)]
:swarm.m.pulse.functioning [as applied 2 AI neural.network.functioning or fun(gible)damental.dis(tance.e)ruption.of.swa rm.manifestations]

_then _
conceptual.re.alignment.made.actual.via.n.tegrative.n otions.of.trace//g _host.memory.m.plementing.in.AI.core.systems.
[ie shifting idealisations.from.androidal>n.sectile>phylogenetic.m .magery]

2. _pulse.netw[are//]or.king _

BMP = biomagnetic.pulse

_if _
:harnessing.of.bio(or non _spiked)magnetic.output.results.in.shifting.2wards .radial.energy.capturing
_then _
spike.reduction+.conceptual.rewiring.of.reverse.wave.
status+utilisation.of.swarm.function.thru.plastic.man i(pulation)festations

–

>non-neural.net.concept.reliance + shift.in[g].worn.control.paradigm[s]
>requires.concept//discovery.chunking.reworking.at.ba se.educational.lvls
[c: _m/pending.notational.educational.movements]

---

terso (2006-06-14 23:44:13) I like this one
Wire me in i m there.

4.6.5 [char]coal.pri|n|ce[s(me-|-agm{i}a)s{ma}] (2006-06-17 09:24)

-

-

-

—-anti _heroin[e].smears.+.co-optive.g[-f|b-]enderi ng—
—
[eye.sme(g {RAM }m)ar[gh].a.duct.ape.ing]
[gree(d)n.smudges.on.c(f)o(ssil.i)nve[r t]x.posturing]
—
—p(r {|sp })e(cious.n {arrow.tive }.te)rcepts+
–long({l }att)it|-n(uminous)|udinal.t(r {el)ig(ious.f|-w|r|ong|ig)htenings]–
-
—
-
-

4.6.6 -t[h]r[ee]i-chambered-ness- (2006-06-21 06:44)

[]
[
]
[
1. ch.amb(l {ing })urr.one:squats+sits.quietly.conscription.wrapped +RIPped
1. blood.m.mag(ic)e.in.great.gasps+screen.(d)riv (en)ulets
1. mortal.e.T[-totalled].drippppp.drippp.dripping
2. im.a.ge[nus].drawing2:scratch.feet.dragging.in.sh adowed.greys
2. f[l]33t.pushing.zipper.torso.fractures.spilling.u p+gut.outwards
2. zip.flipping.in2.morphed.black.cr00[P]n.b()sh)ir(t)dings

3. metal.tr[corpse.v](ip)o(d.loneness)lley.p ushing.a.bone _b(h)ag(gard)
3. screaming.cor[pse.of.white.silence]rid[ing.blac k.leathered.wh]or[e]s
3. grapsing.bluntness thru.pencilled.pretend.gazes[tracing.a.dead.man's.s hapely.foot]
]
[
]
[
][

4.6.7 _ero[tti(c)ng]s_ (2006-06-24 07:08)

#shift.on(e).h[d]ead.meld+snowing.m.motiona l.flakings #

} save 1 + crush 3

#shift.[err]ing[ly].on.the.side.of.meniscus .personas #

sw[-r]imingly poke|dense

#stagna[late]ncy.[c]r[y]u[i]nning.my. best.dress.sense[s] #

–

[m.bod({d }e.ment)y.txt]
.space(-d)furredm[-h]emor[r(-h)age.t]yp eltsmixedslo(-a)thinglyandhypo.
.criticallydi(ver)s(e)membercordsofwantonwort
handpulsingmadov(und)alays.
.alacknessscreamsandslaughtereddream[-s]ingintear nes[-t]sp[-r]ocketpatches.
.[de]to[-u]rnamentalstabbingineyesopenandcaug
hterisedinterpo[-o]l[sof(t)dead]things.
.denou(de)[-v]e[l)op)le]mentingandsorro
wnesspowerpushingthroughpedestalledbl[pr]anketr y.

4.7 July

4.7.1 _dust.b[l*]ow[n*]l[m.media[s*]c[r*]y].eyes_ (2006-07-01 14:29)

sta[o]r[ange.aid].[c*]leav[ag]e*plus* pulse.[s*]ingling*
c.ringe[d*].small.[t*]wink[*]ing.univer. s[ali(ni)ty]es*

thumping.2.a.[b*]rest _feed _breed _ing.[a*r*t(houghtless)*]brutish.beat*

4.7.2 -god[-d]+p-o-i-n-t-i-n-g+ (2006-07-03 06:21)

D _Point— + —-D[u(el)]oo.Pont _ing
Id _Dragged- + —Ego _Po[Queen+Prince]king
End[M.ic]lee + –[Quid.]Pr[Qu]o.p.portioned

4.7.3 _p[bl]a[u]per.l[d]olling_ (2006-07-04 06:24)

—silver.ties.lining.my.f[b]ro[ke.my.]zen.ar .m[brace]s—
—welte.r[hetoric.of(fl {over })]ing.x.clusions—
—[s]h(it)e.art.t[r]ap.+.body.[d]raini ng—-
—r[cr]u[mpled]st[c]ling.of.motor.t[neu -r]onalzz—
—[ram]p[ant.e]lastic.so[ha]rrowing.bl[-|r]ood.ings—

[s.lumpe(n)d.burgundy+blue.i.[x.filter]patc hed]

4.7.4 —-dredge.p.a[da]ste.statements (2006-07-11 19:16)

if[drege.ada]statements

[edit.able]
[edit]reality.fatigue
[(smut)edit]
[edit].con.dew[y].it
[edit]
[edit]concept.phatigue
——————————+ interface declarations
begin.re _rolling
begin.slow.cultural.cr[L]isping
class records
—[and paw] declarations
—[and schizoidal.patterned]declarations
——– declarations
———declarations
—— declarations
[monothetical.breakage]declarations

[soul.de.frag]declarations
[dna | rna]declarations
declarations
[s]el[f]se
el[u]sif Boolean expression then
end sta;
end if;
end da;
end pa;
end ma;
—- end record;
—- end record;
exception.man.dib[s]le
exception.dis.crete.snapping
function sta (parameters : in type) return type meatah4
functions
generic.n.sect.[b]ile
generic declarations
—[mono]handlers
—[x.pression]handlers
if Boolean expression then
package declarations
package Bodymelts is
package GodMiss.ileRetching is
private
private
—statements
cara.statements
pacing.statements
in.statements
pair _bondage.statements

4.7.5 -.-e.sche[ll]r.fingas-.- (2006-07-16 17:39)

-.-rawfleshdrawingbonesbleed.curved.bodymashcyborgani cmelee
-..-signalsmeariverofglistenoceanictearsinvo|u|lcania shamepoint
-...-listlessnessingwrestlewiththefinditeinstitutiona lisedglo|u|ttany
———.
-.po[c]lit[toral]icaul.-whistling-.stiff.-as- .pro[ad]verbial.-bored-
.-g-host.s-peaking.thru.p[l]eak[ed].o[ve(r)][/dev]il[s/null.ed][h]ed[onism].
-.twisted.tipping.points.s-wing-ing.wild.conserve.ah. tiff.loops......-.—
———————————-————- ———-[back.pls]-.-

4.7.6 farm_m.motional (2006-07-18 05:55)

————————golden.streaming.s[f]lip.page
————ec.ho[llo.grammatic].s.tatic.fluff.fol ds
————————red.vision.stagg[reenish]ering

4.7.7 /m[e|a]s[sa]g[e] (2006-07-18 06:16)

/msg e.clipsing.bone.[f]rac[ture]ks.+swirling.milk .structures
+
/msg x.tend.body....shift.dirt.cells+[s]creaming.calci fied

4.8 August

4.8.1 Re: re (2006-08-02 06:46)

[attempts.2.unf(bl)o[ssom]ld.another.disc.u ssion].....

it is n.teresting watching the rants + logs + zipperings +
ova.ton[aliti]es of the mashedup+ova"is net.art dead"
[velvet+satin.potentiality.n.furred] thread.....
–

.............a few [in]part.ially _related tendrils unfurled 4rm my
neck.of.the.proverbial.w.o[od]ulds:

post _hocian judgements + argumentative[ie "discussion"] structuring
breeds tandem|piggybacked|opinionated posturing. reflection +
m.ulation allow 4 the very same.

stoic pro[gr|]fessions regarding the validity of the linear + any
subsequent masquerading of artistic.output diluted as
valuable.only.via.pr[hist]o[r|xy]sperity's.fi ckle.judgement does
not.the.truth.make [+ i don't kno wot _the truth _ is...the
unfinished/unquantifiable holds far more value (purr.sonal.ly) than
concrete, pre.pack(et)ed, right-wrong validations].

labels operate as a bench[big.black.crayon]markers of the known. the
more we m.ploy them [aka as
art/culture/mem.etic(k-toc).agents.in.woteva.guis e.u.care.2.mention]
the more cryst[form]ali[zed]ne they b.come.

i'm currently constructing within the potential of the un[or as.yet]known: i have no idea wot my ARG/wiki/faux.infomorph merge currently _is _ or wot it w[on't]ill b.come. this is the x.citing part - the id[n]e[us]a; the fusing of concept + [mixed.up.cruci(fied)bled]form. hopefully those i'll n.vite along 4 the x.pressive.ride will be just as n.thused. if _how.eva _ nothing is made concrete as observable, label _ish out.put, is my "project" a failure? does it retain a[ny]rtistic value/merit?

4.8.2 -dis-/loc-ated-phrase-shoulders- (2006-08-07 17:23)

/c[r]o[w(o)]ma[n].sitting.in.carved.to [ngue]t(i)e(d)[pide(r)]mi(s)cs

.

.

//displace.me-n-t[al]s.jumping.wave.[afta]blo od.wave

.

–

.

$—[-p-lease.turn(ed.@.the.censored.lathe) .this.down]

.

.

$m[ove.o]ut[ation]e[d].voice.shifting—- ———.now.
$—[myvo|al(ve)|icetainted+birdsongRIPp(l)e(s)d]-

(2006-08-09 23:18:09)
the blue bird outside my window takes flight at the intial wave from the baby in the cubicle to my left. the chorus of reassurance adds the the cacaphony surrounding me in my isolated position demarcated by the bland tones enabled by the deluge of flourescent light. i am a blue bird. i am liar.

netwurker (2006-08-16 02:05:25) _blue.bird[c]age_
.butter[fl]y.soul.shaped.n.jections+soft.[up+life]downy.hand .holdings.
-wishments-=-placements-

4.8.3 _its.the.end.of.the.wor[m|]d.as.we.kno.it_ (2006-08-12 07:24)

+

–

+i.feel+
–

+shi[f]ts.in.the.kn[bl]p[|o]wn(ed).s[h]and[shak(ingly)es]+
+dream.pricks+m.mag[ick.(m) {B }all {ard }]ery+
+titanium.spine.n.s[.it.h]ertz+
+
+bloodied.shivering.lectrod[d]e[n].dawgs+
+
+terr.rawr.terry[towel.snarl.growling.ova.land.spit
s(+molten.political.fizzles)]+
+Cub[ed+crayon.squared]a[hhh].+I[|o]z.(o -ff.the)ra[el]il(s)+
+p(eace.by.jaded.piece)re.empty.em[non.rece]p tivess+
+milit[hex)]a[(b)i(na)]ry[test(os
terone)]backs[pack.mentality].shaved.morals+
–

#i.s.hare(tests.vs.rabbit.chemical.eyed)[pod (s)] #
–

#wilting.[e]m.otion[al].frenzies #
#useless.screaming.sen.sit(ins)[procl]ivi[ti]es #
#sanctum+santit[wh]or[e]ia #
#weeping.cynical.[m]ash[_ups+response.downs] #
#[sub]lime.juice.in.litte|oral.word.cuts #

#

4.8.4 *c[l]ottage*military*cre[d]am[n]* (2006-08-16 06:47)

**********odd***********
*****terr.awe.ist******
*******clottage********
****
cott[ling].cam[bl]o[od]
****
cottage.*war*.creaming*
****
********gore***********
********on*************
*******your************
*******hollow**********
*****democracy*********
*******wire************
****
*****[.-stop-.]********

4.8.5 m[d]e[nial]_construction.1 (2006-08-22 09:36)

_

already feel[er]ing seepages of renewness +
alt _out.looking.creeping.in + settling....it's like my whole
metabolism shifts when i'm left uns _hack _led.....

[dr(unk _like)owning.n.compassing: filterings+omens:
brilliance.in.potted.(d)lite.edges:
reworked.brownian.motions+e.clipsing.playful.(s {i })m {ple }(ile)omen[e]ts]

[have started drawings, watching eps of:
http://bs.brokensaints.com/
n.fusing music, mixing _up n.ternalities + x.ternal spaces, dev.of
feralC projecting, grow(l)ing].....

_

4.8.6 ____glimm[$nutur]er____ (2006-08-30 06:38)

_ _ _ _ $[c]r[e]a[my]punzel
_ _ _ _ $dreaming
_ _ _ _ $c[urved _hair]orrido[o]r
_ _ _ _ $b _loss _oms

4.9 September

4.9.1 –lust.man[a]ge[ment]- (2006-09-06 06:19)

||.thick.hair.curtain.flick.cables.||
.|||suga[h!]r.wate[ye]red.fingers|||.
|.phasing+waxing+weaning+wav[er]ing.|

(2006-09-08 05:41:22)
There´s |||||||||NOWAY..||||||||||||||| _ _ _ _ _.

4.9.2 _ego.flakes.of.the.failed.witch_ (2006-09-08 20:16)

burn: splatting.away.seduction.fl[yers]ies
burn2: moving|shake _blackened|mas[que]ks _

burn3: smooth[bristl]ing.the.throat.coated
burn4: performances.in.boxed.chin[dis]e[a]se.per[a w]formances
burn6: virt[d]ual.sizzlings.on.a.trapped.momentum.pyre

4.9.3 _crowns.of.identity.paw[n]thorns_ (2006-09-11 20:52)

-\dragging.[Korn.Kernel]mazes.—
-\[t {h }ru(e)]
-\nailed.cher[ry]ib.baum.wing[lets]|
-\————-|| -

-

-
]]]

]

[]
[- u.stop.here]

[si(lence-l {van.g }o)gh.letting]
|
|
|
[arcing.br(|h|eal)oken.shoulder.pins+muscLED.ne ed _Ls]
[po(b)ssession.pian(bi)o.pulled.wired.t(| h|)reading]
[goss(l)amer.webs+==============================
====+
st(l)ee(t)ler.than.thou.soc(flip.ur.morbidi ty.d)ialness]
——— -|||||||||||||||||
——\
u.wo(|a|)nder...[b]l[IP]athering+f[ph|r| -]oaming+latency _mouths...
...feeble _c[g]ob[smacked]web _crawling _motion _drunk _+ _ego _spli[t]ffed
.——————.pee[l]ing.rotten.flowering. perls............
....-.. ....-...
....spitting _great[ly] _swollen _punctured.words _+ _ego _structural _gouts

\

httf (2006-09-12 00:35:09)
< %BeginMessage/hurtstotouchfire t[ouch]ing//salut[rel]ations %>

4.9.4 ———-s————having-meme-ories- (2006-09-11 21:44)

———-s——h——————aving.
——s——-t——————ained.
——c——-a——————-rvings.
—-[m]——-b——————ued.with.
—d——y——————ed.
–n———a——————rrative.
-m———e——————mories-
————[
————]
————[........................]
hemo-r———r———h——age—-]

4.9.5 sublimity_[k]nit_pique_ (2006-09-20 06:21)

-
ob[lique]servation _bird _skin:——————
———t[b]r[anch]e[d]e.lined.plastic=o rganic
————————[feathers+vs+leavesuckling]
-
-
[ob]swerved.sculptural.loo[n.test.inal]ping.g aps
——cutt[le.fish]ing.silk.e[go]n.project[tions]
-x.pressions.sunk+s[ur(d)face(d)]pider.sh uffling
-
-
observe[d+anger+ous] _fr+agility _skeleton——-
—-m.magination _exo _clumps+whispering=bio _ness
—-[(transgenic)pig.ment.shattered+broke _ness]
-

4.10 October

4.10.1 _sig.null_sicknes[t]s_ (2006-10-13 21:59)

#cubed/fles[-s]h.found+sl.ic[m]e[th].gagg ed
#squared/omens.running.predicative.101s

#tagged/thru.bov[u/late]ine.screens

broken/[con]nec[t]ks/broker/bleeding/d[f] a[c]tum/backs
head[er]/x.plosions/n.vert/txt/tap[e(volution)]s[tries]

——————————my.queerdom.4.a.h[medi] awse-

sig.nullius:
—-pac[k _try]s.driven.thru.
—-frozen.[lec(hero.us)]trode.blood
—-m[r]at[s.the.size.of.Bow(ie)man's.cats]ta.
—-attach.ments.......do[e.eyes.glitter.here].th ey?

4.10.2 %non-newt (2006-10-14 08:30)

perfectly %20plastic %20 %09strain %20does %20not %20result %20in %20opposing %20stress %20 %09ductile %20metals %20past %20the %20yield %20point %0Abingham %20plastic %20 %09linear %20relationship %20between %20shear %20stress %20and %20rate %20of %20strain %20once %20threshold %20shear %20stress %20exceeded %20 %09mud %2C %20some %20colloids %0Ayield %20pseudo-plastic %20 %09pseudo-plastic %20above %20some %20threshold %20shear %20stress %0Ayield %20dilatent %20 %09dilatent %20above %20some %20threshold %20shear %20stress %0Apower-law %20fluids %20 %09pseudo-plastic %20or %20 %22shear %20thinning %22 %20 %09apparent %20viscosity %20reducing %20with %20rate %20of %20shear %20 %09some %20colloids %2C %20clay %2C %20milk %2C %20gelatin %2C %20blood %20and %20liquid %20cement %0Adilatant %20or %20 %22shear %20thickening %22 %20 %09apparent %20viscosity %20increasing %20with %20rate %20of %20shear %20 %09concentrated %20solution %20of %20sugar %20in %20water %2C %20suspensions %20of %20rice %20starch %20or %20corn %20starch %0Aviscoelastic %20- %20having %20both %20viscous %20and %20elastic %20properties %20 %09maxwell %20material %20 %09 %22series %22 %20linear %20combination %20of %20elastic %20and %20viscous %20effects %20 %09metals %2C %20composite %20materials %0Aoldroyd-b %20fluid %20 %09linear %20combination %20of %20maxwell %20and %20newtonian %20behaviour %20 %09bitumen %2C %20dough %2C %20nylon %2C %20and %20silly %20putty %0Akelvin %20material %20 %09 %22parallel %22 %20linear %20combination %20of %20elastic %20and %20viscous %20effects %0Aanelastic %20 %09material %20returns %20to %20a %20well-defined %20 %22rest %20shape %22 %0Atime-dependent %20viscosity %20 %09rheopectic %20 %09apparent %20viscosity %20increases %20with %20duration %20of %20stress %20 %09some %20lubricants %0Athixotropic %20 %09apparent %20viscosity %20decreases %20with %20duration %20of

%20stress %20 %09non-drip %20paints %20and %20tomato %20ketchup %20and %20most %20honey %20varieties. %0Ageneralized %20newtonian %20fluids %20 %09stress %20depends %20on %20normal %20and %20shear %20strain %20rates %20 %09blood %2C %20custard

4.10.3 [K]RumpPova.T (2006-10-18 20:48)

-jerk.body.C.ment+dream.cor[ality]e.bopping-
-fl.ip[urse.on.all].tw.itch.sw.itch.errors-

#KrumpAllOva.N.Struct #
#PullUrHead.In #
#Cl.ow[l]nishness.cowling #

4.10.4 kisSprint (2006-10-24 08:34)

/1 Pack[D]fragmented.reali(li)t(h)[Y]h.rea ding
/2 thes.pacebtween2spaghettimou[L]th[E]ings
/3 workingMyWayin2oiled[H]2[O]De.sire[N]cr.a cks

/quit aw[WW]e

4.10.5 beardog_conceptual_[pub.lick.(l)ey] (2006-10-25 08:33)

.....
......
....
....
....
....
....
....
......
....

4.10.6 beardog_conceptual_[pub.lick.(l)ey]–2 (2006-10-25 08:44)

.....■beardogpantings■
......■iMaGineFurredTonguesCupsAndSaucers■

........■!–
........This imagination defies the crushing reality mode as Message and
........the conceptualCreditType as LuserNamed.
........–■
........■beardogpanting name="Blackdawg 1"■
.........■crushing reality mode="Message"■
.................■message conceptualCreditType="LuserNamed" negotiateConcreteCredit="false"/■
.........■/crushing reality■
........■/beardogpanting■
......■/iMaGineFurredTonguesCupsAndSaucers■
....■/beardogpantings■

4.10.7 [flip_fl(m)o(_no_li.on)p]page(s) (2006-10-26 13:48)

[lio]N.game:

D[renched]-[foot]pad[ding.of.delicious.r(t)awn(y)ess] –left/right: m[g]o[l.den][no _tonal]vement
D[owny.velvet]-pad[s(hift)] up/down: Stand up/cl[aw.ruddy.l]imb[(ic)s]/crouch[ing.t -igders//hidden.dragnets]
C[xx]ross:[4ward.strained.muscle.ropes+][s (pring)weat]Jump
Circle[ling+(bassline.rumble)grrrr.owling]:Pu nch[drunch.furramonals]/shoot [the.l(v)u(lPine)nar.moon](when drawn)
Square[d.off+musk.scented]:Use[of.arcane.purrin g.s]it[us]em (ladder/lever)
[g]R[rrrrrr]: Draw[n.in.sweetned.honey.pixels]- or St.ow[! those packet claws!] away weapon
Sta[pu]r[rrrrrR]t: [(g)a(me)nimal]Men.u

4.11 November

4.11.1 ** (2006-11-02 06:32)

*

strong
gray
visuals
smudged
across

a

[cheek]bone _sky

4.11.2 [B.Urnt_An]gel.smell:drama_burn (2006-11-03 18:59)

–*flash*
grief.molded[esigned].ash.flakes
–*flash*
snow.wh[t]ite.aqua.flicks.bleeding.through.avian. archi.textures
–*flash*
[l(a)ighta.fum]bling.itchings.sneaking.along [star]studded.spinal.rhythms
–*flash*
destruction.tattoos.as.fingas.stumble.with.[(not)mel(l)o]drama.burn
–*flash*
shaking.n _tent::wonderment.thru.evolution.wingage:ang[l]e
.l.bleeding.in2.earth
–*fl[ick _r]ash*

[post.hoc.d _script:a.humanoid.evolvon.gasps+sh[akes]udder.
[ah!]lites.his.wings.in.an.attempt.2.con|/d _form]

4.11.3 _grav[ity]e.of.response_ (2006-11-12 09:23)

:clickin.thru.res.po[se]nse.actuals:
:mode:1:mode:2:mode:g:*

–m.motional.response.act.[ewe|tiff].ated:
:g1:..n.tensity.of.f[d]o[ona.la]c[ed]used .gaze=loaded
:g2:..response.verb[c]a[nniba]lised+[bird] sh[attered]ot
:g3:..gravity.of.n.tensity.removed.+r.e[ar.blocked]/voked
–
:g[4]lo[t(e)t.(c)al]ball.re.v[h]ers e.all:

4.11.4 _sc[D]ream.ing.n.testines_ (2006-11-14 07:14)

–FOR.E+B.ACK-[E]BO[LA.SIMIAN]DING–

[logic.visceral.loops]
vs
[blood.thumping.beats]

4.11.5 _nteractiventanglementretrocasuality_ (2006-11-20 18:19)

-note: virtual.n.teractive.n.tanglement.can.only.b.verified. retrospec[ula]t[e]ively.

[PST Persona:06] the n.tanglementary has been re _opened to all identity-uSer[vice]s.

[PST Persona:07] identity-uSer[vice]s will be wave.locked _out while x+ytractors attempt 2 clean-up the random causality identity assignments [aka spontaneous gravatar allocation]. particle.self.mmage _momentum is still available 2 identity-uSer[vice]s.

[PST Persona:08] an attack of characteristic _G[l]ue is causing disruption 2 identity-uSer[vice]s, which is ffecting the n.tanglementary. we have rigidity stamped the spontaneous gravatar allocations. check back 4 up+downdates.

4.11.6 diamond()pixel()iz()e(yespls) (2006-11-21 17:20)

()h _over.sn _ow.saline.dust.drip(age)[h(o)w.bathetique]()
()cur(ipp)led.pressure.fur.creepage.in.bare _line _toes()
()drying.ice(land).pats+notes.breaking(h[ilt _filled]earts)
(sy)nap(se)ping.realities.as.drop(e)ping. cubed.pixelize.tears()

4.11.7 – MMO trick.L – (2006-11-30 07:09)

[l]1.bomb[(the.hip-hop)bard.ment] - - soc _x.traction.vi[not]able
———————— - - momentari _n.T.grate.ion.in[evit.able]nit
fixed.+.chilled.stereo.attitudinals- - - my.mouth.fo {gend }(|a)rms.attach.wurds

4.12 December

4.12.1]][s[creen]hot.in.my.(er)god(ic).heart][[(2006-12-03 15:35)

_future||taste.dis.so[|a]lving.on.a.visionary.t ongue _
_b.li[|u]sta[mina].packing.in.padded.amb[ulanc]er _cells _
_[sneak.p][review+]scratching _skin _pads+soft.plodding.h[bio.sp]urts _

4.12.2 /join (br)0wn(ian>n0se (2006-12-03 20:44)

/join doe.nosed.archi->-tech-<-tral.snuffling
/macro skin.wanders.thru.video.sn->-ip-<-pings
/leave juice.gagging.on.p->-(v)o(cal)w-<-er.chugging s
/camp + tingle.sl->-ash-<-ed.with.flick->-ringit-<-ing

4.12.3 Fix[r]e[ality]d # (2006-12-09 06:54)

Fixed #00379, Location.of.torn.plastic _bag.poultry.stuck.dancing.on.fences
Fixed #00458, Problems.with.unspecified.biology.trapped.under.blist ering.heat.co[at]vers
Fixed #17869, Add.[s]late.cracking.in.tandem.chaos[ocial.net].streaming
Fixed #22389, CharcoalLinedImaginations.should.have.a "draw this, please" property attached

4.12.4 ::read/w[spa]r[kle]ite:: (2006-12-12 19:04)

\- - - - - - - - - - - - - - - - - -
st.or.y/mach/1 - - - - - - -
f.air.ree.tailing101
\- - - - - - - - - - - - - - - - - -

my.skull _s[l]i[l]tting.has.reached.a.gnu.lvl.
[n(c)o.ding.Ah.ling.lvl...1...ing.noises, tho].

i.try...2...reach.thru...sparkleite _arcing.nets...2...u.

i.so[|p]w[n].read.glitter[ings.shaved.trip. ..3..le.from.comprehension.eyelids].
i.write.respond[ing!].in.n.tree.cut.d[ripping] na.pack[ette]s...

...3...delves+chest.blown.tendril[ling]s...
m[ellow.dramatic(l)]uck.in.magn[w]ifi[(s)cent]ed.ho[|a]ll[s]o[(c)aring]w .cav[ing]es.

\- - - - - - - - - - - - - - - - - -

4.12.5 ■make.me.look.computer (2006-12-13 15:52)

.C++quined.pix[i]e[s(cher.shel)]ls>stitch
ed+flesh.baked.in2.my.foaming.monitored.skin.......
.resolut[(corrupt)ion]e.bonding.stapled.thru. [agg]re[gation]dness.....
.its.the.edge.of.the.world.as.we.no.it.........

4.12.6 command: d[sh]e[(i)lli]ad-coloured fiction (2006-12-27 07:07)

Ctrl + A Go2.the.beginning+sip.drenched.hawtness.in.coded.vision.[phero]moans.
Ctrl + E The.end:again.in.currently.typed.skin.lines.etched.in.providence.pockets.
Ctrl + L Clears.ur.screen.of.the.clarity.of.c[hest]lutching.an.intent-scorched.body.
Ctrl + U Clears.ur.aggression.throat.of.cursed.bornless.words.
Ctrl + H Same.as.her.backs-tender.muscl[ust]e[r].patte rn.
Ctrl + R Let's.u.search.4.that.fe[|a]tal.mem[e]ory.mark:he[a]ld+rocked.with.post.lovers.sinews.command.
Ctrl + C Kill.whatever.u.r.running[from+2].
Ctrl + D Exit.over+bleed.ur.furred.heart.currency.in2.[s]h ell.
Ctrl + Z Puts.woteva.ur.running[from].suspended:snapped:[back]grounded.in2.process.meat.
Ctrl + W Delete.words.dripping.in2.abs[c]e[ss]nce.spac es.
Ctrl + K Cleared.trap.lines.after.s[ubtly.damaging]ocialis ation-curses.
Ctrl + T Swap.ta[|e]ndemness.in.duel.identity.striking.
Esc + T Swap.2.reddening realities.
Alt + F Move.4ward.in2.s[g]li[johnny.de]pping.in.arme d[+leggish].covets.
Alt + B Move.back[ed]ward[ian]s.one.word.at.a.cruxifi ed.time.
Tab Auto-complete.fingers.track.[n]folding.fiction.pa tches.

Chapter 5

2007

5.1 January

5.1.1 data 6-pheet t[orque]>all (2007-01-07 08:33)

lumberingstangancybreedingincha[r|]ngeshirts+rewi redpants
go4th+moultiplyphasingncasedindroppage=latencypittage

[data 6-pheet t[orque]all + slow moving, leaking in shelled.out
sepia.stainage + go[2]aded by the ever[itable] watch.full]

crownedbinarythornsshiftingentropystrandsinpinkcaseme nts
downhillcovertcommandedgingstrippingovertreebranchlin gs

5.1.2 willowy__[sto]rage_[b]loss[o(h)ms] (2007-01-10 06:18)

da[ta]nk _c[o]r[n[e[r]ep _ _ _ _ _ _di[chotomy]seases
serial.k[l]il[t]lering _ _ _ _ _ _in _ _ _my _ _ _[i].d.reams
purr.petual _ _ _w.ink[l]ing[s] _ _ _ _scarf+shine _ _ _

5.1.3 _Memory_Podd Inc_ (2007-01-13 09:42)

MemoryPodd BETA software [MEMEPODD] creates a user-defined reality version of memory construct files (*.podd) in avatar _compatible models (Tars). Later versions of MEMEPODD are expected to have different reality _layer _field _encoding with AI geared towards autonomy rather re-creation. convertoutpodd is a command line utility to convert *.podd files created with MEMEPODD to TAR manifestations that correspond exactly with a users desired model.

Before uploading the *.podd files, they must be converted to the TAR manifestation format, otherwise your model will operate in a recursion loop [ie non-synergistic and low-reality user response levels].

–

Welcome To Memory _Podd!

Ever felt like your lost true love would always come home? Missing your departed Dad or Mom? Want to have Buster, the dog you had when you were 13, come play fetch again?

Well, you're in the right place!

Memory _Podd allows clients to recreate past relationships with significant others all through realistic state-of-the-art interactive modelling. We strive to bridge reality gaps that allowed people (or animals) from your past to slip out of your life. How do we do this? Through the creation of a permanent remembered version of your Tar (your chosen significant other) through modelling a real-time entity with which you can play, talk, hold and love!

–

Volume 1: Podding Principles and Policies
Volume 2: Creating Your Tar: Will It Hurt?
Volume 3: Tar Driving Operations
Volume 4: Closed-Circuit Tar Creation: Accurate Replication Contract
Volume 5: My Tar is Thinking for Itself! Help!

–

_TarBlog A Entry #45 _

....he keeps stretching my back till it cracks, till it almost snaps.... i keep telling him if i'm gonna be crouched over like this all the time my muscles will do that, but all he can say, over N freakin over, is how _the real _ TarA would straighten up every time, "straight as a sodding rod even after 10 hrs".

–

5.1.4 bio_break[ing] (2007-01-18 06:41)

turn _left: d-ash.bleeding.while.[co]lum(b)inescence.[r e]routing
turn _r[t]ight: [reality.a]bod[e]y.blows+ sing[l]ed[nerfingness].head[line]rs

5.1.5 (2007-01-19 15:54)

On 1/18/07, Melinda Rackham wrote:

■

Hi all

■

hi mel + all.

■

The basic polemic annoys me.. we cant operate today without speaking the language of economics. Culture and commerce do go hand in hand. Are we trying to dive an educative wedge into this ? I don think that's in any way a reality.

■

i suspect those m.mersed in the _production _ [as opposed 2 the codification] of culture cogitate less about their place in the [socio]economic stratosphere + more about the manif[r]e[ali]s[a]tation of their ideals+concepts. the notion of b.ing unavoidably mired in a "language of economics" seems tied 2 a framework driven by certain processes that seek 2 n.stitutionalise these n.deavours via a formal[recogn]ised/parcelled 'cultural' product/stream [i'm seeking clarification on ur use of the term "we" here?] ....

......."we" [as in certain n.divi _duals that /loc.ate themselves (either geospacially or perceptually) elsewhere from a heavily westernised conception of reality that d.fines worth thru capitalistic n.dicators/m.mersion] can function quite fine [thk _u!] in a reality that may b quantitatively different 4rm urs - does this then make it invalid according 2 how u box ur definition of reality?

i find certain modes of cu[ltural]rrency veering strongly _away _ 4rm this top-down/ratified-via-precedent/sanctioned approach x.tremely n.teresting...@ present i'm x.ploring/researching/plotting a faux soc _network project [_feralC] that cs this formalisation as clinging within stratified fibres n.dicative of a close-ended/linear approach 2 weaving acculturation:

"The academy ... is today so swamped by the assumptions and practices of market economics that it is deeply implausible for academics to tell their students they inhabit a postmodern world where a multiplicity of ideologies, world-views and voices can be heard. Their every step hounded by market economics, academics cannot preach multiplicity when their lives are dominated by what amounts in practice to consumer fanaticism. The world has narrowed intellectually, not broadened, in the last ten years. Where Lyotard saw the eclipse of Grand Narratives, pseudo-modernism sees the ideology of globalised market economics raised to the level of the sole and over-powering regulator of all social activity – monopolistic, all-engulfing, all-explaining, all-structuring, as every academic must disagreeably recognise. Pseudo-modernism is of course consumerist and conformist, a matter of moving around the world as it is given or sold."
- Alan Kirby

■

Of necessity cultural producers embrace the language of policy
and the languages of spin.

■

they do? in order 2 have them con[de]fined + validated with a rubber _stamped acceptable sign [ie make it in2 the inner-sanctioned-power-definer's eye _path] i agree....but 4 those not oriented within the "reality" [my definition of reality is more a heavily _variable faceted patterning] of becoming culturally relevant or mass marketed along a e[ducative]conomic axis, i'd beg 2 diffa.....

■

This is basic survival in producing sustainable
"education" and by that i mean cultural events, spaces for dialogue, skills development, introducing new concepts to new audiences.

■

....again, according only 2 those status _quo channels geared 2wards the event/xhibition/object/"the pitch" as defining how cultural landscapes lie....fomenting abstractions currently perceive "education" [as defined thru these means] as essentially perpetuating a dynamic molded within expressive confines out-of-step with the n.credible rewriting of hub _networking or flattening of the creator/absorber/audience [think:myspace, blogging, live-leaking]....in the potentiate infoclimate of social nets redefining m[eme]odes 2wards anything _but _ the sustainable, of rewriting the market/canon from the inside via a removal of the x.clusivity of function according 2 n _dividual creator labels [such as an artist, definer, teacher] education as such ceases 2 b....

[troll _bait snipping here]

■
Dirk wrote that Second Life is harnessing all the creativity out there.. Is that wrong? I used to be highly critical of it, but have changed my mind.
■

i'd b really n.terested 2 c wot in fact changed ur position here mel - if it was the gradual seeping of Second Life as an acceptable platform for corporations/'educators'/other m[eme]ainstream _signifiers?

■
It Performs a fabulous educational and social role in our society. Art organisations are falling over themselves to have galleries exhibitions and residencies there - be part of the culture you've got.
■

bzzzT: i say:m.plode.the.cult[ural].trend

■
Love the one youre with.
■

bzzzT: i suggest: luv.the.1.ur.not

-][m][

_

–LFG Curiosity, Play, or Xperimention PST–

——— http://disapposable.blogspot.com/ ———
——— http://netwurker.livejournal.com/ ——
————sharding.ur.reality.purples-——-

5.1.6 _c[l]a[wed]rved.reality.[n.ter]faces (2007-01-24 07:12)

.post/past[caring]cognitive
..tra[r]c[h]ing.wet.eg[r]o.[s]lips
...sub.stance[dance].leeching
....gold.transform[er].stains
.....skin.s[culpt]often.inter[faced]nals
......RIPple.actuals

(2007-01-23 23:55:06)
.pat .pat .pat, cogs dripping down negative caring]trachea slits aching rose drips]abused ballerina flashing, posing]sweat spotlights flickering twinkles in her eye

(2007-01-24 21:40:45)
.cat.patternings+fe[ra]line.elastic.stretching.
.purring.quantities+soft.cl[p]awings.

5.1.7 jacked[i]Njilled (2007-01-28 14:57)

j _umbled.fop.sitting+limb[ic.systemic]s.creched+d .Raw[l]n.ed
a _p[d]iary _scrabbling.thru.frantic.sw[h]armic.vin[t]e [rface]s
c _auterize[n]d.bl[met]i[er]ndness.thru.v[bin(/sh)]aried.clots
k _ill.s[t]wit[erring.ly.i]ching.thru.gen.der [ma].iden _titties
——————— _[N]in[ja.perfection] _———————-
j _ilted.h[d]ead.slidings.on.bulk.mo[du _lust] _to _red.shouldahs
i _n.spitting.vi[s]c[(f)eral]i['m.jeal)o usness.in.brawn.phrases
l _ong.vul.Pine.st[fl]ares[of.ur.spasming.tale] flickr+faux.flop
l _usciousness.dredged+p[s.alt]i[n(ch)e({ckere }d)]cked.ova+ova

5.2 February

5.2.1 _Utilizing P[os]T[raumatic]S[(ad)hock]:Hell-Reve[r]sioned_ (2007-02-03 10:11)

1. _Lessons _from _*the* _POSt _Modernity _
a. Morality tongue clicking cs reformed static 50's reformu[b]latedless via typ-

ified gender.s[traight _jckting]nap.shots + trap[e.the.]page in monetaried.hells
b. B sure 2 revoke + e[s]c[ape]lipse ur previousness; ethics.do.not.a.post-9.11.world.parse
c. Clued-in systemic approaches leave the weak.weeker + the know[!]n as danger[m]ous[e]

2. _Post _tr[M]ama[!] _[re]Vers(ing _song)e[d] _
a. Focus shattering promo[te]s.distributed attn ext[ra.t]ension = soc _net Mediarenas
b. A preoccupation with the [sound/snap/snippet]bite = rewritten.abs[pr]o[to]r[ece]ption.lvls
c. Bio _artifacts dribble thru the Mediarena as statica; new[mo]bileness.is.the.new.info.gawd

3. _Objects _Removal:[inS]tilling.the.etheral.so[c]i[a]l
a. Beating [y]our prior headness till it bl[r]ea[d]ts in t[d]i[(l)a]m[ond]e
b. Syn[cop(ul)ate] ur way in2 medium bloc.k.ages
c. Personal adage c[ommunication]roo[ms]ning.is.the.Nu.Black

5.2.2 QQ+[T]roll[in.with.the.toon.punches] (2007-02-07 06:29)

/l[h]ook[ed.victim _(r)he(toric)x]ing[wings]
/charge[d.with.st(|l)inky.data.breath]
/cry[ogenically.sp(l)anked+g(n)amed]
/point[blank.affective.r(d)ange(rousness)]

(2007-02-07 02:55:03)
/si(gh)n

5.2.3 _pur[ne]gatory_lives[blogged] (2007-02-08 06:51)

+ c[ruel.n.tentionally]atta.logged + shifted.thru.organ[ic].[heir]looms + do[a]cumen.t + do.cum.ent + doc[ktorr, pls]...........

5.2.4 o/men–l/oops (2007-02-13 06:42)

–

.sticky/corroded/one/[david]lynched/bird/mu[cus
]lch/periph[f]eral/warning/of/dead/bab[i]es

–moved4ward2:
.swivel/headed/twitch/in/alien/dawg/viso[men]n/he
ll/snapped/2/friendly/grids
–staidcontactbout:
.recipr[v]ocal/anima/lface/eye/s.miles/+/crinkle/ cut/human/yearn/turns
–browncoatst[ret(ch)inaln]ipplesbleedingin:
.flitter/organ[ic]s/yellow/feathered/twitterness/
gasp/breath/fit/4/the/taking
–

5.2.5 _[night.m]Aires of[rom] the GeoGraphs_ (2007-02-17 07:18)

1. _Tha Dinna Partaye _
trapped.inna.blood.red.haughtiness.
walls stretched.with.gales.of.[ova]blown.s[creech(i a)]tatus.laugh _barkin. glasses.shift _tinkling+s[ocial _front]pillage. wimmen.shot[hru].in.foul.fashionestas+whipped.per
oxide.frenzies/conCrete.bo[xto]x.fillas.
i.ma[trek]ke.my.otherness.way.2.tha.bathroom.
the.faux.femme.pack.follow+mock; alting.gutted.vitriol.spatter.with.non _word.[di]staining.
i.p[l]ush.the.swirling.perfumed.stinkpack.in2.the .hallway.
stiletto[tter].waspings.as.they.geo _mock+reality.t[sm]ear.

2. _The GeoFear _

esc. tab in2.a.geo.blank.[hi]sts. viciou.s.walled.spaces.bleed.capitalist[-idbits]+r aped.schi[trap.e]zoid.m.mages.

design.b[f]reaks+frenetic.dips.in.main.st[reamn es]s. i.stagger _wander; words.blur+s _pace.s _purrs.in.my.anxiety.skin[s].

Whorling.[anti]c[limax]entre+panic _scrabble _searching. /loc. /loc. /loc. co _ords;

st[d]aggering.in2.train.wreckage.boards+navigatio
n.on.boards.of[canada].frozen.time.stamping.its. [uncompreh(t)en]sable.foot.

3. _The Terrawe[h]izt[ory] _

a.frien[co]d[ed]ly.frantic.Geograph.queries+c

licks.me.in.a.blue.victim.stance[dance].

/loc.promise[ry]+dragging.me.back.thru.l-
[w]ay [.ling]ered.crusts.of.the.physical; i.packet.cringe+follow; all.bumbling.p[erverse]lacement. up.a.set.of.[carto]graphic _stairs; i.[s]t[a(c)tic]remble+[diso]r[i]ent . e nter.tha.[comb.ova]Terr.awe.izt; all.sm[rotted.ch]arm+slave.rhetoric.

promises.of.t[urned-torture]imetables.in.x.change .4.geo _rub-bings+reverse.pleasure.[rum]blings. acquiescence.in.a.d[(h)our]esperation.cr-umb.

5.2.6 –n.terf[ph]a[s]ce.an[at]om[y]ie– (2007-02-27 06:13)

*.[t]a[xo]nomie.sheltering.in.rabid.dreamer.p
ock[Marked+shAved.in.meM]e.ts
.anatomy.of.a.c[ult.B]reeder: running.fr[P.d]ant[e]ically.thru.plummet+melt
.anomie>alien[nnation]>breakage>m.mage.re.c[G
]obbling>h[f]alt[ering].stat[ically]s

trip.wanton.wires+cowering.on.hidden.folk.shelvings:
:bleed.screening.nurses.[vam]pires.scrabble.on.4g otten.eclipse.bedding
ban[a]daged.[engineered]sec.r[h]et[orica -l]s.bleating.on.demo.bio.belt[ings]:

5.3 March

5.3.1 .smudged teats.+.g.lit[eral]ter trees. (2007-03-01 08:41)

.[tr]ac[e]hing.window.snip[pets]=c[c:]o al.c[(h)oru]s.cate]har[acter].trees.
.face[firs]t.running.in.memory.dRIPs:tripping.rem embr[d]ance.veins.
_
+[-]finger.meanders+[y]talking.loud+binary.fa st[ing]
+shuddering.along.with.the.b(r)e(a)st.of.them
_
#c[h]oked.up+ic[icl]ed.down #
#co.[de.pendent]val[v]ence.leaking.in–2 #

5.3.2 aspergers_girls = true; (2007-03-07 07:55)

eye.blink _open;
consciousness.wake _on;

visual.shift = yes;
light _lvl _parse = on;
movement _orientation = true;
duel _geo _concept _function = yes;
think _dissonance = true;
system.[b]o[dy]rientation = yes;

</aspiescripting>

–

#reality _filtering.in.rose.[+goo _packed]foundations+smoothed.orange.hair.-patting #
#shift.internal.states.2wards.–out—(transition al _2wards _pretense = on:) #
#biting.workplace.tongues+watching.distanced.f[ph]a[se.pla]ce[ment.yearnings].[social]fa [i]llings #

5.3.3 _competition m.[d]body_ment_ (2007-03-09 17:26)

competition m.bodies the myth of freedom;
-u r free 2 operate in an open market
-u r free via demo.crazy
.free 2 b smarter than ur neighbours
.free 2 b as sarcastic + pseudo-liberal as u like
.free 2 offer versions as fact
.free 2 present jib[e]s as n.teraction

#u r not free.
#u r not non-controlled.
#u r indoctrinated like the rest of us.

u r:
controlled enuff 2 b cultu[vi]r[tu]ally myopic
controlled enuff 2 denigrate x.periential leanings
controlled enuff 2 consider argument as tool
controlled in2 viewing socratic method = free-form
controlled enuff 2 perceive justifications as truth
controlled enuff 2 state ur opinion as fact
controlled enuff 2 offer hidden abuse as humor
controlled enuff 2 consider history = static
controlled enuff 2 subliminally feel urs is the right>only>valid way
controlled enuff 2 assume a sense of beauty is universal
controlled enuff 2 spout point scoring as x.change
controlled enuff 2 declare arrogance = openess

(2007-03-25 00:56:43) b
[redacted]> arrogance [redacted]< *

5.3.4 [e]mot[ional]e_armo[u]r_101 (2007-03-27 18:13)

[]c[yc]li[c.k.]nical.rigidity

>stitching>freez[.t.y]e>g[b]la[u]nces
[]h[m]o[u]lding[patterns]

>my>m>brace>selves

[]s[h]ombre>[st]ages

>g.assed>br[t]oken[s]>falling.in.r[p]u[d -dles]bble.

[]conscious.[th]ro[a]t[s]

>bark>+>[info]p[h]aste

5.3.5 |-d(sc)ream_borrelia-| (2007-03-31 12:13)

|-d(sc)ream _borrelia-|

-sheen1: skating.[on|the]green-glass.algae:
|-wi[n]t[e(the)r(ed)]hered.plumage
|-caregiver.p[b]ricks[building.regressive.bloc ks]

|-cement.careering.over.skitter.snaps[limb.from.bin ary.limb]
|-bleeding.in2.s[ocial]kitte[n]r[ubs] _jack[in+kin.etic _outs]

-sheen2: cau[terize]ght:
|-drop+plummeting.in.mortar.l[h]oops
|-aviatrick[l]ing.+.clutching.geo.s[tr]u[c]tures

|-hands.tawn[y].on.[mo(u)th]barb[aric]s

-sheen3: sc[d]re[a(lu)m(p)]en.r[t]outing:
|-bitching.wood[p]enn[il]ess.score[d.blank+ analogue]s
|-c.ing.me+suffering.molten.t[al(|c)k]orque. seizure

5.4 April

5.4.1 black_dingo[thic]_n.terf[ur(n)]ace (2007-04-11 06:06)

::blAcK::
-floozy-hair-dream-fwd-w[r]i[th]nding-
–facing-[hir]suit-blindness-with-soft[en]-ch oke+scrape-drowning
—sens[d]uality-[perky-the-]d[uck]owned+ pwned

::DinG!oed::
-gothic[kory]-shakes-in-coded-gamer-dresses
–rhetoric[ketty]-chunks+b[ack]iting-s[g] narl[ed]-spitting

::fUrNa[n]c[y]e::
-ego-n.ter-face-furred+con[ned.lu]scious-dusted

5.4.2 un-[l]aw[l]-[ful.l] (2007-04-13 16:10)

:bloody _[l]aw[l]-[ful.l]
:
:s[pa(nk.a)ge.rank]hits+gag[gle]s
[tite.green]rope[s]+wad[dle]s
::
:moving.in2.ur.[eve-ry-day-mono-working-sp]here.

5.4.3 _Anti-Memoryware _ (2007-04-27 11:40)

——————————————_————-. —-

ReVerb: Anti-Memoryware - [no|wo]Manual Assessment

——————————————_————-. —-

+ Created at: 11:57:02 AM 27/04/2007

+ [re]A[d]ssessment Summary:

:cortext1.1:ID:\Personage\ Memory\Applicant Data\Sensory recallFront\Retrieval\Pro file\egoFilament.default\endcoDependency
:cortent1.6:fluxMatta:\PersonagekslashMemory\Applicant Data\Sweet recallSide\Retrieval\Prog ression\fatherFilament.deadashperpetualAngst
:court1.6:wipeBleed:\PersonallashMemory\Applied+LoosenedslashBurgeoning recallSlip\Reliving\Proce dural\heroFilament.currentshperpetualloop

(2007-09-09 21:25:41) no
trying to fix it

5.5 May

5.5.1 _burrowing.hex[i-deci(grand)mals]es_ (2007-05-02 05:50)

stepA: n.jecting.tint _visual.dermos
[slide.skinning.bloom.p(h)atch(ling)es]
stepB: monitoring.col[d]our.[sn]itches
[blood.p(thr)u(st|)lsings.in.mustyFlowers]
stepC: riding.the.c[bi]oded.h[ova.d]ue.modification. waves
[the.spike.hi(kes).shadeSpiders+pricklingWretch es]

5.5.2 ag[o]nize_n.ternal_ru[scul]pturing (2007-05-03 14:53)

fl[|r]esh[(|j)ack]boot[s]wishing.around .in
_turn.alli[ed=not.x.ternal.eyed.n.e./me!]
i s[the]well+r[p]up.t[ort]ure.f.[|n]fecti veness

smoothing.c[brain.p]ast[ry]es+hyb[good.]r
id[dance].mountain[ted]scape.j[|p]ackets
–

i.ftp.glance[d.glistening.f(hi.fi)lows]

text.pins.in.my.document[v]a[g]r[ant]ied legs

5.5.3 albu[wo]men_skys (2007-05-06 07:52)

-white fur _brushed skies-
–toasted.dove.altitude.wings–
—c[loud]ream.flapping.form[ations]

5.5.4 _bull[terror]gods + br[st]itches_ (2007-05-09 12:46)

::
:

watching:s _port[ing>life>gouges]:
.
:desperation.sitting.in.small _s[mad]hatter _free _zones
:wrapping.myself.with[in].clov[h]e[ll]n _[hoofs+]arms
:brawn.wr[g]on[e]g+test.horrible
.
[biology _lump _chants]
[ns.titutionalised+laying]
[broken _mut(e)tation _gaps]
.
.i.stumble.ova.u+socialised.urs.
.u.flip+stretch.ur.jigsaw.b(end.h)ack.
.shake.my.[t]error.head.
:
::

5.5.5 SocialConnectionAccessProtocol [- SCAP -] ControlVersioningSystem (2007-05-25 09:07)

```
% cvs -d
:codependentserver:internaltripwiring@cvs-mirror.aborti
ve.org:/cvsroot login
(Logging in to
internaltripwiring@cvs-mirror.abortive.org)
CVS password:  [internaltripwiring]
%
% cvs -z3 -d
:codependentserver:internaltripwiring@cvs-mirror.aborti
ve.org:/cvsroot co SCAP

cvs server: Updating abortive/directory/SCAP
Ur abortive/directory/SCAP/NO.pls
Ur abortive/directory/SCAP/YES.dmg
Ur abortive/directory/SCAP/ChangeRealityLog

--
#There are currently 6 SocialConnection release_valves
available.
#Use the main an[ti]xiety_loading trunk:
#Release-1_0: 1st attempt at SCAP. Tremory_+_Shuddery.
#Release-1_2:  1st attempt at the 2nd release.
Thick_womb_music_cables
#unre[a|]eling
unstable_conversation_w[g]r[e|]app[l]ing.
```

```
#Release-1_2_2: The final[ity] + most
stab[b{l}ing_with_ur_g(old)athering_eyes]le
#release in the 1.2 series.
#Release-1_3: 1st 1.3 release with
[g]host_groin_spas[onic]m[ush]s.
#Release-1_3_2: Latest release with some
s[pidery]tone_lizard_clubbed2deathness.
#Release-1_3_3: Latest release with some
st[p]arched_+_sw[|t]ollen_body_w[l]ords
#drenched chemically.
Yearn_f[l]ingers_cup_sh[gl]immer_throats.
```

5.6 June

5.6.1 +cul[robo]ture.[cl]ash+ (2007-06-25 10:35)

+|—-cultural.lashings.against.twi[s|]tter.mechi cals
+|—bot.longings+ro[w(o)].mantising[my.ins ectile.lust.unfurls]

-|—john.doe.[lo(wbie)five.ing.in.millitariesq ue.mash _ups

+|—bli(nd)p.[b]limping.all.the.way.2.the.dr ainless.chromian.bank

5.7 July

5.7.1 _s[p]erver[se]_: 404 poetry (2007-07-04 11:10)

925.has.d-tec[hy]ted:
404.poetry:
that you
redirect the
request for
this address
in a way that will
never complete.

5.7.2 _physical.gl[tw]itte[g]r[ounding]_ (2007-07-05 12:32)

tw[physical _gl]itter.line.1:
[hormone.s]pin _ _pr[odd(l)ing+l](tw)i(n|)cking
tw[h]it[s+soft.misses]ter.line.2:
c[w]racking.open.ur.fawning.desire chest
tw[gu]i[l]tter.line.3:
n _ _tense+spittling.in.lubrication.waves

---

taxi (2007-07-09 17:56:52)
Ossu, Mz. Mez, you don t mind if I add you, do you? Yr speakin my language.

netwurker (2007-07-09 22:24:58)
don t mind @ all! +add:)

5.7.3 copy+p][w][aste_luv (2007-07-13 18:02)

............waiting/][dr][owning/breed/ing:
......sna][ke][pping.2.the.covert.
..b][l][eating.
.................vic/tory.rosings
...........sy][e][mb][yr][o][n][lic.shifting
..co][p][wness.trap][e][ped
......blu][i][sh resp][irati][onse
..............][g][o][o][gling.beatific .smile.h][l][ands
.......with.fin][ne][g][ans][e][ve][redtoes.

5.7.4 d[eep!].d[ark].data.g[aze] (2007-07-27 08:21)

switch.in-2:

{ currency of mention

–current.f(l)ocus.blo(p)wned
–celebrity.d(Pl)an(c)k.timers.set _hailed

5.7.5 (2007-07-30 11:14)

<–[s]have[d]n.blocks.of.connec[k]t.hunke ring
passwordian.tinctures.spitting.on.usernam[ing.day] es

red.blood.bl[ack.p]ossoming.OnContent.c[h]ord s
s.harp _b[r]eaked words+t[m]angled.gl.[inf|l]oss[u]aries

<–real[sh]i[f]ty _angles+tinkle.sentence.ova[ry]tures

5.7.6 [..................poe_box...................] (2007-07-31 20:47)

Edgar Allanesque.

[l _(h)o(rror)s _t]

[......................
no _blood......
no _pix...........
no _thrill[ah]..
no _thing.......
.......................]

5.8 August

5.8.1 _MA[VE]N[TRICLE]_spur[ting]s (2007-08-03 08:52)

```
VENTRICLEPATH="/usrs/ventricle/bleed/st/RIP/pled/CHEST/
meats/in/romance/parts"
VENTRICLEPATH="/usrs/blending/ventricle:$VENTRICLEPATH"
VENTRICLEPATH="/usrs/blending/mysqueeze/ventricle:$VENT
RICLEPATH
VENTRICLEPATH="$ORGANOCHAMBERHOME/ventricle:$VENTRICLEP
ATH"
export VENTRICLEPATH
```

5.8.2 -|-navi[lon]g[ing]at[e]ion-|- (2007-08-07 12:56)

Subject1:
-v[w]o[rd.s]miting.in-	-d[i]r[sCrete.mac -hinim]ama.patches

-al.gore.rhythmic.comfort-|-squeezing.em[neg]oti [ati]onal.blood
-st[h]and.[clutch.n]stilling.-|-nestling.in.b roken.[pair]bonds
-|-[s]and[y].and-and-ness-|-trickle.fre[ima gi]n[ation]zy

5.8.3 agrep|ggation (2007-08-22 06:34)

*grep.gate+dangling.wantons
echoin[gan]gli[o]ng.shivers+black.b[rusied .eg]o _xing
–

:blown.bio.twists+screaming.leavings:watch.the.blood.
+.milk.the.s[ilicon.(s)cr]eed:naturelleness.i n.the.stillness:

5.8.4 –fis-s-ur-es.in.the.–r[a]i[n]-vets.of.l–i–fe (2007-08-25 09:25)

————-[d]rai[l]ment.drifting—— ————-

:pi[xel]ct-tour-this:

:dr[fire.l]ooping.taffy.hair.
:sc[frozen.product]Alp[s]-stitched.2.a.
:bro[pe]ken.backed.
:::VicToryan.g[always.P(ay)]al

:twitching.s[grand]mal[ace]-lness
:we.t[sighted.b]rail[le]s.
:twin[d]n[a]ed.gOlden.scars.
:[raised.in.a.flesh.barn]
:l[g]inger.eyes.on.
::::[l|m]ashed.bOne.[-m]bed.back

:dRop[Ping]:fingers.in.data.pies
:[bon]mot-ions.in.drizzled.mouths
:sIT.cAged+
:::::boVine.d[is.Abled.L]angerous

5.9 September

5.9.1 _Tinker_B[(l)o(ve.l)y.Sh]elles_ (2007-09-03 16:29)

–0–

trip.tinker.][m][Bell[y.warmth.D|w]ishmen t
hawt.b[(gr)a(f)t-h-f]looding
ah, i c[-thing][-ground][-downlings]

round+r[d]o[w.jones]und[ertaker1+2+3]
u 2?de[-part.ickle][-shift]nt[at(d)a(da) !]s
murmur.me+[id]min[o(g)r.itty]e

——[sizzling.u+u[/who]res[ides _(t)here?]

xx

–1–

trip _tinkering. _InB[aby]ellyWArm[s]th
[read.wasp _cauling]
[read: m(t)e(ch)tronic]
[read: blood.(l)Overly]
Bouy _sHells.in.Gal[l(Want:)On].Guns

–1.2–

Tinker _B[all.of.th]e.ll.[w]Rin[k(lin)]gs+raV [an]ishes
HotFlooding _g[Tongue.R]As[Li]ps+gra[vity.li]ftings
Tongue.S.s.s.Li[s]ps.
yes........yes....yespls.

–1.3–

Yes, I see[thing.chords.rippling.in.ur.groundless.hea(r)ts].
I wonder [st]if[fyness+Ju(ng.le)(|a)gulars.In:ten -(si)t(y).st(w)Rangling].

xxx

–1.2.2–

RIP.Bab[le]ywarmth
Wa[(just)Co]s.Pings
[H(G)a(me)nd.On:wet.lip.mouths]
C[H]o[ver(ing)t]bw[br]e[ast]bs

–1.2.2.3–

BloodLover[s.in.(&)still.s]ly]
B[e]uying.u.Se[e]d[Me+Pwne(in)d]uction .Hells
With.GallAnt.I/Want/Guns.

5.9.2 _netwurker.mez is[ez.y]: (2007-09-04 06:22)

:rrringing.thru.f[acebook]lesh
:melting.ego.bone

:cleaning her work paws
:aggro managing to the hilt

:s[eduction].s.s.Li[s]pping
:hovering, edgewise

---

fine_dandy (2007-09-04 03:09:54)
s[m]il[ez] /after mez/ instead, running with dogs... 7:49am not leaping, irrepressible, day... 6:42am cutting mustard... 9:59pm e[a][di]ting her status... 8:30pm reading fractures... 8:18pm Virginia is putting oranges in a bucket, green dust of mold peeling off and sending spores rising spiralling. The grass is bright against the fallen oranges. small suns... 5:44pm Virginia is awake alone, small noises from sleeping animals in the night. the air inside her feels stale, her skin stretching across bones that feel too sharp. lovr sleeps... 9:50pm wondering about the spectacle(s)... 10:22am yoga. baking. moon. teetering. is isn t

5.9.3 c[ru(i)s]he[d]st–[facebook2] (2007-09-11 23:37)

is::—reading.b[l]ooks.that...hurt

is::–facing.the.truth.of.h[l]um[inosity]ans

is::—cupping.tender.vein[cut]s

is::–i.mag[ic]ery _stitching

is::—trea[d]ting.calm.paths.b.tween.the _sparkle _+ _the _cusp.

5.9.4 _silk.pu[ne]rringly_vs_clinic[theory.c]a[u]L (2007-09-22 09:51)

journ[l]ey.[l]in[es]g:

shutte[s(uff.us)ed.ochre]red.skys
broke[n].motions+lilac.h[cl]o[uds]t
atmosphe[fab]ric _r[(i)c(h)]o[lo]u[r]ting
profile _pr[g]o[al]jecting.in.gasps+oh[ms]
bau[row]d[y].dr[t]eamings
slippery.li[nsect.wo]mbs+sl[b]e[gin.twinn] e[d]p _sounds

——————vs——————
Clinic[f]a[ux]l.theor[m]y.bl[r]eed[ea l]ing.
Crossing.bo[unda]r[y]ders.in.st[m]ol[t] enness.
N.stitional.ise[ye]d+bli[ded.in.progress.inte] nded.
Credit.goes.here+[k]n[c]o[ncre]t[ely]. [t]here.

5.10 October

5.10.1 ___i(t|re)n(der)k[ling]___ (2007-10-19 07:10)

-1.0-

sl[h]iding.do[p]wn.cr[h]ush.walls.
..point1.after.point.arg[d(b)o(dy)c]ument .2..
...t[v]o[cal]ngue.w[non]h[a|]ip[pines]s...

#tre[a]mor[(gh)ou(l)]s #
#trem[p]or[ous.marble.flesh] #
#t[p]re[tence]mor[eNmore] #

_

5.10.2 /t ha[rm.a]nd.deep.in (2007-10-19 08:47)

/t n.ternal: [b]itchin.floor[ed.+skinning.my.char.glands.wit h.an.x.istence.knife]
/p zomg! therez a wireframe.in.my.muscles.
/raidchat hold on, something's happening. afk a tic............

[toc]

[toon.memoried+ twitching.SL.breeding]
[afk=kiss.of.integration.death]
[flippe.2.da.[su]re[ly]eeal]:

-white _tiled.alt.lying.on.virt[d]ual.blood.floors-
-knee.deep.in.jointed.versional./cuts-
-scratching.my.left.arm[ies].with.rig[w]h[i]t[eousness]-

/t self: itch.pinning.tails.on.ur.behavi[d]our[al].d[type _wwwriting.m]onkeys
/t slef: therez.re[scape]ndering.dragging.itself.thru.my.s ry.relapse.bones
/t sfel: spewing.crimson.lay[ed]out.drop[era]s
/t fles[h]: watching.frames.crawl.out.my.m[ewling.unc]outh.

---

httf (2007-10-19 07:15:34)
I occasionally wonder about the references in your work. I m currently doing an education project in Second Life, and the SL stuck out. Although, I m probably projecting...

netwurker (2007-10-19 21:55:45)
ur not. >SL< [Second Life]is there 4 sure....afk any1?;) the /t" command is from World of Warcraft [MMOG]...toon.memoried is from both:) thx 4 reading:) *bow*

(2008-01-21 14:44:52)
:III::::M. _M. _ _ _ _ _ _ _
_ _M. _ _ _ _ _ _ _ _ _ _ _ _ _ _ _ _ _ _
_ _ _ _ _ _ _ _ _ _ _ _ _ _ _ _ _ _ _.:: :::: I" II":" :I::M MMI:. :::: "IIIII:. : ..:MI:. :::M
MMI:" :::::. .- -:IHMIHI" : ..:: ::M MM: ::::::::. .. : :I:: :M M. _ _ _ _ _
_ MM:" : ::.:::::::. :.".: ::IHHI.
M. _ .M::::. ::::::I::::: :.
: :: ::::: IIIM: M. _M
::::::::. .::::::::::::::::::. :::: :::::: .:::IMMI. M. _
_ _ _ _ _ _ _ _ _ _ _ _ _ MI:::: ::: ::: :::::::::M. _
_ _ _ _ _ _ _ _ _ _ _ _:::::::: :. ::::: ::::: :::IHMMM. _ _ _ _ _ _ _ _ _ _ _ _ _ _ _ _ _ _ _
_ _ _ _ _ _ _ _ _ _ _ _ _ _ _ _ _ _ _ MI:::.: II:I::::::::: ::::::::::M. _ _ _ _ _ _ _ _ _ _ _ _ _ _
_ _.::::::::IIIII":::: ::IHM. MH :::: IHMHI : " :: ::
: :: ::::II: ":I ::: : ::::IHMM. IMI:: :: :MMI: : ::::II. MH::: :::HM IM :
IMH:" ::":M. M::: ::M IM IM: MHM:: :M I" MM Mpyright</a> |</li><li><a
href="http://www.sixapart.com/about/advertising/">Advertise</a> |</li><li
a href="http://www.livejournal.com/manage/settings/">Viewing Opt ></ul>e
now. skhdl;as E NO EIE EII IJ IJ IJ IIJ I IJ I I JI I JI IJ IJI JI JJ JJ JJ
JJJJJJJJJJ JIJ IIII JIJJI JIIJ IJ JIIJ JI IJJI JI JJIJIJI JIIJOID

5.11 November

5.11.1 #Post_Gendered Sc[(D)R(e)]a(m)pes# (2007-11-01 19:10)

#moving.in.a.tight.stat[e]ic.circle.of.Post _Gendered Friends.

#jac[loc]keted in orange Guantanamo garb.
#Post _Gender1 jumps up + g[j]est[ers]ures
#2 a [consu]m[er]all-like courtyard

#i flounder [(d)unc(e)omfortable]:
#jack-dance-knifing Post _Gender2 joins in.

#joined now by Trend[r]oid[rage].Str[fashion.h]agglers
#all g _litter[ah-rah-T] + shaggy _hair-cuttings.

#Post _Gender1 flits off.
#f[h]ollow + loss.

#[grow(l)ing.firing.shop _masses clogging my path].

#lost then... ....

.....|scrabbling thru concre[am.teenage.babble.li]te flesh 2 find + [k]not| tri-av[lan]e[way]n[h]ues open|m[h]az[y]e-like|2 t[d]ried + 1 leading 2 a blisteringly open land[visual]sc[r]ape with mountains.breathing.with.waterfall.throats + tit[D]e[l(l)icate].ivory.fog.[b]races moving in a -n-ternal-now-x-t[di]urnal space|.................................

#open|so open... ....

.....|ppl here 2|tri[du]a[l]ngled.h[inged]ats protecting against [sky.d]rain[s]|a human _sl[w]a[ge]ve _train inches past|blending f.forts make me offer help 2 the pulley-+-rope man|i'm roped in [literally] 2 narrow _ch[br]an[ded]neled vis[ongs(ens)]uals|b _oiling d[r]ust[ed] skies chewing+sp[l]itting clouds in st[air.w]orm _cups.

5.12 December

5.12.1 Sel[f]e[le]ct>Proc.ess>[1st]S.kin (2007-12-01 09:02)

1. Select

   (a) Self _in _fect.organelles formed by the sub _ego _organs of the first chavatar, if any.

   (b) Visit the psychatomy of the 1st _chavatar.

   (c) Traverse order.in.the.organs formed by the remaining chavatars in the egoplateau, if any.

2. Select>Process

   (a) Assess the st[e]ruc[|p]ture of the 1st chavatar.

   (b) Formulate consciousness _blocks formed by the sub _organs of the 1st chavatar in the thoughtplateau, if any.

   (c) Reverse the cohesion _order of the remaining charvatars formed by the remaining organs in the egoplateau, if any.

3. Select>Process>Skin

   (a) Wireframe orders formed by the sub _ego.ruptures of the 1st chavatar, if any.

   (b) Render adoptive _ordering of the remaining chavatars in the egoplateau, if any.

   (c) Visit the ego of the 1st Skin.

5.12.2 .[dis]tor[t]sion. (2007-12-18 08:23)

.small.su[po]llen.scratch[et]ing.mark.my.[t r](ip)[s]o[ng]d.den.chest.
.long[ing]scrab.blings.
.shi[|a]ft[l]er.markings.on.my.h[sp]a[sm -]ptic.neck.

–

.systematica.in.my.curled.dream.tors[i]o[n].
.wake+watch[er]ing.

–

5.12.3 _s[h|]kyness_ (2007-12-22 03:27)

.he(gg)adp(h)umped.+.s(ocial)harp.toothed .hardness.
.cross-legged.ebony+emotional.arms.ro(w)bo(w) ting(les).

–glance:u|p–

:cloud.mo(lds.o)unds.scraping.2wards.ta[ge]bl eaus
:(soft)b(ull)oil([f]eather) _heads+matado[o]rian
:gold.letter.leeching.in.exqu(id)[pro.quo:dr] istes
:try[sts]ings.with.my.matted.(he)arts
:draw(li)n(gs).within.bodies.b(e)lown+org (l)an(d)s.falling

[re[a]d: (in)al(l)ways.]

5.12.4 _v[H]ex+vix[N]_ (2007-12-26 12:10)

[soft.R(class)ave[N]ings]
[Hex(H)e(LL)n.scr(t)een.lites]
[twi.lightenings+asph(gest)alt>ashfelt>velvet.d arkenings]

#u.kno.knot.wot.u.du #
#here[N] #
#[H]ere[N]now #

[sw(e)i(rd)vel.n(t)e(xT)cks]
[blOw(n)ing.gOlden]
[i.scRabble+h(m)eat.u.in.tenda.(L {H }e {art }y)lines]

---

kochanie (2007-12-26 21:41:07)
does this actually also work as code?

netwurker (2007-12-31 07:42:04)
not functionally, no.

(2008-04-05 14:57:09) YNwabfIbPxOQntIVdeB
gdDKfK hi great site thanks http://peace.com

5.12.5 skel.Et.Al_Etch[ing] (2007-12-31 18:42)

1. p[l]A[ster]ckaging:null

[m({Ro }s {e. })ilked.in.co(Bu {d })ttoned.l(bl)us(h.)tings]
[gRabb(l)ing.+l(scr)eeching.co(lo)urt(s .N.Off.With.Her.Head,Queen)ly]
[i.wonder.+b(sM)ite:sn(gr)a(s)pping.(r)Ows+ trEmb(er)ling.(g)Ahs]

2. -n-s(P)er(m {anent })tingly:yah

#sav[M]a[na]gery.in.a.[drunKin(Ship)] tip[teacup]pling
#sC[limbing.cream.]Alp[s]ping.t[x]X[x] t.hosiery

3. new:Nes[tling]s

} coWe[i]r[d].ing.in.ur.s[h]a[king]Fe[a l]ty.ca[r]ve[d.cOre]

Chapter 6

2008

6.1 January

6.1.1 _skeletal.etching_ (2008-01-04 21:35) [t_ransliteration:1]

:sk:h:el:l:etal:sk:etching:

:in:

:b:road:broke:n:pla:gu:n:es
:t:racings:down:re:moved:h:arms:+:frog:gling:twitch:i ng:le:g:gs
:et::sm:al:lnesses:nestle:+:skin:ur:awkward:t:rap:p:e d:other

:no:pack:aging::here:
:plaster:ed:ova:sen:t:s:meets:phero:monal:b:l:eats
:r:n:ose:milked:blushings:mask:+:moo:tate:
:pok:h:e:r:f:Ace:dr:awn:2:ward:s:mour:nings
:gasping:bitten:words:in:crowl:r:a:ven:nd:dry:h:er:r: s

:permanent:fake:manet:mo:de:mentedness
:managing:teac:up::savagery:
:c:limb:ing:cream.o:varied:sc:alps:
:=::g:rasping:txt:hosiery

:weird:c:l:ow:erings:in:ur:
:h:c:ackling::carv:iolent:ed::c:wh:ore:

(2008-08-11 18:21:16) Introductions
Hello to members of this site please to have joined your forum.

6.1.2 The 10 Best Synapse.Skys of the Web (2008-01-11 20:09)

1. Relapse In Eye.Cav[ity]es
2. Kaleidoscopic.Reality.Ru[i]nning
3. Word _Felt[ing] War[mound]m[ou]th[s]
4. Tracing.Arching.Foo[da]t[a]prints
5. P[c|l]ick Ap[layer.he]art
6. Tease.in2.Answered.Ful[s]l[ow]ness
7. Des[e(e)ductive]ire W[H]eaving
8. Practic[function]al.R[g]ambling
9. Aspergers Ex[l]acer[8]bations
10. P[erspective.silk+]lace.

6.1.3 #.Pls. .Select. .ur. .CHar[r(i)ed.H]Ac(k)tor.# (2008-01-13 13:32)

Toon1:

Name: _DisC[o]ursive _
Class: [B]Ovi[d]ne
Race: Fawn[y+Like]
Hair Colour: Str[L]eaked.Apathy.Brown
Eye Colour: Tinted.Victim.Bl[H]ue[s]
Description: Moves.Heav[y.Txt.S(ubjects)Oil]e(d)n.
........................Is.Obs[(b)e(autiful) quious]cenely.Serene.
........................Promises.Plasti[cine(ma {sk }es)]ques.

Toon2:

Name: _SillyS[H]aus[Fr]a[(f)u]g[u]e _
Class: Pub[l]i[us]c
Race: R[H]Aven
Hair Colour: Saffron.Spew[Au]tum[nal]
Eye Colour: InDi[gg.n]an[t].Red
Description: Crushes.Earth[iness.in.Small.B(l)o(o)dy.Pil es]
........................Runs.In Tiny.Rictus.Circ[uses]les.

........................Connect.[Com(a)]Melts
........................Hands.Out.Fragment.F[W]rac [K.Of.9.Taled.F(S)u]tures.

(2008-01-14 13:29:10) Love this one mez!
Runs.In Tiny.Rictus.Circ[uses]les, in[deed]!
http://packageinsertofsorrows.blogspot.com

6.1.4 .ge[a{s}.phasi(a)]sha. (2008-01-15 19:11)

.
..geisha.aphasia.
...paper.scissors.glock.
....geas, pls.
.....
...
..
.

6.1.5 /dir ect.dis[zy].course (2008-01-17 09:26)

/boot ing.character.stat[ttoo.hew(n)]ues.
/media moss.grown.stone.arch[ing.ey]es.
/sys temic.delv[l]ing.in2.t[gran]ite lips.
/var iance.l[sh]ocked.+symbo[w]l.l[g]oaded.
/bin ding.u.+.ur.silicon.u[who]r[e]s.

6.1.6 [S(il)]enth[Rope]alpy (2008-01-23 08:30)

–Flash: Scrabbling.Shit[f]ting.Clawings–
@freshly.dry.iced.[m.]bodi[m]e[nt]s

[bluewhite.bubbling.skinheats.thru.flown.fingas]
[frantic(kle)s.in.bip(rust.flecked.m)edal.f licks]
[scratching.gelled.entha(|e)lpics]

–=–

[rent1.bleeds.contact.fruit][rend2:pumps.frozen
.singing.bloods][render3:exosquirmickly.slippery]

6.1.7 #dn[p]a[per.cut here.]bird# (2008-01-30 18:07)

BirdF1-TTCTCCAACCACAAAGACATTGGCAC
BirdR1-ACGTGGGAGATAATTCCAAATCCTG
BirdR1-ACGTGGGAGATAATTCCAAATCCTG
BirdR3-AGGAGTTTGCTAGTACGATGCC
BirdF1-TTCTCCAACCACAAAGACATTGGCAC
BirdR1-ACGTGGGAGATAATTCCAAATCCTG
BirdR1-ACGTGGGAGATAATTCCAAATCCTG
BirdR3-AGGAGTTTGCTAGTACGATGCC
TTCTCCA #cut[icle].bird.ACCACAAAG
ACGTGGG #line.here #AGATAATTCCAAAT
ACGTGGG #fe[e]tally.blind #AGATAAT
AGGAGTT #cur[e]ve.d.h.orn[er]y.TGCT
AGGAGTT #bill.on.my.GCTAGTACGATGCC
ACGTGGG #pro[ad]verbial.tab #AGATA

(2008-01-31 03:41:02)
Nice!

6.2 February

6.2.1 531 - (ch) . amber (ed) k (h) e (a) r (t)nels (2008-02-01 07:09)

15($stiff . ening with fea((c))r(eam)!)
5($limb . less f((l))ailings)
53($swelt . (i)ered.fractures
35($uglin((dr))ess(es) (x)
30($denied . (see)d(s)ire
331($snipped-genital-(pup(a))pets x))))))
object
33($rot-cavity-m(f)o((a)rm)ldings)
3($(flesh . g)r(e)ying . orGa(mete)n(Elle)s)
13($let ((form))
13($get* bindings . b(lind)ody))

($define! force-promise
clammered
($if (not?
glamouring

object
(handle-promise-result x)))
hammered
($define! handle-promise-result
amber
($gene (x y)
chambered
((not? (promise? y))
(iambic.pent((up))a)meter
(set-(h)eart(h)! (var x) y) ;
(set-earth! (var x) ()) ; delete y)

exact?, inexact?, robust?, undefined?
get-real-internal-bounds, get-real-exact-bounds
get-real-internal-primary, get-real-exact-primary
make-inexact
real->inexact, real->exact
with-strict-arithmetic, get-strict-arithmetic?

numerator, denominator
floor, ceiling, truncate, round
rationalize, simplest-rationa

make-rectangular, real-part, imag-part
make-polar, magnitude, angle

6.2.2 _7Eve{[D]r[eamic]}N_ (2008-02-12 18:45)

xx7[cu]n[t][wr]ites _N _7daysxx
[7.bags.of.tr(eplete)au(ral.shutting.off,)m a]
[7.wakings+7.dream.dro(p)wn(w)ings]
[7.minute.scream.project(ing)s]
[7.alarms.4.7.doll(jouse)ahs]
[7.night(and daze)mar(h)e(re)s(y)s]
[7.naked.(8min {e }us7th time)whores]
[7.tom.selections+rape.insect.fucking+7x7x7yr(eco vered.ova)s]
xx1fear[egiment]s _N _1abs[c]e[ss]nce.b[h]e[r]erxx
[1.w(alking)oman _glass.(s)entry.hiding.running.stumbles
_deca(pitated+now.de)f[unct]e, pls].

6.2.3 _*Sigh*che_ (2008-02-20 10:59)

*

hAir[bLast]wEt[ted]+dRpwnediNtEnder[lOaded]w]h[ole]Artedness

pSy[i]ch[ing]e*

sTu[Tor]pid+sToo[aCadNemic.s]pider[s.sCrape mYsLashmOuth]
aShmOuth+sCorpiOnt[L]ong[ing.gl]ued+cRackedaT tentionsPines

_mInus _*

gOldenhArrows+dEsp[eciallynOw(l)]ic(k)abl yaBsentfLesh[io(ff)ns]
vEnysjUnocEresvEner[v]ated+ vUln[abLoody]erable+cEr[e]br[al]us

[e _]Ro[s]tically*

6.2.4 .(c)leaving. (2008-02-22 07:10)

.ash[s-odd]en.che[av(ing)y]st
.[w(p {wned })ollen]urveillance.eye
.glu[at]t[achm]en[t].thread
.[t]ox[ic(ky)].heart

_i.will[i(-)n(illi)gly].[(k)not]. hurt.u _

6.3 April

6.3.1 In this album: (2008-04-01 09:58)

_bee.st[h]ung.in.[se(a)rgent]corporality _ (photos), _cob.webbing.vs.brick+batbones _ (photos), _t[oon]a[i]rred.brush[er]ings _ (photos), _scaling.d[rag+(o)n+drop]own[ed] _ (photos), _eng[ame.adrenal]ine.drones[+zerOOOOhs] _ (photos), _Bi[|u]tch[er]Rings, pls! _ (photos), _smells.of.r[a|]op[e]ing.burns _ (photos), _booty.+.teh.+bullet.b[r]east _ (photos), _embryotic::narc[r]otic _ (photos), _real.le[state.b]ase+run+bac? _ (photos), _flashed+shaved.danger[m]ous[e.ova.here,geneti cally?] _ (photos), _body _m[virtual.lust.y]ode[s, p]ls _ (photos), _c[visual.animus.tw]rittering.just..here.. _ (photos), _salt[ernate] _[c]lick _tangs _ (photos), _crowd.down+prey.2.ur.interrrrphaseplacement.gawds _ (photos), _[uber(na {<ur>scent<on.my.shimmer.finger> })wings _ (photos), _m.b[p]urring.eyes _ (photos), _inse|[hu]rt.ur.gau[slea]zy.pres[ci]ence, here _ (photos), _sliding.on.Erosity, than[atos]kfully _ (photos)

6.3.2 _trEm[d]o[lls]r_ (2008-04-26 17:29)

```
doll_tre[ru]mor[s] = <<TREMORS
<tremor name='the_5th_world'>
<fracture>
<fracture name='post2charinscription'>
<polymers>
<polymer var='user' val='YourDollUserName'/>
<polymer var='3rdperson' val='Your3rdPerson'/>
<polymer var='location' val='YourSoddenSelf'/>
<polymer var='spikey' val='YourSpiKeySelf'/>
</polymers>
</fracture>
<fracture name='post2skin'>
<polymers>
<polymer var='user' val='YourPolyannaUserName'/>
<polymer var='msg' val='YourPleading'/>
<polymer var='lastword' val='YourLastword'/>
</polymers>
</fracture>
</fractures>
</tremor>"
TREMOR
```

6.3.3 bet[t]a[living.thru.brutal_ness] (2008-04-29 11:21)

Congratulations!!

You have been selected for early beta access to [x(butter)scotch.h(r)ead(sux)+milken-meann cssesx].
As a user, you will have an opportunity to use [xash.hu(lk)ffing +(f)lick(er)ing.(co)gentle.tonguesx] before the rest of the world, as well as shaping the [x(t)railing.print(debauch)ed.f(l)ingersx].

[xf(t)awn(y).skinned+arcing.(/w)ho(?)rmo nal.mea(s)tagex] is the first [xcarbon.scr(e|l)atching.on.my.evolu(ddi)t(e)ionary.back(page)x] which allows you to view all of your [xbrittle.word.(fl)axesx] in a single secure place.

Thanks and welcome to the [xf(d)e(Sire)athering.ur.caballed.(n)ESTx] community!

The [xTrickling.D(CL)o(P)wn(ed).Ur.Marketing.F acex]Team
[1]www.Trickling.D(CL)o(P)wn(ed).Ur.Ma -rketing.Facex .com

1. `http://Trickling.D(CL)o(P)wn(ed).Ur.Marketing.Facex.com/`

6.4 May

6.4.1 _white.shud[t]d[t]er:me>m[ind]y>social>i> (2008-05-19 12:45)

.[sore]ca[u]lling.u.in.blinds.of.velvet.socia l.melt.
.rib[caged]bing+[finga.raw(r!).d]rubbings .
.u.shout^up^+>arrow<s [oul.t]ilt.down.

<snap[i]?>
<sinkage.in.the t[m]umble[core(d)].m(des)ire>
<re:if[f](r)y.+vomit.s(l)o(mo)cial.coda s>
<lick.ur.pre-sett[messy.canon.dress]ages>
<@howl[site+nuanced.nite].newness.in.gr[e]at [me.in.ego-gulps]eness>

@buttermilk(ed).c(k)ara]pacing, pls.

.caked.in.small.[tri.me, pls?]angular.fuse[ething]s.
.[liquid.con]fusion.sp[l]eak[s]+dribble.s hine.g[ro]ut[er]tage.
.chit[terlings.pinging].[th]ruinous+chat[ho llow.Gs][b]lathering.

@ownership[Page 1>Chpt Tw(h)o(a)]: x.clu[de.u+bloat.me(a)]s(ure)ive.

6.4.2 –desk.s-cra-b-bling+cl[h]a[nd]w.scr[l]atch[key]ing– (2008-05-29 07:06)

[tinkling.sloth.spin[k]s
c(l)aving.d-rain-ing.bucketing]

————————————-————- —IF-
:tappity _wrapping[txt.(blown.XTC)pup(ils)ae]:
:crawling.tip.f[inga]licks:
:boss:IN:boss:OUT:

:focus[sing.internal.blogs.of.capitalistic.paint] :
-THEN—————————————————- —-
:w[pr]o[cess(pit)ed]rd.herding.scre[ams] ened
:shimmer*stop**my**bland**hand*:
:i.[wh]o[pping]ffice.ch-air-.spin:sudden:
:+gel.stretch:arms:UP:mouth:O-PEN:

[clavicle.trickling.thru.broken.c(p)av(ement)ing.bones
i trip.(sw {p })o(llen)va.+screech.th(memb)r(ane)u.u]

6.5 June

6.5.1 _gr-owl.body.in.slicked.fingas_ (2008-06-08 11:35)

[.]u suc.
[.]u b(l)ond+brea(p)k
[.]in-too-.
[x]ARG(h).

[x]f.lick.(r.look!c!)
[y]D(rink.E.dink)NA.u.

[.]flesh({l }ions+tigahs+bears)
[.]oh.
[x]-m-y.

#
#wrong.
#bi-pedal.
#way.
#
#go!
#Back!
#

[x]gr.ow.l(wings)
[xx]junk.
[.]f {l }eather(man+rubber.women)s(es).

#
#u.
#stupid.

#funking!
#b[w]ench!
#

---

thewarinkansas (2008-06-11 07:03:50)
you get a hell yea

6.5.2 Twitterwurk 1: @grappling @on @ov[um]a. (2008-06-29 09:58)

netwurker @grinding @tec[h]tonic @hips. @grave @cars @vs @binding/@reaping. about 16 hours ago from web in reply to grinding

netwurker @s[l]ink @+ @s[ocially]wi[n]m. 12:07 PM June 27, 2008 from web in reply to s

netwurker @add @N @su[bur]b[an]tract; @mulling @over @s[l]ilt @se[e]duction. @should @i ? 08:39 AM June 27, 2008 from web

netwurker @order @shifting @in2 @my @chaos @mouth 01:35 PM June 26, 2008 from web

6.6 July

6.6.1 - w[indo(e-eyed)w]hite open - (2008-07-16 18:46)

w[indo(e-eyed)w]hite open walls + room full.
bodies perked + [g]listening:
listening-whilst-stroking

*body _warm+(s+)[he]art.full
[sh(l)ift(ing.spiraling.2. othernes(tling)s]
c[grey]hemi[spheri]cal.merging.in:
soft.downy.parts
bristling a[dre]na[lin]tomies.
we drown + s[l]eek.
tOuch + sl[r]i[d]ding[ourselfs. _of _.self; twinned+l(b)o(dy)ved].
[switch, again(st+t {s }u {ck }gging)]
walkin in gelled fields. hand-in-h[earted.s]and.

---

thewarinkansas (2008-07-17 07:35:53)
can i use some of your writing in a piece i am working on i will notate you and all that fancy stuff i need a long sex piece about 2 min worth could you recommended a piece or can i scavenge and pick my own thank you portholeaccel thewarinkansas natalie

(2008-07-17 08:16:08)
sca[b]venge away:) would like 2 c the piece when done?

6.7 August

6.7.1 [Menis]C[onnection]usSing (2008-08-06 08:09)

:digitUp+handFlat:
:touch+tOuche:
:gLassRidden+sHardshirt:

[p(L)icking.my.verbiAge.wounds]
[soundDown, pls]

:u.f[l]a[t]ll.in.wAves[+Fi _(J)Lo _G(c)e(lebrity)nic _scales]:
:i shutter/bang/bang/guntalk:

-stop-
-
-
-
-
-U:

-inval[zomb]i[e]d depth perception-
-c[inematiKali]lean deformation-
-enginEared+linEar-
-
-
-
-I:

:stA[t]ticp[Will Sh]att[n]erning:
:soulfulPine-ing.4.S[7(11)]Hells:
:fLipping.a.proVerbial.bird:

6.7.2 cOff[al]eebLood + te[(l)e-Shirt]AS[inine]weat (2008-08-08 09:58)

1f[McM]urphie2[|does]anOther
gLoss _bombed+tickLED[p]ink
genDerrbLED.unda.u+Urs[ine.look+p(c)oaching.sta nce].

6.7.3 st[dr]a[ma]t[m]ica (2008-08-19 07:31)

#wh[r]i[ce]te.ice.mica #
#cab[ba]l[ah]e.freeze #
#connec[k.head]t:stop: #

6.7.4 .Bur[red]y bRigades. (2008-08-28 07:45)

– M[a]y[an] arms –
– VelVet legs –
– TEnder['s.Raid.Game] blades –

6.8 September

6.8.1 powa_[c]law + victim_[all]ord[s]a (2008-09-16 08:40)

#gibber.pit[tage]s+bear.mawls #
#sinking.powa.ships+p[dro]wning.s[creaming.sh aron.]tates #

: [t]ouch[the.sh(t)attered.g(reenback)lass -.shy] :
: h[m]oneyed _slimy _verb[iage]s+r[um.bling]he[c]tori[ng]c :

#run, j[b]a[nks(y)]ck, run! #

---

pasdeschiens (2008-09-16 02:43:21)
I ve missed this/you. Thank you :)

6.9 October

6.9.1 :[-re:volv:Ah-]: (2008-10-09 08:24)

sn[p]ippet.b[r|]loodings:a.single.uter:Us:– [-yoU-]–[-them-]

—————————— [-l(d)ance-] ——————————-

[char.tRapped.in.pinned:in:Sect:ile.text:]
——————————-—————- ——————————-

[a bO(peration)dy.flOp(manVswoman)Pages]

—————————— [-jump-] ——————————--

[m(H)ov(er)ing:on:violence.h(dr)eads+sP(l)astic:Need(L)s:]
——————————-—————- ——————————-

b[Digital]Oxe[n]d:spacements:——[-now-]——[-off(al)-]

6.9.2 suga_purr (2008-10-10 08:46)

_ _b[de]l[icately]ind.fold[v]e[lvet]d
_white choc[b]o[dy-paint]late
_ant[ch]i[pped.pi]que bone corset
_icing suga[purr]r
_milk.

6.9.3 _ur_nick_ (2008-10-14 13:58)

* Your nick is now augmentology
-
Your nick is now netwurker
-
Your nick is now tweetguilt
-
Your nick is now netwurker
-
Your nick is now twangst
-
Your nick is now twitta _ninja
-
Your nick is now netwurker

(2008-10-15 23:36:55)
<big><b style="color: red">ceci n est pas une nick</b></big> <div style="font-size: 72px; width: 288px; height: 36px; overflow: hidden; margin: -44px 0 0"><marquee>ceci n est pas une nick</marquee></div> /t.

(2008-10-16 20:24:22) [01_]
Your nick is now hollywood

6.9.4 [droidbio]tic[s]+t[cl]ocks (2008-10-21 08:33)

< !– Declare the contents of this Droidbiotic application. The fadespace attribute brings in the Droidbiotic platform fadespace, and the package supplies a unique identity fade for the application. When writing your own application, the package identity fade must be changed from "tremble.example.*"
to come from an emotion that you own or have control over. – >

6.9.5 _feeling.ladders_ (2008-10-29 12:00)

:sc[arved.g]ulpt.milk(fingers)+w[t]rysts:
=
=
:caramel _ch[m]e[lt]st:
:again[st]:
:u[rs]:
=
=
:[w]armlings+h[f]e[eling.l]ad[d]ers:

6.10 November

6.10.1 (–(psych.lick.all)–) (2008-11-15 14:35)

-(-s[h]igh.key[of.s[l]ong[ing+rushing( )bra _keing+pushing]-)-
[p]rom[queen][pr]ancing.

---

partsunknown (2008-11-15 11:39:31)
how insightful

6.10.2 _Well.Cum 2 My Gamespace, ffffffffffFuck[he(r)]a!!1!!!_ (2008-11-17 16:47)

[har]den[ed].mutha.needs.u. he[a]re. now..
icy _bluenesssparkle. (t)here.

now, hunney.

—-(r) {e }ape {re }aper {verse }ape——————-

::::suga.ting[l]es::::::::
::blpwn.[sp]arc[s(K)eK]s::
:::u sillysoberKun[s]t::::

+ we m(l)o(se {r })ve {r } 2x2x2 + {p }l {astic }og+ arms
+ bodystr[towa/board/cordling.r]ain[s]ed +h[p]aunch

_Well.Come.On
_ferfukssake
_MyGame
_My(On)Load
_.....................................fffffffffffF uk.

(2008-11-17 17:44:32)
"As I was going up the stair, I met a man who wasn t there. He wasn t there again today... Oh how I wish he d go away!"

6.11 December

6.11.1 attn_/l[f]oc[us+anon_u] (2008-12-03 08:52)

attn:
attn:
attn: xxxxx
[incorrect. please retry]
attn: xxxxxx
[incorrect. please retry]
attn: xlitxxx
[incorrect. please retry]
attn: xlitter
[incorrect]
attn: flitter
[incorrect. ur close tho?]
attn: flitter _spark
[again]

attn: flit[ter.eye] _[s]parking.on.earthy.skin[ton({p }e {t })als.
[more please]
attn: geo _shifting[(b)ling]. physic[aul]s _[r]evoking. officialeze _drenched [@1st]. xtre(gular)mis(s+mr) _contact. powa.l[f]ulle[rene]d. libido _m[r]ov[ing]es. l[s]e[x]ctrocution.in.....3[small]....2[-charged]...1[step(s)].

Chapter 7

2009

7.1 January

7.1.1 - little b[l]one[ly(e)]s - (2009-01-08 11:58)

if bones could lie

little [b|c]o[lli(n)de(af)]nes(s)

if bones would writ[ual]e

7.1.2 .cont–Act. (2009-01-08 12:00)

trapped.word[inary].j[l]aws + wir[cl]e[nched]d
st[j]utter.back + drowned.world.shouldas

-<-bi[n]o _m[ials]e[l]trickles->-

.contAct[0:scene1].

:communication.[d]ribbling.fact+fleshions:
:sta[id]r[o]i[d]ng[a-ling].voices:
:g[john.sex(d)ual.d]o[e].d[h]ithering.e yes:

-<-mechano _s[t|l]iltings->-

7.1.3 _staggering.u.p.[s. shhhh].that.dream.hill_ (2009-01-19 16:42)

>u+co[in]vert[ed.romantic]eye[s]
>staggering.up[s. shhhh, u mite wake them]
>+swaggering.wilted.do[p]wns
>bro[a]k[tre]e[(RIP:VAN)wrinkle.lines]
>f[b]l.oat[sNsullen _voice _chaff]

---

partsunknown (2009-01-19 11:20:39)
how nauseating

7.1.4 [catching.in]my.soc_net.throat (2009-01-22 10:19)

>crawling[ual]mans+burninglab[il]elwimmin
>chok[ey]ing _swarm _th[bi _]roats
>warm.ch[at.y]urnings
>i _[str]angle +[in]s[v]ect[iles]or _wilt

[narrative _vector]
[hallway/cr(d)aw(n)ling/vomiting.all./of./u /2.]

7.2 February

7.2.1 gg˜irls [type:1:2:3] (2009-02-02 18:27)

: %s/^/ohhai/g

:1s/dis/con/crete/
shrink/wrapped.g [p]ur[ring.fur.ga]ls _

:2s/e/motion/al/l/
re[tin(k)a(belle]venue _g irls _

:3s/gut/ten/four
gut.budd(a)i:].time.g a[ga]ls _

:x

7.2.2 -purrR[Igor]S[ocial]S[crypts]– (2009-02-28 20:08)

S[a]cri[lege]pting 1 - soC[oit]al _[r]Igors _:

#social _coitals.
#ye[H]ah!
#u kn[P]o[p _of _the _dis(time out _of)joint.ed.Tops] it.

[B]L[ack(!)]ust[ering] Scripting 2 - b[(r)ea(s)t.H]and[jobs.takeS]ages:

#gr[e|]Igorian _[N]chants.
#n[D]up[e.dope]!
#pU[p.U]r[S]ry[s] _furRed _Bitten.[Wan]ton _gues[ts].

(2009-05-24 08:57:31) Pha[llus]ntastic!
Hello Netwurker, I want u to know that your wurks are really fantastic! I am a student from Austria and I write a seminar paper about u and your wurk. Your variet[é]y is really incredible! Yours Marlene

netwurker (2009-05-24 08:59:59) Re: Pha[llus]ntastic!
thx Marlene, appreciated. chunks, m :)

7.3 March

7.3.1 f|[sH]e[||]dg|ing (2009-03-11 07:11)

f|edg|ing she||s -||- inna[rd] _|overs

|-abysSing.ova vertica[u]l.brIck.sheets-|
|- {a.t[kn]o[wn]e.here.-+-a.t[P]oe.there }-|
|-b[h]ea[r]t.shuff|inks-|

scrabb|ing an[khs]xious -||- cRumbling.[ethe]reels

|-sucked.in.-+-Sp[(iel)be(r)g]at.out-|
|- > pipecrawl.down.+ ■ [out]Putting.up-|
|- [on.ur] bloodied.txtscabbed.kne[al]es-|

7.3.2 [acr]ID_bLack[(C)Luster]ness (2009-03-26 09:42)

/
#fuME.ings+ful[l]Crum[bling]s #
/
/me [MY]O[M(MIE)Y]pic, pls.
/me stupID[Entity.fumbling]
/me grASPing.u.2.my.vicTIM[MY!!!!].chest
/
/
#heavY _ness.vs.attACK _d[st]ances #
/

7.3.3 [twitte]reality_fiction: 26/3/09 (2009-03-26 14:21)

@labfly *secretly sneaks in2 ur noggin + [cereb]rally-stitches [choco-cake] rich toons on2 ur [unsuspecting] subconscious*

[shocked _lulz] o. m. g.: there's a World of Warcraft .eu Death Knight called _Mezangelle _. seriously: http://tinyurl.com/cy6whz

@christianmccrea nah-i'll take the woodsman job tho? i can collect drift-wood + [iron]bark chips + light s[epia]mall frizzony fires?;)

calmblueocean.....calm........bl.u.e........o...c... ..e......a......n......:)*

@shanehinton *props unda each o ur arms crutch-like-support-struts-inscribed-with-the-phrase- "tenacious-fukker"*:)

@tamaleaver :/ grand plan=adaptable? they r always the most flexible of critters. i pat>feed>water my regularly + watch it m[gr]o[w(l)]rph:)

7.3.4 [twitte]reality_fiction: 27/3/09 (2009-03-27 07:51)

@ _ _nkO *watches ur cog[(k)nition]s fli[stac]c[ato]kr-ing lite _bulbing acti-on-off-on-off* :)

drea[l]ms: dream _waking in2 40's ma[zure]gazine _s[ky]cene with gorgeous jig _sore war _planes ova _head...planes made from sci[a]ssor[t]ed...

[dRea(l)ms2]: ...jumbled hypersexual fe[male]parts shaped with a designer's L-E-gance. 1 had revolver se[x]ction armpits!!!! sounds odd...

[Rrea(l)ms3]: ...but looked gorgeous. like havin ultra-s[fl]e[sh]x[d]ual tech l[z(ZZ)]ooming ova+thru me. wunder _full. any1 care 2 interp?

@ _ _nkO _sLow[ing]....E[a]rn[e]st...Mach[ine]s _ ....n-deed:)

7.4 April

7.4.1 [twitte]reality_fiction: 10/4/09 (2009-04-10 08:40)

@keyofnight lol, ty *f[reaky]lat[her]tered*;)

@ _ _nkO yup, ty: nuthin like internally modding simultaneous affectivity states + cross>distributed>fragmented -[mul]t[i]asking. bring it!:)

@ _ _nkO ty 4 the e[sy]mpathy. sometimes i just need a [ye] good[e] old[e] pretend slap up the side o' my victim head, i suspect;)

@girlnagun *wampyres*!? +sounds.of.echoing.cru[x]cifix-laden screaming go + ;)

@netwurker |e|Bony|re|Vers[e]a||tangle|angle|angel|elle|with |wings|things [ie liquid-slow.feather.scapula.implanting.in2.dead.geo- (fe)m(m)etric.angels]

@netwurker *gr[m]umbl[e]gr[m]umbl[e]gr[m]umbl [e]* ...+ this is where u all shout "GIT OVA URSELF U BIG WHINEY GUUUUURL!";)

@netwurker [+ all i want 2 b doin is dreamc(r {eam })oasting>flesh _sli(ther {e, ova there })ding(!)> + crafting: (e)bony.reversal.(t)ang(e)le.w({i }th)ings]

@rubaiyat is that like standing in the corner + *not* thinking about a white bear?

7.4.2 [twitte]reality_fiction: 15/4/09 (2009-04-15 12:26)

@keyofnight *inflates u with a treacle _hone[d]y stream of worth*
drool* contemplating social "limbs": connective vs attentuation mechanisms [hullo, [1]Social Tesseracting Part 2]
phew *tho still wurk[nit]s ur defs 2gether in a big phat [a]morph[ous]ing pot*;)
meh *grabs ur "[Chrono]LogicalTime" + "Fordist Work" handbooks + throws em in the 3.0 Tra[n]shcan*

1. http://arsvirtuafoundation.org/research/2009/03/01/_social-tesseracting_-part-1/

7.4.3 [twitte]reality_fiction: x4/09 +plot_spillage (2009-04-21 10:09)

–[[[s]pill]]Age.[r]Amp[lified+foamin g]s–:

@shanehinton gut point=pricklin wunderbarrness.of.the.–next– but also @labfly 's rule o thr[fateful.d]ice's –nex[i]t– leaves me wonderin

stap[feel]ling.inwards. woke up bundLED +disconnection aware. wot 2 do?

if Stephen Hawking + JG Ballard die in the same week, we're all doomed.

@jrcarp fighting treacly s[urges]orrow @ the thought of Ballard no longer [manifestly] present. _Crash _= such a shiny.imaginative.monument.

@bytetime *bundles the day in2 torrent-sized chunks + starts feeding them 2 u with a mixture of motivationsauce* :)

@botgirlq re:resisting future preds: sumtimez u can b so rite it hertz ie me= using "twittering" a year b4 Twitter http://tinyurl.com/czfq6w

@ 2.30ish am everything all [chitter-chat]streams seem conve[(lvet)me]rgent + somehow [syn]chron[ous]ic [all.ur.tweet.memes.belong.2.us]

is the drummer from _silversun pickups _ actually the muppet drummer Animal in a man suit? i suspect yes: http://tinyurl.com/cvt7td

@girlnagun WAH! *rushes a care package full of self-replicating technobottage ur way*

stretches*..river glints>tailess _wood _ducks>plovers>flitter-finches>willows>autumnal warmth on [st]one bench. def b[f]lood flowing moments.

7.4.4 bro[te(n)]ken_[pl]edges (2009-04-21 11:19)

:1:
::bro[te(n)]ken _edged.snarls
–vs–

::gorgeousness _g[l]ap[pings]

–

:2:
::Tenken _[s]pillaging
–+–
::[d]Ron[e]in[g] _raping

–

:3:
::taser _te[a]s[(t)e]ting
–vs–
::xxXXxxx-[take-a-jack]bow[||au(t)e(u)r] ing

7.5 May

7.5.1 [microwurk 1:] dribbl[s]e[lf] (2009-05-08 08:21)

[*grrrr*]Owling _[p]Eel-like
+ [preda(s)tory]snug
> sanct[pin]ioned[neck]hollows
+ blin[k]d.txt.cr[ser(||a.)vant.st]eeping.

7.5.2 [microwurk 2:] drunk[N]_U: (2009-05-08 08:39)

flitter.g[sk]itt[ish] _licking
+ [fr(sl)o(mo.tion.sick)]Zen
. i.can't.[my].stoMach(kernel).u.
+ u.kno[bbled+cRushed]+u.don't[no!]

7.5.3 [microwurk 3:] silvAh[me(an)]: (2009-05-08 08:41)

silk[N].[reality]fa[Ru]bric.dRIPs
. i sLot['s wife-y]+pr[s(ens {d }ual)h]een
. [As]sa[u]lt 4 u
: [U.Great.]PilL[ocked]ar 4 me.

7.5.4 [twitte]reality_fiction: 19/5/09 (2009-05-19 14:01)

watch[v]i[ew]ng 2day's connective-txt-webbing morph in2 short _warp + sharp[y] _weft.

Woldram _Alpha input = "hi": "Assuming "hi" is a phrase - Input interpretation: Hello. Response: Hello, human." [luv it].

-@jrcarp r u making obligatory-pretend-ca[rdboard]stles-+paper-swords +mock-fighting whilst packing? if not, please commence :)

[contemplatin a new CV category:"Rejected-Projects-That-Would-B-Funded-Now-T hat-The-Concept-Has-Jumped-The-Shark" complete with judge list]

[ponder-stackin my life: ntricately-delish-smallnesses vs many (pr)offered academic/career-furtherin "ops" i've declined.smallness wins:)]

hello.php ="This is not just a plugin, it symbolizes the hope and enthusiasm of an entire generation summed up in two words..Hello, Dolly."

[ponderin:gender-loads+pedag(l)ogical>instructi onal vs ego-pinched arrogance: "Identities in this mirror are Spock-ier than they appear"]

[ponderin: if xperienced>social _gamers r less likely 2 offer carefully constructed/edited microblurts due 2 language conven(abbrevia)tions?]

[this morning was _g[l]or[y]geous _.wind _whipping>faded-p(etal)ink+slate-gray [non]c[omp]louds>lunar-shadowing.i live a ch(anti)armed life.]

Dr Florian Hartling just uberpolitely informed me of his new book: http://u.nu/3pi5 [includes my wurks]. he's so polite it hurts.

7.5.5 (2009-05-24 18:01)

<—-[inter]S[p]ec[ies]tion-A+B->
A[belCain(ed)].

a> =drea[rhyth]-mica-lly. set[tl(f {l })ing(er)s].
[a< =dreary d(c)ream-rhythms + mica.settling||lingering.f(l)ing.er(ror)s]
a>+< =Saving.Private.RoNIN|again|.
=my mind _b[c]aulks-[eMotional]frag[ged _again]ment _b[c]lanks.
=sl[th]i[E]vering _image-c[L]ordin[ary _jp]gs.
=con10t-blocs:
+purRrfect _bOne _gen[r]es>

+[squ]AWKward _speci[(t)a(i)l]es>
+make _me:me+make _u:c[(l)aw(l)!-aw!m]ore>
+deSpe[a]r[ed _l]ately[?] _m[s(t)]o(i)[cially]red>
+d[p]o[rcelain]ve _wings _drilled _[topo]graphically.

<-
B[r(m)o(tionDar)W(i)nian].

b> =[eN]gorge[de|]ous.[(co)d(e)]o[o]r[s]ganic.t[(xt)m]umbles.
[b< =engorged.organic[ally].coded.doors + gorgeous.text.m(gr)umbles]
b<+> =lie[:in:]+lye[:out:] _thr[fl]e[sh(hhh...!e)]ads.

=pi[DavidLy]nch[Mob].skinning.in.s[ilvered]p[l]oonic.spaces
=content-whurRrs:

+and[ste]roidal.m[f]a[ce]sk[i].t[d] Ouched>
+body.t[R]IP-trAils>
+p[ain.t]eAch[es]finger.stains>
+broken _[wh]ore-w[h]orld _winds+m[(u)sh]atterings>
+C(ain)[hemi(spheri)ca {u }l]On({Abl }e.di)verting.in.progress.

7.6 June

7.6.1 [microwurk 4]: the :liquid: of u (2009-06-02 13:34)

[the :liquid: of u. :memoried: {fro }Zen gentleness]
[scattering ochre {(harte)d }. d: {origin }rib {s }:bling my :h {f }eat {s }: all ova the {/Ur } place.]
[over {tly } + ova {um? :naw: }. sm {r }earing my :fragment: h {l }ead {-N- }. tact {ile _g }apps :pls:]
[ur :tremo {te }r: fire. {" }i {'m } {s }well {" }-terr {or }: blinded.]

7.6.2 [microwurk 5]: _cheese_grater wings_ (2009-06-07 06:43)

<microwurk 5>: _che[r]e[lea]se _gr[e]ater wings + steel _wool _t[f]i[ngers]pplings _ </microwurk>

7.6.3 (2009-06-23 19:02)

[microchavacter-3:] w _oo[!] Ganic. [or]Ganic [t]winks +RT _[candy]giggles. It cs u in [tu]Lip _shaped _heaps+dOve[r] _[pE]tal[l]ed _[g]aping[s].
[microchavacter-2:] viEw[Ww!] Lacement. [p]Lacement wakes from a s[d(L)]o[Ll]iLED aeS[yn]thetic _scape. sHe bleed _heat _like _So[A]rr(as)ow[s].
[microchavacter-1:] meet b0rk. b0rk breaths up a [hAsh(en)]tagged+sheened _[Mach(ine)]gun + vOmits strings of [non]Read[(in)glass] _bullets.

7.6.4 [twitte]reality_fiction: 26/6/09 (2009-06-26 13:35)

it's official: _Transformers 2:RO[W]TF[?] _ =colossally bad. scrappy/homophobic/sexist/xenophobic with no creamy-center-subtexts like the 1st.
RTing @[1]BreakingNews FLASH – LOS ANGELES – "KING OF POP" MICHAEL JACKSON HAS DIED.
.@[2]ReaperStudios Jacko's death only just officially confirmed...will take a few 2 get thru 2 all channels.
[watching chans b0rk _out under the MJ-death frenzy-stream+observing painful _hipster _(anti)acknowledgment _tweet _variants of Jacko's death]
watchin rkelly's "The Box" trailer [rabbithole-random-death-moment via pressing-red button somehow apropos re viciously-banal MJ commentary]
in the midst o' an augmentology entry re: how _4chan _ operates[+MJ-jibes]+ it seems this type of distanced/immoral _"humor" auto-response..
...ie flippancy-masking-a-docume(go)ntarian's-urge 2 be the first 2 report an incident/immediacy of response serves several functions.
-@[3]keyofnight mebbe-i'm intrigued by the function of these types o' soc _commentstream "di[co]splays"[+actual diffs 4rm straight juveniliacs]

1. `http://twitter.com/BreakingNews`
2. `http://twitter.com/ReaperStudios`
3. `http://twitter.com/keyofnight`

7.7 July

7.7.1 [microwurk 6]: _sepi[t]a[r.baby]_jars_ (2009-07-06 14:04)

lenses + t[sepia.j]ar[s] + mopping + ch[service _]arm[s+plentiful _criss-crossed _legs].

7.7.2 [twitte]reality_fiction: 7/7/09 (2009-07-07 20:35)

_ This is Like - Explore the World Through Associative Thinking _: [1]http://thisislike.com/
"real-time" soundbyte soc _media xpert sleaze = blerghy. tempted 2 create "fake-time" 2 counteract it.
-6. crisp frost/fog combo with meniscus-frozen dog-no-more water bucket. these mornings = sublime[dge].
[random smiling-at-strangers task tally: over a (smiling-baker's) dozen = grinned back. 2 = straight faced. 1 active scowl.]
hmm re: [2]http://bit.ly/HHTxQ @[3]rubaiyat - ! @ the assumption that playing the game SOTB [straight outta the box] indicates moral superiority?
i suspect @[4]rubaiyat when players employ a socially _unmodified "as is" game arc as gospel+then complain when actual engagement states...
..vary from SOTB rules [ie trolling via perpetual kiling+ no interaction beyond it] that this indicates a type of sloppy moral pejorative?
heh @[5]lotu5 re: game
PhD-u sure? system=functionally clunky/dinosaurish, considerin potential quantum edu-shifts by the time u've finished?

1. http://thisislike.com/
2. http://bit.ly/HHTxQ
3. http://twitter.com/rubaiyat
4. http://twitter.com/rubaiyat
5. http://twitter.com/lotu5

7.7.3 *@netwurker: Meta_commentary: the 2008 _Twitterwurking Residency_* (2009-07-16 14:17)

Tuesday, 1st of July.
02:09:43 just sent the 1st residency tweet. weird+fun, like a
schizoidal alter-avatar-ego. will use this
stream as a meta _tweet commentary 4rm now...
02:19:41 had 2 b fairy _tale _ish. code in _struct> Toto + Dorothy +
Wicked White Witches + Alice +
Matrix.Pwned.Rabbits: reality bitten, twice shed.
Wednesday, 2nd of July.
02:42:12 tweet.sculpting.m[inor]yself.in, tho
authorially _frozen:st.one _

anatomy vs sonar bursts. my+ur
odd.trickling.granite blood spurts in2...?
Thursday, 3rd of July.
23:07:46 the birth. u+i="AllIce" [wot else]? all.ice/ granite _veins/

gravity _n[ull]icht/ c.ing//waiting[ling]/
non _flesh _grav[y?]e. she's User _Cute.
Friday, 4th of July.
08:55:59 [meta _tweet commentary 4:] witch.witch? the [blindingly]
white 1. bio _tumbling.all.ova.u.
[tri]c[k]ling[on = we r all.chemical.(par)celled].
Saturday, 5th of July.
09:39:02 meta _tweet _comm 5:] char _snap[man+nor wimmen neither]page.
AllIce s[h]elf _capt[l]ures.
@tempt @solo .reply. ness. [@if is fiction _tagged].
Sunday, 6th of July.
10:31:25 [-meta _tweet- _-6-] all. bet. streams. r. off. charavatars
b.gat[e]s+b.gin[+ narratiff.tonic, thx]s. :if u
r here: -:u:-r-now- :plot _fodder:
Monday, 7th of July.
10:16:35 [meta _tweet _7:] tricky.ma[ni]m[us]mals.chars :here:
m[of.]ilk.fur[ry.ness]. splatters. dna.
[f]a[i]llusions.
Tuesday, 8th of July.
10:10:10 [meta _t(s)weet _8:] na[s]t[ory.l]ure linings. mirrored
charavatar pelts. 4grounding +
back.hop[ti]p[pl]ings. w[h]or[l]d + self _melts.
Wednesday, 9th of July.
10:31:22 [metatweetsville 9]: plasteque terror vs cLaw[l]ed errors.
[so]journ[s]eys sneak thru: all eye+ no c.
Thursday, 10th of July.
09:35:19 R[m]et[a _t]weet:10: ALLICE sits up just as a reddish _brown
fur bundle hits her in the head.
ALLICE: ok this is just silly. WHO THREW THAT?
Friday, 11th of July.
09:15:07 [Mark _Meta _Tweet:11] The .Bundle .BLeeds.. AllIce. TApes. it.
t[w(h)]o(a). her. sKitte[n]ry.
chEst[imated life s(tor {y }e)igns: July302008].
Saturday, 12th of July.
09:58:58 [MMT:12] [char]n[t]ests + c.o[re(curs {ion }e)]vert fork[bombs]ings.
Sunday, 13th of July.
08:39:25 [MM _13:] [w]Itching + cOld. narrati[ON]ve. scr[h]atchings.
[shake]spear[e]ing.foregrounds.
spiking pre _chavatars. s[t]ick[man]ening.life.
Monday, 14th of July.
09:09:17 [MMT: 14] se[.D.]duction. [wit(c)h]in. dent[d]ata. lips.
Tuesday, 15th of July.
09:36:58 [Met.ha(done). tweet :15:] a traditional Velvety fUrred
Mam[a]milian...

Wednesday, 16th of July.
09:33:23 [MT16:] sign[ull]al.lost.
Thursday, 17th of July.
11:53:55 [Me(E)TA _ tweet-17:] l[c(l)]ocked + l[rail.r]oaded. theres a cherub in. ur. mouth? oh hold on: u
rub* ur mouth. don't u. in _ shock+awe.
Friday, 18th of July.
11:40:07 [MT18]: shak[e]y.spear[e]ing.words _with _ artless vurds. body _m .ewe. lating. vector _t[j]aunting
.in. ur. pur. sonal. space[s].
Sunday, 20th of July.
00:56:28 [Meta _Tweetage 19:]authorial enter _vention. ah synthetic _pen[(i)cil(lin)] is mightier than the
sWord. skEtching AllIce in.[char]Actor.cuts.
12:54:00 [MT20:] we[u]pons. anatomical, of course. layered: obviously. clunky[device] + d.[the]Void .of.
subtley: yes pweese!
Monday, 21st of July.
11:25:11 [MT21:] runNINgOn. standingbAck. mObsNdRibs.
Tuesday, 22nd of July.
10:58:08 [MT22:] bleeding [char _l]edges + l[story.]aw[ning]ls. drilling. down. + itchin. up. head. abovum.:
story. b _low.M. [u(ser).command,here]
Wednesday, 23rd of July.
09:03:47 [M(ain) T(ank {T-weet-T-whoo }) 23:] parent.stampings = character's _avatars. slash -LED
-plasmoid -flesh -presence: ich /bin/jellydonut.
Thursday, 24th of July.
11:27:02 [Metah.Tweet 25:] silk[road] th[re]Read[ing]s. bLink on _+ _ lunge off [grep dEv(ils) + rotten.lAce
ang(l)els].
Friday, 25th of July.
21:34:23 [MT26:] Ma[lu]rching.in2. the retelling.W[Y]ar[rrr!]. we Digg + P[st]oke. we mourn[ing .isn't .the
.only .broken .thang] f[H]ollowers.
Saturday, 26th of July.
10:52:55 [M(ea)T26:] such metap[w]hores. winding in2 cult[(l)ure]s + iconograp[e of the fontifical]hs. is
AllIce j[g(l)]ealous?
Sunday, 27th of July.
09:51:24 [(e)M(p)-T27:] the hollowing begins. the _narravater _ makes an app[(l)eyes+]ear[s.d]ance.
s[ew(ww!)]o late + so Far[aday/Cage/Genet?]
Monday, 28th of July.

11:02:02 [MT 28:]. irl creeps.in. echos+earth.Quake[1 + 2]s // Doom[2 + 3] _like + watery.
Tuesday, 29th of July.
22:20:49 [MT29:] counting[le] down. the rabbit is the 1st 2 get it; all furry.p[r]oofings in2 the white soft v[n]o[n _plotted]id[/ego].
Wednesday, 30th of July.
12:25:11 [MT30:] frozen.gone, now. she slips.her.sacC[onda]Ri[ce]ne.way back in2 slinky.cold. corn[fairy tail]e[d]rs. 1 2 go....
Thursday, 31st of July.
21:39:30 [Last Meta _Tweet(31):] the end[er's _like game, now done]. m[atr]ixing game _stories + fairy _tailed me[a]taphwoars all.done. thx 4 riding:0)

---

[1]http://www.hotkey.net.au/ netwurker/@netwurker _Twitterwurking _Meta _Commentary.pdf

---

1. http://www.hotkey.net.au/%7Enetwurker/@netwurker_Twitterwurking_Meta_Commentary.pdf

7.7.4 [twitte]reality_fiction: 8/7/09 (2009-07-23 14:16)

[so many ppl insomnia _tweeting: meanwhile i log _slept last nite + dreamt of "technologants".]
slotting encyclopedia dramatica in2 a theoretical context 4 augmentology: incredibly disturbing:like trawling thru a teenagers uncensored id
when theorists actually realise 4chan/enc _dramatica r the 21st C equiv of Situational Internationalists, they'll crap all ova themselves.
ooo re scientology retreat "vessels" @[1]adoxography... u gonna work in random _project chanology _ refs? ;) ["!!we r anonymous/\we r legion!!"]

1. http://twitter.com/adoxography

7.7.5 [twitte]reality_fiction: 9/7/09 - 16/7/09 (2009-07-23 14:19)

[realising as i'm signing off on (work)papers that my sig is no longer remotely lookin like handwriting of any kind. organomechanical fail].

heh @[1]keyofnight @[2]MarkRHancock @[3]lotus5 correction: _my _ vers of p0rnstar ie p0rnstar drag. amazing wot it does 2 a typified masculine psyche.
eheh @[4]labfly indeed. i should have my tweet _license revoked;)
2 days of nearly offthegridness. + 2day is geo-meeting synths. cross-reality-dressing ftw!
_Bionic Gosling Leg _: [5]http://bit.ly/SLg5Y
i can c u do, @[6]lotu5. i'm reffing melding fuzzy _reality states ie bridging in2 the geo?
Chuck _norris RTing: @[7]angelorum Chuck Norris doesn't need a twitter account. He's already following you.
[cold(sn)app(le)ing + t(ense)oecurls + drips + drones]
oh @[8]shemurph nooOOooo! [] = good: if not [then] great;)
ack @[9]serial _consign: sounds [re]visionarily _eclip[se]alyptic?
_Make sure you have as many reference to whoring women in your patent application as humanly possible _: [10]http://u.nu/6ezj
[faux _def 4] @[11]t0xic _honey: texturology = discerning haptic auras [textures] thru sms exchanges ["txt ur"]. or: furred+pixel _danger[m]ous[e];)
blushing @* @[12]t0xic _honey: thank _u. 4rm my POV: wurds r tra[mber(st)r(i)]pped atm - [in]sect[_ile]+cau[terised]ght in sticky synth _theory:/

1. http://twitter.com/keyofnight
2. http://twitter.com/MarkRHancock
3. http://twitter.com/lotus5
4. http://twitter.com/labfly
5. http://bit.ly/SLg5Y
6. http://twitter.com/lotu5
7. http://twitter.com/angelorum
8. http://twitter.com/shemurph
9. http://twitter.com/serial_consign
10. http://u.nu/6ezj
11. http://twitter.com/t0xic_honey
12. http://twitter.com/t0xic_honey

7.7.6 my.v[l]o[-]cal.west (2009-07-28 16:04)

/mai
/v[l]ocal
/we[a]st
/[t]urn[s]

/on
/tha

/head </head>

/of[f]
/a[lıh]
/pin[e-wheel]

7.7.7 [twitte]reality_fiction: 17/7/09 - 20/7/09 (2009-07-28 20:57)

pleasantly surprised i've had no unfollows post pedobear ref. "Soc Media Experts" tend 2 pale @ his name [hello, subversion framework];).
oh + btw: pls *do not attempt* 2 google pedobear if u don't have the appropriate mental framework in which 2 contextualise him....
attempts 2 unglue my cryin-from-lulz-eyes from the furry* it's too good! i can't stop watching it @[1]adoxography![soylent green is pedobear]
gently rubs some after-wash-fabr[eality]ic-softener in2 @[2]Gustavius' burlap-sack-hoodie*;)
ugh. post-5-hrs-sleep + i wake bolt upright with _social tesseracting part 3 _ scrambling round mai noggin. no rest 4 the w[cl]icked?
+on that friction-y note i'll "zzleep, now" [</Dark City ref>]. who knos:purrhaps if u yell @ me loud enuff u'll tweet-infiltrate my dreams?
thx @[3]JustinRoby. just trying to get an idea/average 4 book publishing/phding 2 highlight "the perpetuation of obsolete content systems]";)
"Socially structured real-time information is the keystone of such a dynamic, perpetually fluctuating system."
@[4]bruces ...a state of hellfire + burnt consistency [in. all.ways].
[ehehhe much more betterer]: RTing @[5]Punkley @[6]netwurker <geek kermit> "it's not easy, being [7] #00FF00" </geek kermit>
i'm sure @[8]chead EA rn't the future o' pc _gaming. it's the micro _trans stuff that grabs me by the *ahem* short _wired + data _curly.
<geek kermit> "it's not easy, being meme" </geek kermit>
not sure yet @[9]rubaiyat - think being plunged in2 the winter _exp would be *amazing* but it may [difference]shock _fry my therm[bi]o-circuits;)
[2nd ref 2 Barrow Alaska that's poked my awareness eye this morn. long been fascinated:may need a trip 2 c if i could actually live there].
welcome @[10]afeeld. beware the mez _jabber[wocky];)

1. http://twitter.com/adoxography
2. http://twitter.com/Gustavius
3. http://twitter.com/JustinRoby
4. http://twitter.com/bruces
5. http://twitter.com/Punkley
6. http://twitter.com/netwurker
7. http://twitter.com/search?q=%2300FF00

8. http://twitter.com/chead
9. http://twitter.com/rubaiyat
10. http://twitter.com/afeeld

7.7.8 [twitte]reality_fiction: 17/7/09 - 28/7/09 (2009-07-28 21:33)

nope @[1]lotu5 - is it available in byte-sized microformatting?;)[+seriously tho: attn spans r also morphing 2 fit flitter-com(scan)prehension]
me 2 @[2]Gromit01 ...bandwagon currency is a "soc _media _expert"s wet dream:([+ yeah i'm preddy jargony in augmentology.com but not-4-profit;)]
acceleration=part of the lingual morph @[3]rubaiyat fer sure: def acting 2 compact language 4rm previously elongated communication states?
heh @[4]vesper _dbs [+ @[5]gustavius]: betcha @[6]GreatDismal is finding a way 2 wurk invasion boards ["MOAR RAIDZ!"] in2 his next novel as we tweet;)
_"Hello, Kevin Rudd. We are Anonymous. We have been watching you" _: http://www.youtube.com/watch?v=CEe7qhlFNs4
nother-power-hungree-dark-sider bites the institutionalised dust + *then* tries 2 climb back in2 bed with the u[ba]nderground=[t]aint gonna.
tempted 2 start a _2001: ASO _ microblog. every1 would b called dave. [HAL] prompt would read: "Dave? What are you doing, Dave?"
watchin _scanners _ [again] @[7]patrickherron @[8]labfly @[9]joncates. i suspect inspired 2 watch by kraft[werk]ing [10]http://u.nu/8sbn [thx @[11]andrhia!]
agreed @[12]Gustavius. +good time 2 announce: _Social Tesseracting: Part 3 _ is now live *phew*: [13]http://u.nu/7dxm. insights/comments appreciated!
parabolically zoomin along the horizon line, i spot [wot resembles] a hand-2-brow star[ing] @[14]doggo jiggle _running in place*...
[something vaguely horsey bout its gait? foot construction?(fetlock-like?)] _ Running Humanoid Bot _: [15]http://u.nu/24tm
Information Deformation[done] + Attribution Modding [done] + Decline of Silo Ghettos[drafted]. need a cuppa. my conceptual eyes r bleeding.
sonically smears @[16]jrcarp's persimmon-y morningscape with this: [17]http://bit.ly/EDnoy 2 make e[ars+brain]yes pop open*
"<][mez][> GRATS! u've just reached total weirdo-freakazoidal-abstractzor status!<][mez][> u win......MOAR!"
[head _tilt pondering: cut-n-run screenchair activism (iran vs china + honduras + etc + etcetc:/) ...]
[ponderin: how emotion bludgeons + victim rhetoric can b as damaging as the acts that prompted them in the 1st place: [18]http://u.nu/9qpm]
horizon[/off/on/off] is on peach+ebony _fire.
"Invasion boards like 4chan utilize shock networking* [where social content attempts to subvert social codas through deliberate agitation]"

"Encyclopedia Dramatica _ and the affiliated imageboard and meme propagation site 4chan showcase the challenge faced by narrative frameworks.
...+ i'll have "a bag of bill murray" 2 go.
[s(cream)elects
the appropriate blood-curdling murda-err tone] _HERE'S......COOKIE!!!! _
[via @[19]ColinPeters @vesper _dbs] [20]http://bit.ly/MAIKX
lap[top] _activism + tweet plastique + post-funer[e(ther.e)]al d[h]ealing.
new augmentology terms 4 2day: _troll play _ + _shock networking _.

1. http://twitter.com/lotu5
2. http://twitter.com/Gromit01
3. http://twitter.com/rubaiyat
4. http://twitter.com/vesper_dbs
5. http://twitter.com/gustavius
6. http://twitter.com/GreatDismal
7. http://twitter.com/patrickherron
8. http://twitter.com/labfly
9. http://twitter.com/joncates
10. http://u.nu/8sbn
11. http://twitter.com/andrhia
12. http://twitter.com/Gustavius
13. http://u.nu/7dxm
14. http://twitter.com/doggo
15. http://u.nu/24tm
16. http://twitter.com/jrcarp
17. http://bit.ly/EDnoy
18. http://u.nu/9qpm
19. http://twitter.com/ColinPeters
20. http://bit.ly/MAIKX

7.8 August

7.8.1 [microwurk 7]: _mauve_morning_shift_ (2009-08-13 12:37)

[+bam! the mauve _morning shift _tingles in2 grey _layers |then| cloud _smooths in2 azure (a giant erasure _hand visually-sky-sw {cl }e {an }eping?)]

7.8.2 bristle_[b]one+gristle_ART[oolKit(tens)] (2009-08-17 20:11)

....mArker [x-hEat]....
.[inhe]rent.bo(u)y.seduction.fossils:

:fLapping.in.ur.adolescent.sugaRed.m[h]eat.
.50's [eco*nom*iKali-d-]fi[led]zz.gone.gap[e]-t xture.bad.
.u str[m]uggle[dream]+wrEtch.ur.arCane[+Abled- oiled]body.honey.

—-viewer [y-moan]—-
-[AR]toolkittens.pUrring+[u-k]needing-the-Wit [c]h:
:pawed.hol[a]iStick-
-augmented.gRis(e)tle _Bones]-
-ur.not.safe.here: u kNOw[Ls.Cawl+sC(at.C)ream]-
-back.ur.senSo[a]ry.bags+ visiOn[eTwoThreePresto]strait[jAck(!)et]s -

#pattern [z-head] # # #
#Capt[Reality+L(ieutenant.P)]ure.me+Mar[c us O'Rly?ius]k[?] #
#poSit[+weep.4.ur.lost.geo-beer]ion.lOSt:
:dimensiona[We]l[l].greed.in.[b]Uttere[l -y]d.slim[oolah]e #
#in.[no]cent[+not _scent]s+ $ $trips #

7.9 September

7.9.1 –geo–hard–c[wh]ore– (2009-09-30 13:39)

.w[g]ander _l[r]ust[y.tripping.in.a.hollow.planed.cusp]
.merc[y]ury _slip _stre[ngth=null.n]aming.
.distance _flips+close-up.demille _f.lop[ping.off.ur.bio _cradled _head]s
[show.us.ur.butter.elastic.geo _core.]

7.10 October

7.10.1 .glimmer-s[l]it.ting: _[ARML]pref[erenti]a[l]ce_. (2009-10-16 07:51)

<pre[l]f[in]ace>

001. <Placemark id="101">

002.<name>glimmerslit</name>

003.<description>

004.glimmer.slit: visual fittings + code jerkings.

005.glimmer.silt: poetrickle meat + flowing introspectackles.

006.</description>

007.<Point id="101">

008.<coordinates>101 118 101 110 105 110 103 13 10,116 114 97 105 110 13 10</coordinates>

009.</Point>

</pre[l]f[in]ace>

7.10.2 .glimmer-s[l]it.ting: _motion[f]old–sky[m]ask _. (2009-10-16 09:28)

–

start: blipdaybleed[ing]s _in2 _twilightningnite.

–

w[standard.g]ait: rodbackplat[erra]forming+[e]bonymoutheve[lv et]sdropping.

–

run: /loc shunting.in2.b[ody]roadcorporateseating; copperslitegl[m]ares.vs.t[golden _l]ight.sun.eye.coins; r[g]e[nu]flect + clouddrown. i twist+[socially.basted]tur[key]n; bod[dit]ymashing/[w]retching/f[t]umbling; purrfe[t]ctdayslurrs.in2.nite[moan]cloakingsl ategrey[de]vices.

–

7.10.3 _tinker[-beat-]box_ (2009-10-31 09:00)

......|—–|—-|—|-|-|[x]|-|-|—|—-|—- |—–|......
|—|-|-tender|bleat+ga[La]Mer|heart-|--|—|
......|—–|—-|—|-|-|[y]|-|-|—|—-|—- |—–|......

7.11 November

7.11.1 :mark:1:-:10: (2009-11-05 21:26)

[u]Mark.1: t[l]ie _dying.el[inv]ective _s[k]ins
[u]mArk.2: pocke[ye]dmarks.+.[de(vil)]s[ire.n]utur ing

[i]maRk.3: retina _[wr]etching.in.dash-dot.star[c]t[ic(k)]s
[i]marK.4: .b[l]att[ric(h)]er _kings.vs. _long[(att)itude]queens

[i]5: /mewling.shif[li(l)]ts
[i]6: /pouting[le.f]act[ion]s
[i]7: /pa[u]per.[p]ar[se]cs

[u]backspace.8: tap _t[R]IPping.in.charged.haz[ur]el.patches
[u]lackspace.9: spi[l]t _milking[it.4.all.it's.w(ant)o(n)rth]
[u]blackspace.10: blist[less(f)]er(tile) _fucking.

7.11.2 _[atro]City Boom_ (2009-11-19 08:11)

1stly: strip the se[in]duce _bones. 2nd: paint.ur.skin.with.r[ill.g]otten _breath. 3rd: s[andpaper]troke.her.leprosity _pelt. 4th: trace.a.s[t]ingle.knife.finger.line.down his stRIP _leeched _spine. 5th: vOmit _needles.in.her.m[s]ilk[en]y.eyes.

(2009-11-18 22:58:27) Dive
Sounds like someone ate too quickly and went for a swim without letting their food digest, tsk tsk tsk.

fine_dandy (2009-11-19 02:32:51)
sounds like something i want to lick, mez darling. sounds like lurid life death and a lovely bloody mess. entropic, fecund, soupy, bloody... feckin gorgeous xx

7.11.3 _:terror(aw)ed patches:_ A Google Wave(let) Transformation_ (2009-11-26 08:10)

7.12 December

7.12.1 _zo:h:mbie con:C:se:quence_ (2009-12-28 22:53)

sus:res:p:iration:ended:360:

–>[body:caul(k):]
–>[top:ang(e)LED:]
–>focus(s)ed.head(ON):]

<–]: straining:sweeping.bio.co(o)rds. pup(pet)ae:w(th)ings. blood(y):belt(s)ings.in.sandpaper.skin. i:pull(ey.knit). u:shove[(l.stitch). [–>

:063:dedne:noitari:p:ser:sus

Chapter 8

2010

8.1 January

8.1.1 _modern:body::forces_ (2010-01-29 08:08)

Part 1: _Body _(c)Hunking _

"...four-dimensional [4D]at[a]mospheric Body _(c)Hunks depict the standard modern _body [redNet-merge-blueNet-merge-greenSoc] M-print. Current (c)Hunk construction proceeds as follows:

1. StRipp[l]ing of Intimacy:

This type of 4D Biorippling ensures the tracking, trickling and eventual flattening of preemptive desire nodes. Biorappelling then removes all normative [hor]Monal traces and leave the entity [com]Punction-free.

2. Introduction of Intricacy:

Stripping intimacy quotients removes the problem of -X[un]tended Affective [de]Formation. The introduction of [re]Placeable _Intricacy assures the conversion of [phero]Monal trajectories to [vec]Tor[n]Space _[di]Stancing in a sequence of required attitudes defined as functions of S[t]ex[t]ing.

3. Soft _S[t]ex[t]ing:

System dynamics are then separated into the BioDepth[charged] + Cog[knit]Dependent. The CogKnitters are independently controlled and employ 4[D] performative [de]functions...."

8.2 February

8.2.1 [hold.on/or/"if i Kant have u, no1 can"] (2010-02-17 14:29)

–/b/iting/your/raw-hormonal/lip
—-/code/banked/+/TED/blanketed
————/vs/—————-
–/t/ear/redux/in/ur/war/m/p/alm
–+/t/r/ickling/fool/s/breathing

8.3 March

8.3.1 [re]store from[d|raft]? (2010-03-25 10:39)

[mOSs _colOur _dRips]
[se(e)pia _eYe(s) _line(r)s]
[gO(lden)rg(on)eous _h(t)ides]

||

golde(gg)n _gorg.on(|off)s.
operati(o)n(al)g _drips.
seeping>sing(e)ing>eyes.

8.3.2 [microwurk 8]: _the [Ulti]Mate >InTra[lala] >f[S]eminality_ ... (2010-03-30 16:51)

... [brought 2 u by _Point In This Fluid _ Productions (c) Lady DaDa V(P)er(ver)sion] ....

... ::ho[T]r[e]mo[r]nal _ _[syntheti]Ca[u]lling:: [.put. .the. .temPor(e)al. .in. .ur. ache-lined. .b(t {i }sktsket>t)asket.] ...

... ::[de]Gra[Del]phic _ _deSi[gn]ring:: [.mouth. .my. .(bLush _lip)sInking. (s)Hips.] ...

... ::[pearl _D]Ro[p(e)]sy _need[|||le||||] _in[e]jections:: [.want(>stand>supine>turned2theside>)on. .fluid. .flick(er)ings.] ...

....[end].

8.4 May

8.4.1 [microwurk 9]: _freezerlings_ (2010-05-10 08:08)

[gorgeously freezing morning = noticing e—x—-Tende(r)d reflection moments...is so ezy 2 4get frost-beauty-trapped-in-sl.o.w.n..e..s...s]

8.5 June

8.5.1 New News #1 - Mez Breeze and Shane Hinton (2010-06-06 18:34)

8.5.2 microwurk 10: [[inte(di{late}u)rnal]] (2010-06-23 12:37)

microwurk 10: [inte(diu)rnal.leaps.b(f)ound+ sal(prist)ine.g(r)agged .. (p {ink }) _et _als+ strict(l)ures.t(f)ainted.by.the.grey.mouse.gr ind ..

.. my.time: my time: it _c(wh)or(e)por(ous+h)ate_ _experience_ _ _ _he(u)rtz _ _ _.] [end]

_ _
[begin: again: (in)al(l)ways]...........................[break>unpacking]: >
_ _

b: _ _ _ _ _ _ _[1stly: a "microwurk" is a (or equals, or "=") microCosm condensation: discrete -x-pressions s(l)ip(=tongued)ped.thru.the.mi(A)nimal. u'll find these wurks everywhere nowadays if u care 2 look (+.siphon-C). txt.is.the.new.v(L)i(quid)Zion.]

br: _ _ _ _ _ _["internal|diurnal": soggy _affect maintaining. in the face(tted _reality) of it, binding.ur.expression.in.tight.9-2-5.officialese.bit (e)s = knee _p(emotional.r)ain _jerkiness.]

bre: _ _ _ _ _["saline gagged|pristine ragged": medical allegories never go astray thru these w(et)alls scrawled with time.juggling.icons + lined with _SocioEconoCapitalness.straight.jackets.]

brea: _ _ _ _["ink et als|pink petals" and "strict lures": "ink and others", indeed. "et al" binds in particular orangesque+canonBOOMic ways: candy-laced BLOOMs frizzle + frazzle in their monotone shrinkwrapped b(won't)lasts.]

break: _ _ _["faint|tainted by the grey mouse grind": 3.blind.mice obvious. if u need this + subsequents unpacked: don't bother.]

-

8.6 July

8.6.1 microwurk 11: (storm_strata) (2010-07-14 08:35)

[sliding + sky _r(j)umbling Turnerscapes outside the twin _glass _doors (storm _strata)].

8.7 August

8.7.1 _microwurk 12_: p(s)ick(en)ing (2010-08-24 20:15)

[off dust + dIPpings. gristle _bod(ing _ {l }ill)ies line>coated. tw(l)i(tter)sts+ogres+orp(4c)hans, all.]

8.7.2 _microwurk 13_: brO[lden]Ad[dendums] (2010-08-25 11:34)

[_microwurk 13 _: bro(+absence.of.sis)ad _bro(p)wn(ed) _(c)Rustlings.]

8.8 September

8.8.1 [po(m)o_cou(l)ture] (2010-09-01 14:33)

[po(m)o _cou(l)ture: dec(adent.sh)ades o' bringing u orgasms instead of enlightenment]

8.8.2 _Ding[leveling||pairbond]Mirrors_ (2010-09-03 10:48)

|||||||||||||
[sli]Ding[!lvl!]mirror.face[t]s
|||||||||||||||||||
we life _t[Ashes]Urn+experient[point+tWis(h)t]
|||||||||||||||||||||||||||||||||||||||||||||||||||| ||||||||||
gRad[i]a(n)tions+time _(c)hops.in.POI.otHer[e]ness
|||||||||||||||||||||||||||||||||||||||||||||||||||| ||||||||||||||||||||||||||||||||||||||||||||||||||| ||||
...+ spoRadically:a s(ynched.)low.gleaming.slide.wHere.we sLot[s.Wife] _meet + r[g]e[nu(ine.in)]flect
|||||||||||||||||||||||||||||||||||||||||||||||||||| ||||||||||||||||||||||||||||||||||||||||||||||||||||
|||||||||||||||||||||||||||||||||||||||||||||||||||| |||||||||||||||||||||||||||||||||||||||||||||||

8.8.3 [AD]Sum[m]er_Melt[BC] (2010-09-13 10:08)

[these season(all) changes]>
[all bluster+sic(kness||ADjustments||fever _cauls)]>

{+meanwhile i'm all: "crow counting: 1/4 of a murder" + tracing gorgeous _dream _scars down tender _drenched _stomachs. }

8.8.4 [glittErringly feathered: all glut + shatter (2010-09-23 11:42)

INT: Bio _Tarred [(protect)feath #Er(ror)ed]

the stuff of eb #O[ily]ny _resi[dual]n. f #Licker _brain+deadpan. c #Racks+ tarred internals: bio+by[te]rot.e. b[s]lack _garroted _body _slush. my organs, [corrupted+]full[erenes]. my head, bl #O[wned.in.Fragonard-ness+ el]ated. my moves, bLAN[keted+conventionally-corrosive]d.

BUT: sur #Face[t]-y...

EXT: [f(w)rac(ked.e)tal _coated sunshine] Day

swan[song]NINg.in.C-qu[p]ins. g #Litter _fr[L]ost lAwn[ing]s + neut #Ra[re]l _bare feet. d[t]res[tles]s: c #R[uched]eam+milk, in staggered s #Hades. s #Tartle-co[(lo)u]r[Sing]sages + c #Ris[que]p bouffants. tink #Elle _f[h]eathe[b]r[onze]s d #Rift+pi[que]ck...

_

[SUMMARY: bio _corrupt images>rotting internals vs EXT: gorgeously

[cris]porcelain feathers>image-purrings]
–

8.9 October

8.9.1 _+3[_gorgeous_]bio_ (2010-10-04 20:18)

_+3 _

blue[wren(che)]d+porous.
d[wr]angling _f[l]eathered _hope.
hop[+scotch]ping _[f]ever _[b]right.

_+2 _

[f]lash _4ward _in _c[d]ream _sn[p]atches.
furred _flick[]r+paw _rush.

_+1 _

w[l]o[ne]lf _dog _asks: _follow?

8.10 December

8.10.1 xXh[K]is[S]toriesXx01x (2010-12-02 13:52)

xXbare _leg[al] _melt[pair _bond _bait]+twitchXx

>a needle _poinT[ime]<
>regurged+intestinal _fashion _[Augustus:G]looping<
>i _rememBurrRRRRrrr _+ _f[a|]eint _meme.ory _left<

>thin _[drip]tubed _skirted+ _tied _mono _aches _+ _80's _pains<
>b+w _stripe _shorts+ _ferret _hair[Spray]de[a]d<
>u _knew _this _all _along _, _huh?<

8.10.2 —Dear Mr Mis[ogyni]s[t]— (2010-12-06 14:27)

–PurrRRRrrrrAcccckkkkkk—-
—Pure–stop–Attack–stop–

—Dear Mr Mis[ogyni]s[t],—
——BabyCa[c]k[l]ing+——-
—Victim[orous-sha]Making—
-Idol-ly[s]ing + B[rR]awling-
-Ur.fear.is.s[lips]ho[d]wing-

—[att(n:me-me-me)]Ack is—
—no[t, u coward] defense—
–nor el[egant|C]oque[T]NT—
–u.stink.of.the.abort _drink-

–convince ur sAlted s[h]elf-
-in ur crippled con[ned]cave-
-of S[ouL]anc[ed]Tit[ties]y–
-u slip + feminine Shee[p]n–
–all divine + [paci]Fisting-
-[com]Passion.is.not.[f]urs–

-Sea _s[Pine]erpentLurkSwells-
-RIP[oiesiS]ing off[ence]+in-
-Ur voice is bald.+Ur senses-
–...[not]B[ut]alder>ugly.—

—or——————————————- ——
u Purr + Ack.
Pure: stop.
Attack: stop.

–

Dear Mr Miss>Misogynist,
Baby-Caking>Cackling and Victim(timorous>sham)Making: and
Idol-lying>lysing and Bawling>Brawling: equals
Your fear is slip-shod-wingless>showing.

Attack and attention "me"meing is no defense>(you coward!)
Nor is it eloquent(>TNTish)>elegant>or coquettish.

In short: you stink of the abortive>anti-drink.

You convince your salted>alternative(shelved)self which lurks in
Your crippled conned>cave
Of soul(lanced)+sanctity, of titty-lessness.
You slip + feminine sheep>sheen
All divine + pacifist>fisting, while
Compounded>passion *is not yours*.

Sea spines and serpents lurking in repressions swells:
RIPping>poiesis off and in:
Your voice is bald. Your senses
...not like Balder: and or but(t ugly).

Chapter 9

2011

9.1 January

9.1.1 _Kal[e]i[d(R)o(tor)sCoping]_ (2011-01-07 16:37)

:Kali _time1:

}body _[bAshed+BL]Us[h]ed
}tran[blood.ink.]quil[l] _bruised
}ur.hands.on.my.rotor.thr[sc]o[pe]at

::Kali _time2::

/awkWard[of.the.flesh.state]+l[w]ilTing[les]
/[c]Rushed.[p]Etal.dam[n]age
/like.a.[RageFace]bOSs.

9.1.2 _microwurk 14_: Mr+Mrs Kin[g].Glasses (2011-01-10 07:54)

[swirling.ice.chIP.hearts + fawn.down(y).thoughts.thru.(d {ist }ance {d }.looking.)glass(es)]

9.1.3 _microwurk 15_: f[L]ingerNails (2011-01-14 07:46)

ur.[st]Raw[berry].blood.unda.my.blAck.pudDing .f[L]inger _nails.

9.2 February

9.2.1][L][.A.M][bast][.be[r]ing (2011-02-10 22:47)

....i.am.a.AM][ber][|P][olymer][M.being .....

.][t][ra][p][ped.like.manning.
.][s][Exe.d.like.b][y][urning.nokia.
.][dr][unkled.like.][L][EG][i][O][n]plogy.

9.2.2 _ab[rev(S)o]lution[b]a[be]ry_ (2011-02-16 20:37)

:imma free biatch, babe.E:

[transliteral _coDe(a)d _via _pop _cult(man)ure _read]:

_imma.p(E)lastique.
_imma.deLic[k.Vic]ious.
_imma.M(ark.eted.Tr)u({P }e)t {ul }ant.

_imma.bloN(ull)de _skinned.
_imma.wh(t)ite _t(S)eethed.
_imma."frE(asy)e".

_imma.G(L)a(dy)gged.
_imma.straP(U)p(Pet {[i]t })ed.
_imma.vanilla _(d)Emo(ed).....

[meanwhile, in.the.Reality.forEST]:

_they're _a:cOn(ned)Crete.
_they're _a:(h)Armed.['S]up.
_they're _a:rev(S)olution _(h)airy.

_they're _a:domino _(t)Ripped.
_they're _a:socially _(s)piked.
_they're _a:Gre([D]ece)ased.

_they're _a:Tun[isia]E[g(ypt]d.
_they're _a:S(Y)eMened.
_they're _a:(Jor)da(n)maged.

9.2.3 .rabBit_frOSt[ing]. (2011-02-19 09:01)

{ yea(bU)rn

.

{ fRo(bert)st

.

# #
# # # # # # # # # # #
#robert _frOSt _ST: do.u.live:tHere:? #
# #
# # # # # # #

{ kill(zOne)

.

{ souled

.

{ (rab)bits

.

# #
# # # # # # # # # # # # # # # # # #
#kill _zOne _bits: Ra(re)bb(s)its.+.sIlK(en) #
# #
# # # # # # # # # # # # # #

9.3 March

9.3.1 |L[D-F]ACED_LIPS (2011-03-14 20:31)

|B.URN.ISHED _G[L]ORY _HOL[D]ES||PER[IN]CEPTION _WINDOWS||[D]REAMING.IN.SODDEN[S]KILL.SETS|| BRAWN _+ _T[ECH>Y]AWNY||G[S]OLD+O[UT]LDEN|

/[y]earn.ur.vicious.h[bl]ooded.keep
/keep.it>solid[ded+capped].it>progress.it:[d] own.
/o[p]wn.it>p[l]unch.it>push.it:[dr]own.

.lil[']Ting[les].
.Stagg[H]er.
.Plum[s+apples,both]me[e]t.
.[d|p]Ru[n|]ched.
.Fr[sw]o[llen|]zen.

_

|L[D-F]ACED _LIPS _+ _SWOLLEN.CLOSED.MOUTH[INGS]|

_

_Foot[fall]notes _:
|U C| burnished glory holes.
{I C } urns+mantles, dust _grey. gore _holes+dished _conventional _[l]awe, please.

|U C| perception windows [+ maybe] inception winds.
{I C } faces+feet[notes],[cRest]fallen. w[r]eSt[erling]+easterlys, [b]low[rippled _calf.furr]ing _softly.

9.3.2 _microwurk 16_: *smoooooooO[h]O[wl]oooooooches* (2011-03-14 20:39)

[....cRumble _heArt + brEa({w }r {a })th _in.flUX...]

9.4 April

9.4.1 _r[l]ush + p[l]inch luv_ (2011-04-06 22:07)

grInd[ie].hOPped+ [p]lucked
str[z]ipper _ling+ f[merc]ury
l[|f]eather _m[a|]usk+ br[h]o[bo]ken.

—

+++++s[i]L[k]ips++++++++++

+++++deSire[n]++++++++++++

+++++ach[E.z(y)]ing++++++++++
—–

suck[h]er.p[l]unched+ uSed[iment]
slow _drip _launch+ taunt[ing]
d-fined-squeeze+ gRip[ley]s.

9.5 May

9.5.1 The Sit[M]u[rder.Aggreg]ation Room (2011-05-07 11:03)

][the #SituationSkinny][

-:-imp-:-formation
-:-nympho-:-mation
-f[#Blo]o[D]rm #A[ge]tion

][hell _coated.break.in.the. #DailyWeatherPulseAndSmileGrind][

@netwurker

www.ingramcontent.com/pod-product-compliance
Lightning Source LLC
Chambersburg PA
CBHW031250230426
43670CB00005B/124